GENUINE PRETENDING

HANS-GEORG MOELLER
& PAUL J. D'AMBROSIO

GENUINE PRETENDING

ON THE PHILOSOPHY OF THE *ZHUANGZI*

COLUMBIA UNIVERSITY PRESS   *New York*

COLUMBIA UNIVERSITY PRESS

Publishers Since 1893

NEW YORK   CHICHESTER, WEST SUSSEX

cup.columbia.edu

Library of Congress Cataloging-in-Publication Data

Names: Moeller, Hans-Georg, 1964– author. | D'Ambrosio, Paul J., author.
Title: Genuine pretending : on the philosophy of the Zhuangzi / Hans-Georg Moeller
    and Paul J. D'Ambrosio.
Description: New York : Columbia University Press, 2017. | Includes bibliographical
    references and index.
Identifiers: LCCN 2017003660 | ISBN 9780231183987 (cloth : alk. paper) |
    ISBN 9780231183994 (pbk. : alk. paper) | ISBN 9780231545266 (e-book)
Subjects: LCSH: Zhuangzi. Nanhua jing.
Classification: LCC BL1900.C576 M64 2017 | DDC 181/.114—dc23
LC record available at https://lccn.loc.gov/2017003660

Columbia University Press books are printed on permanent and durable acid-free paper.

Printed in the United States of America

Cover design: Lisa Hamm
Cover image: Creative Commons

CONTENTS

Foreword by Chen Guying   vii

Preface   ix

Introduction: A Joker in the Fold   1

1. Sincerity, Authenticity, and Ancient Chinese Philosophy   19

    The Dialectic of Sincerity and Confucian Ethics   19
    Authenticity, Irony, and Daoism   30
    On the Ascription of Authenticity to the *Zhuangzi*   34

2. The Confucian Regime of Sincerity   41

    The Rectification of Names, "Dual Correspondence," and
        Role Model Ethics   41
    The Fear of Insincerity and the Moral Ontology of Sincerity   49
    Alternative Readings of Confucianism and a Preliminary
        Conclusion   53

3. Philosophical Humor and Incongruity in the *Zhuangzi*   59

   Toward a Daoist Theory of Humor   60
   Parodies and Tricksters in the *Zhuangzi*   76
   The Incongruity of Names and Forms   113

4. Smooth Operators: The Arts of Genuine Pretending   123

   From Dissonant to Empty Role Models   124
   Zhenren: The Zhenuine Pretender in the *Zhuangzi*   126
   Social Survival   138
   Drunk Skills: On Contingent Excellence   151
   Where We Come From: On Rambling and the Art of
      Philosophizing   164
   Sanity and Health: Immune to Afflictions and Conceit   171

   Conclusion   181

   Notes   189
   Bibliography   195
   Index   211

FOREWORD

Chen Guying

THE ZHUANGZI IS ONE OF MY MOST BELOVED TEXTS. IT IS an abundantly rich resource for reflecting on nature, the human world, and spirituality. History has given us many different interpretations of the *Zhuangzi*, and yet its philosophy can never be exhaustively explicated. With today's convergence of cultures and increasing communication among world traditions, it is natural that scholars from around the world should come to esteem this great book of Daoism.

I have known Hans-Georg Moeller for a long time and appreciate his work on the *Laozi*. I am delighted to find him working on another Daoist text. I have come to know his student Paul D'Ambrosio as well, with whom I have had many pleasurable exchanges on Nietzsche, Zhuangzi, and other philosophers. Their work on "genuine pretending" is an inspired new take on the *Zhuangzi* and engages in comparative philosophy on the highest level.

Scholars today need to be steeped in the philosophy, language, culture, and history of more than one tradition in order to make significant contributions in philosophy. Genuine pretending is a perfect example of how cross-cultural philosophy can develop valuable new perspectives on the history of philosophy, society, and human spirituality. It shows how Zhuangzi's freedom occurs at the core of our daily lives, and how it is accessible even in its most mundane aspects.

Truly, Zhuangzi's writing is characterized by humor. Scholars have often noted this fact, but few have undertaken serious philosophical investigations into the implications of it. The reflections on humor developed in this work bring to light important aspects of Zhuangzi's teachings.

I am delighted to invite readers to join on this path of reading the *Zhuangzi*!

PREFACE

IN THIS BOOK, WE ATTEMPT A READING OF DAOIST PHI-
losophy that departs from more common spiritual or metaphysical frameworks. We approach the *Zhuangzi* as a sometimes biting and provocative
sociopolitical critique of its times and reflect on its often comical expression
of a subversive existential mode that allows one to better endure or even to
thrive in adverse circumstances. For us, this text, among other things, advises
against the common human tendency to develop an inflated ego in reaction
to success—or to lose confidence in response to failure. The socially induced
identity one adopts may turn out to be an ominous chimera. For the sake of
maintaining sanity, the *Zhuangzi* undermines rigid beliefs, judgments, preferences, and dislikes by fostering a humorous attitude toward the world and,
in particular, toward oneself.

When we arrived at the idea for this book, we first imagined it as both a
study of the *Zhuangzi* and an outline of a New Daoist philosophy.[1] Eventually,
we decided to rein in our ambitions and focus on the first goal only, saving

the second endeavor for another occasion. Still, we hope that a sympathetic reader may be able to infer a trajectory toward a potential New Daoism from the gist of our interpretations.

We would like to express our deepest gratitude to the eminent New Daoist philosopher Chen Guying—a role model for us—for contributing the foreword to this book. We are indebted to Seth Crownover and Mike Ashby for editing the text and correcting many mistakes and to Christian Schwermann for providing much-appreciated sinological and otherwise knowledgeable input. We pay due respect to Brook Ziporyn for inspiring much of our understanding of Daoism, and we are grateful for the advice on genuine pretending, as well as general comments, to Sarah Flavel, John and Mary Jo Maraldo, Michael Nylan, Julia Jansen, Henry Rosemont Jr., Rolf Trauzettel, Andrew Whitehead, Trenton Wilson, Yang Guorong, and Ellen Zhang. We thank Robert Carleo for inventing the term "zhenuineness," Robin Wang for living and sharing her own version of being a New Daoist, and Hans-Rudolf Kantor for nothing in particular. We wish to thank Wendy Lochner at Columbia University Press for her support, and we extend our gratitude for permission to use some revised excerpts from our other publications to Roger Ames (*Philosophy East and West*), the University of Hawai'i Press, Huang Yong and Springer (*Dao*), and Livia Kohn (Three Pines Press). As is academically customary, we accept full responsibility for any errors and shortcomings of this work and assign all the blame for them to the respective other of the two of us.

GENUINE PRETENDING

INTRODUCTION

A JOKER IN THE FOLD

Daß es mir zum Beispiel niemals zum Bewußtsein gekommen ist, wieviel Gesichter es giebt. Es giebt eine Menge Menschen, aber noch viel mehr Gesichter, denn jeder hat mehrere. Da sind Leute, die tragen ein Gesicht jahrelang, natürlich nutzt es sich ab, es wird schmutzig, es bricht in den Falten, es weitet sich aus wie Handschuhe, die man auf der Reise getragen hat. Das sind sparsame, einfache Leute; sie wechseln es nicht, sie lassen es nicht einmal reinigen. Es sei gut genug, behaupten sie, und wer kann ihnen das Gegenteil nachweisen? Nun fragt es sich freilich, da sie mehrere Gesichter haben, was tun sie mit den andern? Sie heben sie auf. Ihre Kinder sollen sie tragen. Aber es kommt auch vor, daß ihre Hunde damit ausgehen. Weshalb auch nicht? Gesicht ist Gesicht.

(To think, for example, that I have never consciously registered just how many faces there are. There are a great many people, but there are a great many more faces, for every person has several. There are people who wear the same face for years on end; naturally, it shows signs of wear, it gets dirty, it cracks at the creases, it splays out like gloves worn on a journey. These are simple people, practising economies, and they do not change their faces or even have it cleaned. It'll do fine, they insist, and who is to prove them wrong? The question, of course, since they have several faces, is what they do with the others? They keep them for best: their children can wear them some day. But it has been known for their dogs to go out wearing them, too. And why not? A face is a face.)

—Rainer Maria Rilke, *Die Aufzeichnungen des Malte Laurids Brigge*
(*The Notebooks of Malte Laurids Brigge*)

"Genuine pretending," the notion introduced in this book for the purpose of representing our take on the philosophy of the *Zhuangzi* 莊子, is not an altogether new idea. It connects with the "wild card" metaphor employed by Brook Ziporyn in his concise and subtle account "Zhuangzi as Philosopher"

(2015). What distinguishes our approach from Ziporyn's is perhaps best summarized by saying that, rather than as a wild card in the general sense, we see the genuine pretender more specifically as a *joker card*.

Following Ziporyn's metaphor—and playing with it—the *Zhuangzi* can be understood as presenting a view of life, or, for that matter, of the *dao* 道, as a rather absurd card game. People play this game without knowing why or how; and there are competing, conflicting, and contradictory claims as to what the rules of the game are and how best to play it. The value of each card is permanently disputed. Therefore, the game—which has no rules as such—includes a "metagame" about determining the rules of the game. Now, two types of players emerge: First, there are those who are drawn to the rules of the game and spellbound by the values of the cards. They are convinced they can know what the rules are and what they ought to be. They set out to defend and argue for certain guidelines and values, intending to make everyone else adopt and follow them. Naturally, they'll win over a good number of players. In this way, various groups of rule-and-value believers emerge, endlessly applying, amending, renegotiating, rebelling against, or consciously breaking the rules. Second, there are players—or maybe a voice inside each player—to whom the rules appear utterly contingent. These players do not argue for adherence to this or that rule, or demand changes to the rules, or revolt against all rules whatsoever; instead, they sneak in a new kind of card—the wild card. The inventors of the wild card, to echo Ziporyn, differ from the rule-and-value players in that they do not attempt to "see through the surface" of the game in order to find its foundational rules and values therein—which, as the rule-and-value people may believe, would resolve the conflict over the game once and for all. They acknowledge that "this conflict itself" is part and parcel of the game, or "of the surface itself" (Ziporyn 2015). The wild-card people thus do not come up with any further propositions about values or rules, or reasons for them, in order to bring the game to a definite conclusion. Rather, they contribute to its continuation by introducing the wild card—a card that *represents the permanent openness and contingency that lie at the heart of the game* and constitutes its empty center, the hub around which it endlessly revolves. The new wild card differs from all the others precisely by being the only one that can be the same as all others. It thereby manifests as a Daoist "zero perspective" on and in the game. It can playfully assume all the values represented by the surface of the cards, but it cannot be identified with any of them.

Eventually, as Ziporyn (2015) points out, the "metaphor of the wild card begins to break down, as all metaphors do somewhere." This is certainly so, but before we leave it behind and turn to the actual metaphors and allegories of the *Zhuangzi* (which are of course also doomed to meet a similar fate), we would like to take it a little further. The notion of the wild card nicely illustrates what our oxymoron genuine pretending is supposed to convey first and foremost—namely, that something or someone, on the one hand, assumes a role that it (or he/she) is not really. But, on the other hand, it (or he/she) thereby does not act in any way falsely, hypocritically, or in deviation from any authentic essence, since there is no such essence to begin with. The wild card's true value in a card game is that it can be played as any card, since it is not and can never be valued *as itself* (or *in itself*). Precisely because it has no specific identity or essential value assigned to it, it can actually and with full validity represent, assume, or "pretend" to be whatever it is supposed to or wants to be. It always enacts its roles "genuinely," but never "authentically."

Genuine pretending is real, but not determining; it neither violates nor constructs identity. Wild cards and genuine pretenders actualize their roles temporarily without forfeiting their nonidentity. The wild card is never tainted by the roles it assumes: it returns to the deck of cards as if nothing had happened, with none of its roles sticking to it. Just like the notion of the wild card, our idea of genuine pretending is thereby associated with what may be called an existential mode of play. In this mode, as in child's play, roles are not assumed to deceive others or ourselves for the sake of personal gain, nor to eventually make one become something that one is not (yet); instead, possibilities are momentarily or experimentally enacted, experienced, or engaged with, all without any essential commitment to them.

If David Parlett's *A Dictionary of Card Games* (1992, 104) is correct, a peculiar form of the wild card emerged only recently in history: the joker was introduced around 1860. However, we think that it may have a philosophical ancestor predating it by about two millennia. The image of a jester or medieval (moral) fool on the faceless wild card reveals not only its strange otherness in relation to all the other cards—an otherness that always evades identification—but also, we think, its most interesting peculiarity: it is a funny thing. Humor is often based on incongruity, on the reversal of expectations, on dissolving something into nothing; it has a relieving and relaxing yet simultaneously bonding effect, both psychologically and somatically. This, too, is what the joker brings to our slightly absurd card game. In life, a joker makes us laugh about ourselves and the world; in the card game, it reveals its utter contingency, it befriends us; we consider ourselves lucky to have a joker in our hand. It is, ironically, our highest trump. Rather than fueling our existential *Angst* and *Sorge* (to speak with Kierkegaard and Heidegger, those two mistaken brothers of Zhuangzi), it makes us smile and *fröhlich* (gay), to borrow a word from much closer kin. If not for the joker, the game would be much more boring, and maybe even unbearable in the long run. The joker does not save us, for sure, but it keeps us cheerful and playing. What more could one ask for?

We consider humor just as crucial for understanding jokers as it is for understanding the philosophy of the *Zhuangzi*, and thus also for understanding genuine pretending. This is why the section on the art of genuine pretending in this book is preceded by one on the philosophy of humor. And this ordering has to be kept in mind. However, the notion of genuine pretending can also be understood "soberly," much like the wild card is a more "sober" variation of the joker. Abstracted from its humor, genuine pretending can be envisioned metaphorically with the image of the wild card, but it can also be illustrated by reference to a concrete example taken from human experience. When watching a movie or a theater performance that stirs our feelings, we enter a state of emotional genuine pretending. The joy, sadness, or anger we feel is real and actual. It is, often enough, accompanied by immediate and involuntary physical reactions such as a faster pulse rate, laughter, sweat, or tears. There is nothing fake about these feelings and their bodily expressions—they are genuine. At the same time, however, they are not personal. In a strict sense, the happiness or anger that we feel during these times is not really *ours*. We do not relate these feelings to ourselves but feel them, so to speak, merely by proxy. In the theater, we experience happiness or sadness playfully (as children do perhaps much more regularly) and thus, in a sense, only pretend to be happy or sad. Soon after the show is over, the feelings subside and we forget about them. The experience does not afflict us; or perhaps, as Aristotle thought, it provides us with a *catharsis*—a form of emotional release or cleansing that, rather than filling us with feelings, actually *empties* us of whatever residual emotional ballast we may be carrying. If Aristotle's conception is true, then in addition to illustrating how common genuine pretending is, this concrete example also demonstrates its importance for maintaining sanity.

The single most famous allegory in the *Zhuangzi*, the butterfly dream story at the end of the second chapter of the book, illustrates genuine pretending as well. A major point of the story is that during the dream the butterfly "has no knowledge of [Zhuang] Zhou" (*bu zhi Zhou* 不知周), the dreamer. Only this complete cognitive disjunction between the butterfly and Zhou allows the former to fully enjoy the experience of fluttering around "free and easy," as a

Daoist may say. Just like the feelings in a movie theater, emotional or existential experiences in a dream can be highly intense and real—as, once more, physical reactions undoubtedly show. A wet dream is genuinely wet. At the same time, the dreamer merely plays the role he or she adopts in a dream—it does not essentially define him or her. Once we awaken, the dream existence often fades in an instant, only to be forgotten forever—although this was more commonly the case prior to the flourishing of psychoanalysis. Here, we do not wish to delve more deeply into an interpretation of the butterfly dream allegory but would like to maintain that genuine pretending is one of its central philosophical themes. The butterfly in the dream exemplifies at the same time true actuality and nonauthenticity; it represents radical transitoriness and existential contingency. Once more, in the allegory, the nonauthenticity of the dream is by no means experienced as a lack of identity or a pathological fugue state. On the contrary, it is experienced as an intensely joyful and healthy "wholesomeness." As we will try to show, the wholesome but simultaneously incongruent state of genuine pretending in the Zhuangzi, as exemplified by the state of the butterfly in the butterfly dream allegory, is depicted in the text as zhen 真, or, in our rendering, as "zhenuineness."

As our slightly modified version of Brook Ziporyn's wild card analogy shows, the philosophy of genuine pretending does not come from nowhere—it is a response to a "game" that is already going on. It is a philosophical position emerging within a discourse to which it reacts and in which it contextualizes itself; the philosophy of genuine pretending as it is developed in the Zhuangzi is historically grounded. It is widely acknowledged that the Zhuangzi incorporates a number of explicit and implicit criticisms of, or reflections on, rival philosophical schools of the time, most important the tradition we now call Confucian (rujia 儒家) or, in the terminology of some scholars, "Ruist." A number of prominent figures from the history of ancient Chinese philosophy, such as Confucius (Kongzi 孔子), Liezi 列子, and Hui Shi 惠施, appear in the narratives and dialogues of the Zhuangzi and are famously mocked or otherwise debunked. The thorough historical anchoring of the text is, last but not least, underscored by the fact that the final chapter of the book constitutes what could be called the first history of philosophy in China. For us, therefore, in a somewhat Hegelian fashion, the Zhuangzi can best be approached by situating it within the historical framework of "disputers of the Dao" (Graham 1989).

Given the materials excavated in Guodian 郭店 and Mawangdui 馬王堆 in recent decades, it can be reasonably assumed that both orally transmitted and early written versions of the Daodejing 道德經 also predate the composition of the Zhuangzi as we know it. As we will show in our analyses of many sections of the Zhuangzi (e.g., the Hundun 渾沌 parody), the Zhuangzi makes frequent use of the Daodejing's imagery, as well as the philosophical ideas associated with it. At least some parts of the text can therefore be read as narrative and discursive elaborations on segments of the Daodejing. In particular, the Zhuangzi draws upon anti-Confucian tenets in the Daodejing that attack the validity of the philosophical vocabulary associated with Confucian texts or representatives—concepts such as de 德 (power, efficacy, virtuosity, health)—and then sets out to twist, reverse, or otherwise subvert this terminology. The fictitious depictions of meetings and dialogues between Confucius and Laozi in the Zhuangzi represent the relation between the text and specifically Confucian teachings or ideas. Typically with a strong dose of humor, the Zhuangzi "deconstructs" the dominant ontological, epistemological, and—perhaps most important—ethical vocabulary of its time.

We think that the idea of genuine pretending should be understood as evolving through a dialectical process of engagement with (not only, but importantly) ancient Confucian ideas and language. Therefore, we do not claim that the Zhuangzi's engagement with Confucian notions represents a correct or complete or coherent picture of Confucianism—whatever that may be—or of the philosophy of the Confucius of the Analects (Lunyu 論語). It is not our intention to defend or otherwise assess the "accuracy" of the Zhuangzi's presentation of Confucian teachings with respect to their "true" nature. What interests us is the way in which the Zhuangzi distances itself from what it depicts as Confucian. While it portrays Confucius differently in different passages, it often either critically distances itself from what it presents as Confucian or it makes the character of Confucius a spokesperson of views contrary to what he is commonly associated with. Our understanding of the philosophy of the Zhuangzi as emerging from a critical (and often humorous) assessment of Confucianism is historically grounded and reflects the text's original reception as early as the Han dynasty. In its short remarks about Zhuang Zhou 莊周, the Shiji 史記 (63.9) notes that "he mocked the followers of Confucius in order to illuminate the arts of Laozi" (di zi Kongzi zhi tu yi ming Laozi zhi shu 詆訿孔子之徒以明老子之術) and "flayed the Confucians and Mohists" (piao bo Ru Mo 剽剝儒墨 [Nienhauser 1994, 23]). Judging from this rare early comment, it seems that Zhuangzi was indeed perceived as an anti-Confucian "dissident" at the time. It also seems that he developed his own "brand" of Daoist philosophy as a practitioner of the arts of Laozi precisely on the basis of his anti-Confucianism. Our interpretation of the Daoist philosophy of the *Zhuangzi* follows the assessments found in the *Shiji*.

To acknowledge a critical attitude toward Confucianism or Confucius in the *Zhuangzi* is not to deny, as has been done, that its philosophy may be read in the end as quite compatible with a "better" version of Confucianism, one that is deprived of its "bad" misappropriations and concerned with preserving its "good" essence. Such synthetic readings, which can be found today, for instance, in the works of Chen Guying 陳鼓應 (2012) or Yang Rubin 楊儒賓 (2008),[1] may indeed be valid and justified. However, our aim in this book is not to unearth some common ground between Daoist and Confucian thinking in general but to explore the interpretative potential of what we believe to be a particularly Daoist take on the *Zhuangzi*.

The picture of Confucian philosophy that the *Zhuangzi* paints often revolves around a philosophical program of a rectification of names (*zheng ming* 正名) and certain ethical demands attached to it that focus on a correspondence of names and actuality (*ming shi* 名實), or of forms and names (*xing ming* 形名). As texts such as the *Analects* and the *Mencius* (*Mengzi* 孟子) show—and the depiction of Confucius in the *Zhuangzi*—the early Confucianism to which the *Zhuangzi* critically reacts highlights the moral importance of a correspondence between, first, the designation of social roles and relationships (or ranks or titles, or "names") and their enactment (i.e., "forms"), and, second, between this performance of a role or relationship and the inner mental and emotional self of the person who performs it.[2] We use the term "dual correspondence" to refer to the early Confucian command that one ought to *sincerely commit* to one's roles and relationships not only in one's actions but also with one's heart-mind (*xin* 心). Speaking in the vocabulary first suggested by Henry Rosemont Jr. (1991) and later stressed by his collaborator, Roger T. Ames, such a dual correspondence requires one to "*live—not play*" (Ames 2011, 96; emphasis in the original) one's roles such that, for instance, a father not only acts as a father should but also eventually becomes a true father with his whole heart and soul.[3] The early Confucian insistence on dual correspondence has been embraced and creatively adopted by later champions of a Confucian ethics, but it also originally gave rise to anti-Confucian ideas and sentiments, both of which are on full display in the *Zhuangzi*. Here, these sentiments work toward a "rehabilitation" of a playful enactment of social roles and relationships.

In modern Western philosophical terms, the dual correspondence implicit in an early Confucian ethics can be addressed as an issue of *sincerity*. A seemingly good person may fulfill his or her tasks reliably and correctly. However, from a dual correspondence perspective, this is not good enough. Mere correspondence between role and action smacks of, as Hegel puts it, "the heroism of dumb service" (der Heroismus des stummen Dienstes [Hegel 1986, 378; see Trilling 1972, 35]). One may enact one's roles without cultivating a corresponding identity and thus lack a sincere commitment to them. Accordingly, a Confucian dual correspondence ethics, as well as a modern ethics of sincerity, is constantly concerned with potential fraud and false appearances. It questions people's true ethical motives and requires real intellectual, emotional, and existential identification with one's actions. The constant suspicion of sincerity that haunted many modern Western philosophers had already been aroused in ancient Confucians. Early on in the Analects (1.4) we learn that we cannot trust ourselves morally and so have to double-check our commitment to do and ultimately be good every single day on various levels: "Daily I examine my person on three counts. In my undertakings on behalf of other people, have I failed to be dedicated (zhong 忠)? In my interactions with colleagues and friends, have I failed to be true to my word (xin 信)? In what has been passed on (chuan 傳) to me, have I failed to make it my practice?" (Ames and Rosemont 1998, 72; translation modified)

As we attempt to show in this book, the Zhuangzi finds the permanent suspicion of oneself and others entailed in the categorical imperative of Confucian dual correspondence disquieting and—perhaps more problematically—creating an impossible task. As the antimoral criticisms found throughout the Zhuangzi show, the text assumes that the very insistence on Confucian morality brings about what it tries do get rid of—namely, falsity, hypocrisy, and selfishness. It creates the very problems it claims to resolve.[4] Confucian moral demands are, to use more contemporary parlance, tied to social constructs. And rather than simply demanding conformity with such social constructs, a Confucian ethics demands the impossible—that one "naturalize" the social by personally substantiating family relationships and political roles established by the structures of a social order. This impossible demand is to sincerely make one's own what is not one's own to begin with, or in the words of the Analects, "what has been passed on (chuan 傳)" (1.4) to oneself.

From a Daoist perspective such as we find expressed repeatedly in the "primitivist" sections of the Zhuangzi (as well as their corresponding passages in the Daodejing),[5] the acts of civilization enforced through the imposition of social divisions, ranks, and institutionalized human relationships as hailed in the Confucian texts and celebrated by the establishment of exemplary models are acts of wei 偽 (Daodejing 18)—literally, acts of "human making." In other words, they are inherently artificial or, to put it once again in contemporary language, social constructs. From a Daoist perspective, Confucian ethics is profoundly paradoxical, or to use another contemporary term, it is built on and proliferates a giant double bind: it is aimed at a sort of a posteriori verification of what is essentially socially enforced and learned as being actually natural or personally sincere. What is external is supposed to be matched and grounded internally after the fact, as demanded by the emblematic maxim "inner sageliness and outward kingliness" (nei sheng wai wang 內聖外王), which, notably, first occurs in section 33.1 of the Zhuangzi, though it later became a paradigmatic expression for the Confucian ideal of personal cultivation. The supposed moral grandeur of one's social role—"one's kingliness"—is to be founded on one's personal virtuousness or "sageliness." Or, speaking with Mencius's (see Mencius 孟子 2A:6) famous organic imagery, one's ethical excellence in the social dimension is supposed to "sprout" from one's true inner nature. Everyone is thereby called upon to supply with sincerity the social roles that one finds oneself entrusted with, and to meet moral expectations with a purported inborn identity. According to a most crucial passage in Zhongyong 中庸 (22), while the dao of nature or the world in general is supposed to have been "sincere" (cheng 誠) from the start, humans are singled out with the task of making sincere whatever they do. This is what the text calls the dao of humankind: "Sincerity is the dao/way of nature/heaven; making it sincere is the dao/way of humankind" (cheng zhe, tian zhi dao ye; cheng zhi zhe, ren zhi dao ye 誠者，天之道也; 誠之者，人之道也). The Zhuangzi, we submit, rejects this impossible Confucian categorical imperative of making sincere what is not so from the start. Instead of simply adopting the Confucian "game plan," it inserts a joker into the fold—the genuine pretender.

The Zhuangzi's reaction to the impossible Confucian demand to make sincere one's social persona is not, we believe, to replace a wrong Confucian notion of sincerity with a correct or even better Daoist one—that is, a kind of authenticity. On the contrary, the genuine pretender, as a reaction to the Confucian sincerity claim, diverts from sincerity and steers toward an altogether different direction. Therefore we believe it is unfortunate that in the context of an "age of authenticity," Heideggerian and other notions of authenticity have been ascribed to Daoism and, in particular, to the Zhuangzi. One of our intentions in this book is to liberate Zhuangzi from Heidegger's all-too-tight and all-too-constraining—and, even more uncomfortably, all-too-German and all-too-serious—embrace.

We think that Heideggerian readings of the *Zhuangzi*—which have been a major force in both Western and Asian Daoist philosophy for at least half a century—are anachronistic and eisegetical in that they are more responsive to the present "age of authenticity" than to the "disputers of the Dao" in ancient China. However, any contemporary interpretation of ancient Chinese philosophy, including ours, will inevitably be anachronistic and eisegetic to a certain extent, because it must necessarily reconstruct past meaning within a present semantic framework in order to connect in a meaningful way with contemporary discourses. Still, there are differences in degree, and interpretations can be more or less historically sensitive. The intention to ground our reading of the *Zhuangzi* historically has led us to pursue an interpretation that is diametrically opposed to the Heideggerian approach to the *Zhuangzi*. For us, the *Zhuangzi* reacts to a postulate of sincerity, or rather to a more or less analogous ancient Chinese version of it in the form of a Confucian ethics. And it reacts to this ethics by deconstructing and undermining notions of sincerity through humor and other means. Rather than asking for a "better" sincerity, it invites readers to distance themselves from its idealization and to see through its fallacies and flaws, as well as its more sickening aspects.

Nonetheless, we do not wish to imply that we find Heideggerian interpretations of the *Zhuangzi* entirely unacceptable. We generally agree with the hermeneutic position of a reception theory that sees meaning as an emergent product of the interaction between a text or work of art and its interpreters. According to the representatives of the so-called Constance school, such as Wolfgang Iser (1989) and Hans Robert Jauss (1982), meaning as such is not already originally contained in a text but is constructed through the process of interpretation. There is no doubt that Heideggerian readings of the *Zhuangzi* have been able to produce understandings of the text that many scholars find valuable. We may not be among them, but of course, we, too, are able to see how the text could be read from a broadly Heideggerian perspective, and we will discuss this later in the book.

In accordance with an hermeneutics of a reception theory, we acknowledge the potential multidimensionality of any text or work of art. The *Zhuangzi* is a particularly complex and rich work, and therefore its multidimensionality is especially obvious and relevant. As many commentators have observed, it makes use of a wide range of literary and rhetorical devices and genres, inviting different modes of reading, ranging from poetic reveling to logical rumination and humoristic relaxation. The reader is constantly drawn back and forth between different interpretations of the text, finding it difficult to settle down for long with any one in particular, except perhaps for an ongoing hermeneutic of "rambling without destination."

Moreover, as many commentators have observed, the *Zhuangzi* introduces a large variety of philosophical and religious perspectives. This has led some (among them still most prominently A. C. Graham [2001] and Liu Xiaogan [1995]) to identify different strata of the text that can then be ascribed to different authors or groups of authors. For us, the multidimensionality of the text goes even deeper and does not merely reflect a complex editorial process during the course of which materials from various sources were collated and grouped together. We think that not only each single chapter but most (if not all) individual narratives, dialogues, and poetic passages as well are polyphonic, so to speak, and lend themselves to multiple readings, depending on which "key" one reads them in. For us, the often acknowledged yet philosophically neglected *humoristic key* is especially relevant. The humoristic key has the hermeneutic advantage in that it resists dogmatic reification. It inserts a certain irony into the text that renders any understanding provisional and adds a grain of salt into the mix. Consequently, it defies the reduction of the message of the text to a single message or maxim. The often noted "perspectivism" of the *Zhuangzi* is not only—and arguably, not even primarily—a philosophical position but also a methodological tool of this text. It allows ten suns to rise at the same time, to speak with a famous image of the *Zhuangzi* (2.10), and lighten up the scene from multiple angles.

The multidimensionality of the *Zhuangzi* allows for readings of the same passages in different keys and with different foci of attention. On one level, one can read the text in a propositional key and isolate or abstract certain positions, arguments, or viewpoints from within it. Influenced by conventional philosophical methodologies, some current academic interpretations of the text operate accordingly and have ascribed various isms to it or to some of its sections. Thus, the text or its presumed author(s) can be labeled, for instance, as a skeptic, relativist (see Kjellberg and Ivanhoe 1996), or whatever -ist may be regarded as most fitting by an interpreter subscribing to this sort of analysis.

Alternatively, the text can be taken more comprehensively as a kind of canonical scripture, or *jing* 經, as reflected in the honorific title *Nanhua zhenjing* 南華真經 (Classical scripture of southern florescence) conferred upon it by Emperor Xuanzong of Tang 唐玄宗 in 742. Read in this "sacred key," the text is seen as providing a profound, all-encompassing vision of the world; it can well be regarded as a compendium of enlightening stories about extraordinary humans and wondrous creatures initiating its readers into views of the world that remain otherwise inaccessible, obscure, or secret. Not unlike many texts associated with the Confucian tradition, under this reading the *Zhuangzi* can be seen as presenting a long parade of exemplars that one ought not only to revere but also set out to emulate if one intends to attain a higher stage of being. It can be read as a guidebook for spiritual, physiopsychological, and moral cultivation. The reception of the *Zhuangzi* along these lines has a very long history and is closely intertwined with the development of Daoist practices and textual production commonly associated with the *dao jiao* 道教 tradition, which one may or may not want to label as Daoist religion. In her book *Zhuangzi: Text and Context*, Livia Kohn (2014) presents an elaborate and most instructive overview of this dimension of the *Zhuangzi*. A practical and at least partly soteriological approach to the *Zhuangzi* depicts it as promoting the enhancement of human capacities. This enhancement can take the form of greater mental and bodily health, but it can also be extended to a spiritual elevation into a mystical union with the Dao or the cosmos.

In our readings of the *Zhuangzi*, we try to do some justice to *dao jiao* approaches, particularly because of their substantial historical and contemporary relevance. It is clear that the *Zhuangzi* provided fertile ground for religious or spiritual interpretations and continues to do so. The very short, but nevertheless semantically dense, allegory of Hundun at the end of the Inner Chapters, for instance, is rich in mythological and mystical allusions. As Norman J. Girardot (2008) has shown in his book-length study on the Hundun symbolism in Daoism and beyond, this brief narrative can be understood as encapsulating a whole Daoist belief system built on intricate cosmological conceptions and expressing profound hopes of salvation. The story therefore archetypically represents a larger network of meaning that gives sense to the world and one's existence in it. At the same time, it points toward a promise of salvation and a potential religious goal of attaining a transcendent level of spiritual existence.

We agree with Girardot's (2008, 33) verdict that the "best way to characterize the Daoist idea of salvation is to see it as being fundamentally 'medicinal' in intention and structure." And we acknowledge that when the *Zhuangzi* is read in a sacred key—a reading often encouraged by its imagery and style—the "healing" that the text promises takes on the form of a mystic ascension toward a higher spiritual dimension. However, we do not think that such a reading is in any way privileged over other, more this-worldly interpretations. Particularly when one directs one's attention to the humorous elements of the text, "devotional" readings of narratives such as that of Hundun, the Emperor of the Center, can be diverted and undermined. As we try to demonstrate in our analysis of this story, a twist in perspective allows one to suspend one's awe of the strange protagonists in the stories such that one can see them in the light of a different "sun"—namely, a carnivalesque one. Instead of venerating them, one begins to laugh about them.

The humoristic hermeneutic does not, however, take anything away from what Girardot has identified as a "fundamentally medicinal intention and structure" of Daoism. For us, too, the *Zhuangzi* represents a Daoist quest for health and sanity, although we understand this quest as emphatically *mundane*. According to our reading of the text, it employs humor in order to de-deify its protagonists and thus to secularize itself. At the same time, it thereby secularizes its medicinal strategy. The sanity it promotes and imparts is not a transcendent spiritual blessedness but instead an everyday mental health that allows one to cope with stress, anxiety, and the challenges that both social success and social failure can present. For us, the *Zhuangzi* allows for but by no means requires a reading in a sacred key. While, unlike Chen Guying (2012), we would not like to use the term "humanist" for our interpretation of the *Zhuangzi*—given, in particular, the nonanthropocentric leanings it shares with the *Daodejing* and other Daoist texts—we follow Chen as well as quite a few other contemporary Chinese interpreters (Wang Bo 2014) in reading it as decidedly existential and inner social rather than politically escapist or spiritually otherworldly. This focus does not diminish but arguably only increases its therapeutic potentials, and particularly so in a present-day secular context. Consequently, our reading, we think, offers some form of compatibility with philosophically distinct but similarly mundane approaches to Daoism, such as Edward Slingerland's (2014) recent attempt to marry it with cognitive science. Likewise, it connects well, we hope, with Barry Allen's (2015) "applied Daoism" as described in his philosophical exploration of the psychosomatic and social practices of martial arts.

By affirming Girardot's approach, which tries to grasp a basic intention and structure informing a philosophy, religion, or book, we follow him and many others in suggesting what may be called a *comprehensive* philosophical reading of a text in recognition of its historical context. Rather than engaging in a kind of propositional reductionism, we try to make sense of the semantics and rhetoric of the *Zhuangzi* as a whole, including its narrative components, imagery, core notions, as well as its stylistic and poetic devices. In a sense, we thereby try to reconstruct what is in Hegelian terms the "spirit," or in

Chinese terms applied by Chen Guying (2012) and others, the *jingshen* 精神 of the text. We thus connect methodologically with traditional forms of writing intellectual history, or the history of philosophy.

For us, the spirit of the *Zhuangzi* is emblematically represented by the figure of the genuine pretender. As we try to show throughout this book, we believe that a philosophy of genuine pretending can open up many of the core allegories and tales that constitute such a large part of the *Zhuangzi*. At the same time, we also think that the core terminology of the text, including most prominently such notions as *you* 遊 (rambling, roaming), *zhenren* 真人 (zhenuine person), or *de* 德 (power, efficacy, health, virtuosity), reflects a philosophy of genuine pretending and can be comprehensively understood from such a perspective. Last but not least, the text's ubiquitous humor can be made sense of once it is seen as an appropriate communicative medium of genuine pretending.

Speaking with Hegel, we assume that "the truth is the whole." This does not mean that the text expresses one and only one idea or propositional truth claim coherently throughout the whole work. On the contrary, it means, as we said, that it is not possible to identify one single statement or ism as the final verdict of the *Zhuangzi*. The whole is instead the complete discourse of the text operating on the propositional, narrative, terminological, and stylistic levels alike and embedded in and informed by the historical context to which it responds. A comprehensive reading of the *Zhuangzi* looks at the text in the way Richard Rorty conceived of philosophical writing—namely, as a kind of intellectual literature complementing other genres of literature, such as prose or poetry. A philosophical book thus represents not so much one particular explanation of everything, or one foundational maxim or Archimedean point upon which everything that is good or true can be grounded with certainty, but rather a way of life and thinking. It presents, metaphorically speaking, a host of characters involved in a common plot who thereby shape a historical moment or period. To speak in Hegelian terms once again, the whole is concrete, and not abstract; it includes that which is true as much as that which is false, it is dialogical and dialectical, and it is evolving and changing, rather than a lifeless final conclusion or a priori axiom. In other words, we think that the *Zhuangzi* expresses the spirit of genuine pretending and that it does so via a wide variety of philosophical and literary forms, none of which constitutes the last word on or the ultimate definition or contradiction-free formula of genuine pretending.

Genuine pretending is an incongruent and so potentially comical notion, given the important role incongruity plays in making things funny. Precisely because of this, the notion lends itself to expression in the form of humorous tales and remarks as well as in ironically ambiguous statements and commands. For us, reading the *Zhuangzi* as a book on genuine pretending also means reading it in a humorous key. This humorous key, we believe, provides a route to philosophical interpretations of sections of the text that are rarely read as humorous, such as the Hundun narrative or the various stories about cripples in office in chapter 5. According to Kant's definition in section 54 of the *Critique of Judgment*, which we discuss in more detail in our analysis of philosophical humor in the *Zhuangzi*, laughter results "from the sudden transformation of a strained expectation into nothing." We agree with Günter Wohlfart (2010) that this definition provides a clue as to the function of humor in both Daoism and Chan Buddhism. Humor de-essentializes its subject—in the double sense of the term "subject"—and thereby produces relaxing and healthy effects. If this apophatic function of humor is understood and appreciated in a thoroughly mundane, secular, and nonmystical way, then the spirit of genuine pretending comes to the fore.

In line with our comprehensive hermeneutic approach, we have used as our source text the *Zhuangzi* in its textus receptus, or standard version, commonly regarded as having been edited by Guo Xiang 郭象 (d. 312).[6] As mentioned, we are of course aware that the text has not been authored by a single identifiable person and presents a collection of materials from unknown origins. We also acknowledge the presence of different philosophical trajectories in the text, which have been variously classified as Zhuangist, Primitivist, or Yangist. We think that these different strata cannot be separated as clearly from one another as suggested, for instance, by Graham (2001). First, there is, for example, a considerable element of Yangism incorporated in Primitivism, and many Primitivist ideas, too, are readily compatible or interchangeable with Zhuangist thought. Second, from the perspective of a multidimensional reading, these different strands can be identified as simultaneously present in the same chapters or sections of chapters in the *Zhuangzi*. For us, a philosophy of genuine pretending can be expressed in various contexts, including those that may be labeled as, for instance, Zhuangist, Yangist, or Primitivist. Therefore, we do not wish to claim that every single passage from all thirty-three chapters of the *Zhuangzi* is best understood as intentionally or unintentionally outlining a philosophy of genuine pretending. Instead, we believe that, just as it is possible to read many passages in the book that are normally not read humorously in a humorous key, it is also possible to read these and other passages from a genuine pretending perspective. In other words, we believe that significant parts of the text do come to life and make sense when seen sub specie genuine pretending, and that this is so for the whole range of the book and not just for specific passages, chapters, or groups of chapters.

We share the doubts of other researchers about the widely held belief that the Inner Chapters represent a fully coherent segment of the book written by only one author—namely, the historic Zhuang Zhou. These Inner Chapters skeptics include, among others, Ren Jiyu (1963),[7] Feng Youlan (Fung 1931),[8] Yan Beiming (1980), Zhang Hengshou (1983), Chris Fraser (1997), David McCraw (2010), and Esther Klein (2010). We agree with Klein (2010) and assume that there is no clear evidence that, for instance, the Robber Zhi chapter (chapter 29) is historically later or less authentic than any of the Inner Chapters, or the Inner Chapters altogether. Of course, there is also no clear evidence of the contrary. We believe that the issues of authorship, date of composition, or the "authenticity" of the text and its parts more generally remain very much open for discussion and may never be sufficiently resolved.

However, this philological quagmire does not present a severe hermeneutic obstacle for us. The oeuvre of basically every single philosopher has evolved and changed over time. That there are substantial differences between the early writings and the later writings of, for example, Martin Heidegger does not mean that the earlier works are more or less authentic than the later ones, or that Heidegger was a more or less true Heideggerian at different stages of his life. On the other hand, there may well be writings by Heideggerians other than Heidegger himself that are closer in style and content to (say) Heidegger's late writings on *Gelassenheit* than to Heidegger's own early book *Sein und Zeit*. The very concept of an authentic core of a thinker or oeuvre is problematic. As we said, it is not our intention to reduce the philosophy of the *Zhuangzi* to a presumed innermost or authentic essence. And much less do we intend to make any claim about any single individual's thoughts in ancient China. We do not know if Zhuang Zhou wrote the Inner Chapters or any other part of the *Zhuangzi*, and we are not even sure if he ever existed. But there certainly is a multidimensional text bearing his name, and this text, we hope to show, can be made sense of when read as a response to other texts of its period, particularly those commonly associated with the Confucian tradition. Furthermore, we

submit that it is possible to read significant parts of it—if not the entire text—
in the spirit of genuine pretending and in a humorous key.

When referring to passages from the Zhuangzi, we cite the chapter and section number as they appear in the online version of the text at the Chinese
Text Project website (www.ctext.org/zhuangzi). This website is now widely
used and provides easy and instant access not only to the Zhuangzi but also to
parallel passages in other texts as well as lexical information. Therefore, it is
particularly useful for an intertextual reading of the Zhuangzi, which we com-
mend. It also includes cross-references to the Harvard-Yenching concordance (Zhuangzi yinde 1956), which had previously been the most common way
to refer to the source text in Western academic studies.

1. SINCERITY, AUTHENTICITY, AND ANCIENT CHINESE PHILOSOPHY

Les hommes sont toujours sincères. Ils changent de sincérité, voilà tout (Men are always sincere. They change sincerities, that's all).

—Tristan Bernard, *Ce que l'on dit aux femmes*

THE DIALECTIC OF SINCERITY AND CONFUCIAN ETHICS

Despite the considerable impact the modern Western discourse on sincerity and authenticity has had on contemporary scholarship on ancient Confucian and Daoist philosophy, Lionel Trilling's (1972) seminal and immensely influential book on this subject, *Sincerity and Authenticity*, seems to have been largely ignored by scholars in the field of Chinese philosophy (exceptions include, for instance, Blum 2007 and Chen Xunwu 2004.) Arguably, the most important work among the many inspired by or written in reaction to Trilling was Charles Taylor's (2007) *A Secular Age*, which, it is probably quite safe to say, also did not have much of an effect on the study of Chinese philosophy. Taylor's book includes a famous section on what he calls the age of authenticity, which connects with Trilling's earlier work. Along with a more recently published trade book by R. Jay Magill (2012), simply titled *Sincerity*, Trilling's and Taylor's works provide us with some of the central vocabulary for our present investigation—namely, with the notions of sincerity and authenticity. In what follows, we outline why the semantics and the ideas of sincerity and authenticity as discussed by Trilling, Taylor, and Magill are highly relevant, if not for obtaining an understanding of ancient Confucianism and Daoism "in themselves," then at least for acquiring an understanding of the history of their reception in the past one hundred years, and in the past three or four decades in particular.

We do not wish to engage here in a metadiscourse regarding the current conversation on Chinese philosophy and its often unreflected upon semantic and intellectual resources and socially conditioning contexts. Instead, our aim is to present a book on the philosophy of the *Zhuangzi* and its historical environment. However, we want to provide at least a brief overview of one of the major conceptual frameworks that has been applied explicitly and implicitly to the literature. We argue, broadly speaking, that Trilling's distinction between sincerity and authenticity reflects distinctive intellectual and cultural trends in Western modernity. These trends have also permeated modern representations of Confucian and Daoist philosophies. Confucianism has typically been understood as representing an ethics of sincerity; and we think that this understanding fits the traditional reception of Confucian ethics quite well and, in particular, the depiction of Confucianism found in the *Zhuangzi*. Correspondingly—or alternatively, however one may like to see it— Daoism and the philosophy of the *Zhuangzi* have typically been identified as representing a philosophy of authenticity; we disagree with this identification and suggest a different one: genuine pretending.

Trilling begins his reflections on the history of sincerity and authenticity with a remarkable and beautifully phrased reflection on the hermeneutics of a history of ideas. It has lost nothing of its validity and simple profundity and indeed has become only more relevant in the context of the ongoing methodological debates in comparative philosophy. For this reason, it is worth quoting in full:

> We read the Iliad or the plays of Sophocles or Shakespeare and they come so close to our hearts and minds that they put to rout, or into abeyance, our instructed consciousness of the moral life as it is conditioned by a particular culture—they persuade us that human nature never varies, that the moral life is unitary and its terms perennial, and that only a busy intruding pedantry could ever have suggested otherwise.

And then yet again, on still another view of the case, this judgment reverses itself and we find ourselves noting with eager attention all the details of assumption, thought, and behavior that distinguish the morality of one age from that of another, and it seems to us that quick and informed awareness of the differences among moral idioms is of the very essence of a proper response to literature.

This ambivalence I describe is my own as I propose the idea that at a certain point in history the moral life of Europe added to itself a new element, the state or quality of the self which we call sincerity.

(Trilling 1972, 2)

Although Trilling speaks here neither of non-Western cultures nor of philosophy but rather of Western literature, he addresses with disarming honesty the central antagonism of universalism versus relativism that still haunts what continues to be called comparative philosophy. Trilling exposes the core of the debates about contrastive or comparative approaches in East-West philosophy by indicating that the ambiguity between these poles never truly vanishes, at least not on a personal level, if one is honest with oneself— or, to put it less morally and thus probably more correctly, if one is a good reader. In the end, one has to take a leap of faith and go one way or another, either in the direction the winds are currently blowing or not. Clearly, for Trilling, sincerity is an exclusively modern (and European) phenomenon— in texts and culturally, though not psychologically or cognitively—and accordingly authenticity is too, since it develops out of sincerity. With respect to China, we make a different observation in this book, but not without feeling the very same ambiguity that he describes so aptly. We do think that it makes sense to detect, as so many authors have, more or less the same problems of sincerity that contemporary society wrangles with, if not in the *Iliad* or the plays of Sophocles, certainly in the *Analects* and the *Mencius*. But then again, our leap of faith is a split one, and we jump right back in the other direction by assuming that, unlike in modern Europe, the "dialectic of sincerity" (Kelly 2014) in ancient China did not—or at least not in the case of the *Zhuangzi*— result in the transformation of sincerity into authenticity. Instead, we argue that it took a different course toward what we call genuine pretending.

The following quotation leads us to the heart of Trilling's conception of modern Western sincerity, albeit in an indirect way, by approaching it from the perspective of a postsincerity era that has already lost its former trust in sincerity and moved beyond it. True to Hegel, whose spirit is present from the first to the last pages of *Sincerity and Authenticity*, Trilling seems to suggest that the dialectical negation of sincerity begets a more complete grasp (or *Begriff*) of its essence. After all, the "essence" (or *das Wesen*) is, as Hegel explained famously at the beginning of the "Doctrine of Essence" in his *Science of Logic*, that which is *gewesen* (or *vergangen*)—that is, that which "has been" or "is gone." Once we have critically distanced ourselves from sincerity, we understand better, in hindsight, what it has always essentially been: "If sincerity has lost its former status, if the word itself has for us a hollow sound and seems almost to negate its meaning, that is because it does not purpose being true to one's own self as an end but only as a means. If one is true to one's own self for the purpose of avoiding falsehood to others, is one being truly true to one's own self? The moral end in view implies a public end in view, with all that this suggests of the esteem and fair repute that follow upon the correct fulfillment of a public role" (Trilling 1972, 9).

Sincerity basically means "being true to one's own self" by doing what one does and saying what one says honestly. It means that one's actions and words are backed up by one's own internal feelings and convictions. At the same time, the vector of sincerity points from the inside to the outside, from one's true self with its convictions and emotions toward the public sphere, where these are represented and where they manifest themselves. This is the sense in which Trilling speaks of sincerity—in hindsight—as a *means*. The purpose of the correspondence between one's inner self and one's public persona is to support or to guarantee the latter by means of the former. The inner self legitimates the outer self. This is to say that the morality of sincerity is ultimately a public morality: its purpose is to provide a moral foundation for social agency and interchange. It allows for social trust and other components of social order such as—to use a word that is currently quite popular in China—harmony (*hexie* 和諧). This is also confirmed by the "reward" one can expect for being sincere—namely, "esteem and fair repute," which can be bestowed unto the sincere person only by others and is thus once more clearly of a social nature.

Trilling is keenly aware of the crucial importance of a word that, as he says, he initially used only coincidentally or for matters of sheer expedience but that actually turned out to be most significant for his understanding of sincerity—the word "role":

> I did not deliberately choose that last word. It came readily—"naturally"—
> to hand. We nowadays say "role" without taking thought of its original

histrionic meaning: "in my professional role," "in my paternal, or mater-
nal, role," even "in my masculine, or feminine, role." But the old histrionic meaning is present whether or not we let ourselves be aware of it,
and it brings with it the idea that somewhere under all the roles there is
Me, that poor old ultimate actuality, who, when all the roles have been
played, would like to murmur "Off, off, you lendings!" and settle down
with his own original actual self.

(Trilling 1972, 9–10)

Trilling here exposes the essential interrelatedness and interdependency of
the concept of sincerity and the wider genre of an ethics focusing on social
roles. Given the outward direction of its vector, inner sincerity is always not
only tied to but also geared toward and directed by public roles. Not without
paradox, its very point is therefore to reduce the difference it produces between
the inner self and its public role, if not to nothing, then to a minimum. Paradoxically, the "invention" of sincerity, which demands a full correspondence
between the self and its role, creates the very split between inner self and
outer self that is supposed to be resolved by reinstating conformity between
the two. The demand for conformity produces an awareness of a distinction
that could not have been communicated, and so become socially relevant,
without that very demand in the first place.

The notion of sincerity implies that our concrete social personae, the persona of a father, mother, teacher, and so forth, are not merely a theatrical
impersonation, not merely histrionic, as Trilling says, or played. The "original
paradox" of the notion of sincerity—that it produces the split between an
inner self and an outer self that it then purports to close—is mirrored in the
wider conceptions of a relational ethics, no matter if it demands a full identity
between personhood and roles[1] or if it allows for the two to remain distinct
as long as they are in sincere congruence (as for many Confucian thinkers, including, for instance, Tu Weiming[2]). An ethics focused on roles or relations presupposes a division between persons and their roles and relations
and then demands that the role or relation does not merely remain a role (or
relation) but becomes a true expression of the person as well. Once "father" or
"teacher" is understood to refer to a role that one plays, one is asked to play it
sincerely and therefore no longer only to play it. The "old histrionic meaning"
of a role is supposed to be transformed into a new ethical meaning of a sincerely adopted or expressed or—in more radical versions of Confucianism—
lived role (see Ames 2011, 96). In short, and reiterating what we said in our

introduction, what interests us in a reading of Confucian ethics as relational or role oriented is not the now much-debated question of whether this conception does or does not allow for autonomous agency (though we do not think that this question had much influence on the *Zhuangzi*) but rather that in any case it has been typically understood as prescribing sincerity.

Regarding the task of establishing personal identity, the notion of sincerity presents as much a solution as a problem. And the same is the case for an ethics that is tied to it. But, of course, from a Hegelian perspective, this could not be otherwise and is by no means a unique property of sincerity but of all formations of the spirit; however, since we are not writing a book on Hegel, we will not pursue this issue any further. Instead, we return to Trilling and his discovery of the "Me" that the idea of sincerity inserts into ethics and that also imbues it with a fundamental and irresolvable suspicion: if I fulfill my roles properly, am I playing them insincerely or am I sincerely enacting them? The distinction between the self and its role is the semantic condition and social framework of the moral distinction between sincerity and insincerity. The categorical demand for sincerity breeds an equally categorical suspicion of insincerity. Or, in the logic of the *Daodejing*, sincerity and insincerity generate each other. You cannot have one without the other.

When the Me is burdened with a constant effort to "make sincere" (*cheng zhi* 誠之) a role it finds itself *facing*—or, in other words, when it is asked to constantly make sincere a social face that is imposed on it—it may eventually become fatigued. At some point, it can no longer play the teacher or the father convincingly for others and may feel that it has failed as a true teacher or father. In the end, it may cease to believe in its identification with its social role. The latent and unavoidable inbuilt suspicion of insincerity cannot be voiced only by society but also by the Me against itself. It can become the subject and object of this suspicion. And at this very point it can finally cry out in desperation, to quote Trilling, "Off, off, you lendings!" When the "dialectic of sincerity" has come full circle, the Me tires of the constant suspicion it is exposed to and has a fortiori been led to inwardly adopt and practice. It wants to shed its roles altogether, to return to itself from its alienation (if we may speak once more in Hegelian terms) and to *come back to its true self on its own*. At this point the Me reverses the vector of sincerity with a strenuous effort of self-empowerment and points it toward itself. It revolts against and negates the whole role and relational ethics framework along with its ethics of sincerity and replaces it with the new notion of *authenticity*, so that a new ethics of individual uniqueness and freedom is born. In early Confucianism as it is represented in the *Zhuangzi*, this turning of the vector that transforms sincerity into authenticity did not take place. But according to Trilling, it did take place in Western modernity and led to, as Taylor would put it, a new "age of authenticity."

The turning of the vector begins with an inversion of the suspicion of insincerity; that is to say, it begins when the self no longer questions its true commitment to its roles but rather questions if any commitment to a role can ever be true. It is asked if the quest for sincerity implies a betrayal of the self: Doesn't the commitment of the self to a role other than itself betray the essence of this very self? Or, in the new language of authenticity, is it not the case that "a judgment may be passed upon our sincerity that it is not authentic?" (Trilling 1972, 11). Or, to use a previously quoted formulation by Trilling, "If one is true to one's own self for the purpose of avoiding falsehood to others, is one being truly true to one's own self?" Being true to one's own self should be an end itself and not just a means of achieving public honesty, order, trust, or harmony. The self must be cultivated not by sincerely becoming its roles but also, to the contrary, by revolting against social hierarchies or orders that may suppress it. By liberating itself from a determination by its roles the self sets itself free, transcends its roles, and creates and re-creates true and independent selfhood and autonomy.

Trilling illustrates the revolt against a role and relational ethics of sincerity and the breakthrough toward a new ethics of authenticity with a subtle discussion of Hegel's "creative" interpretation of Diderot's dialogue *Le neveu de Rameau* (Rameau's nephew), as found in a section of the *Phenomenology of Spirit* on the "world of self-alienated spirit" ("Die Welt des sich entfremdeten Geistes"). To cut short Trilling's rather complex readings of Diderot through Hegel, it suffices to say that these readings revolve around the character of Rameau, whom Trilling (1972, 44) describes as a "buffoon, flattering parasite, compulsive mimic, without a self to be true to." In the dialogue, Rameau stands in sharp contrast to the character of Diderot himself, who represents— in Hegel's terminology—the "honest consciousness" of an ethics of sincerity. Rameau, the "compulsive mimic," is a thoroughly insincere character. His blatant nonconformity with the imperative to fulfill one's roles honestly is highlighted by one of his "operatic performances," which culminates in a "momentous abandonment of individuated selfhood to become all the voices of human existence, of all existence" (44). The description of Rameau's performance, which both Trilling and Hegel quote at length, has him singing in all kinds of different styles, moods, social roles, and the like. He can impersonate any role while not identifying with it. Thereby he not only flatly contradicts but also mocks the attitude of the "honest soul" represented by the narrator, Moi (Me), and consequently appears as a "scornful nihilist" (29).

According to Trilling, the dialogue is ambiguous in meaning and can be read in at least two ways. "In its first intention," Trilling says, it "passes a direct and comprehensively adverse moral judgment upon society. It lays bare the principle of insincerity upon which society is based and demonstrates the loss of personal integrity and dignity that the impersonations of social existence entail" (Trilling 1972, 31). Read in this way, the dialogue criticizes society for having corrupted sincerity, and Rameau represents this corrupted sincerity. Me, the "honest soul" in the dialogue, is accordingly the "good guy," and the whole work becomes a moralist denunciation of insincerity and amounts to a call to restore true sincerity in society and in ourselves. Trilling, however, does not sympathize with such a reading and thinks (and we agree) that neither did Hegel. He therefore elaborates on a "second intention, which is to suggest that moral judgment is not ultimate, that man's nature and destiny are not wholly comprehended within the narrow space between virtue and vice. From this comes the sensation of enlargement, of delighted liberation, that the dialogue affords" (32). Seen from this perspective, Rameau represents the first stage in the revolt against the inauthenticity of sincerity. He is not merely a nihilist but suffers from the impossible demand of a moralistic sincerity that stifles true uniqueness, creativity, and the independence of the self. He represents the "disintegrated consciousness" that has been produced by a role-based ethics of sincerity and exposes the latter as "regressive and retrospective" (47). His performative rebellion against sincerity—its negation— is essential for self-consciousness, or spirit, "if it is to develop its true, its entire, freedom" (47).

Read according to its second intention, *Rameau's Nephew* is a call to arms against a modern Western role and relational ethics and the first breakthrough in the development that leads to a replacement of a moralist focus on sincerity with one on authenticity. Summarizing Trilling's distinction between sincerity and authenticity, Orlando Patterson (2006) has defined the first intention as requiring "us to act and really be the way that we present ourselves to others," and the second as aimed at "finding and expressing the true inner self and judging all relationships in terms of it." Very much in line with this definition, Rameau ceases to strive to really be the way that he presents himself to others. According to Trilling and Hegel, he thereby paves the way for a new quest that will eventually allow people, and specifically artists like him, to express their true self and judge all their relationships, and consequently their social involvement, on the basis of this newly acquired authenticity. The reversed trajectory of the new ethics of authenticity as opposed to one of sincerity is summed up by Allen Kelly (2014), who writes, "The goal of authenticity is self-examination rather than other-directed communication."

For Charles Taylor, the revolt against an ethics of sincerity as described by Trilling has led to nothing less than a whole age of authenticity that has deeply shaped modern philosophy, particularly in the forms of existentialism, literature, art, and politics but also "culture" more generally. Taylor (2007, 473) speaks of "a widespread 'expressive' individualism" and a "culture of 'authenticity' " consisting of an "understanding of life . . . that each of us has his/her own way of realizing our humanity, and that it is important to find and live out one's own, as against surrendering to conformity with a model imposed on us from outside, by society, or the previous generation, or religious or political authority" (475). Taylor himself is basically sympathetic to this age he finds himself in. However, as many before and after him, he is also very much aware that authenticity, too—just as its historical predecessor, sincerity—is dialectically challenged and challengeable, and so he suggests his own *Ethics of Authenticity* (1992) in order to set it morally straight. He intends, on the one hand, to preserve the Enlightenment values of freedom and autonomy that are entailed therein but also to shield it against selfish individualism and the antisocial tendencies that come with it. Accordingly, he distinguishes between legitimate and illegitimate strains of authenticity and, in line with the current mainstream view on the benefits and harms of authenticity, states with analytic precision that, "authenticity (A) involves (i) creation and construction as well as discovery, (ii) originality, and frequently (iii) opposition to the rules of society and even potentially to what we recognize as morality. But it is also true, as we saw, that it (B) requires (i) openness to horizons of significance (for otherwise the creating loses the background that can save it from insignificance) and (ii) a self-definition in dialogue. That these demands may be in tension has to be allowed. But what must be wrong is a simple privileging of one over the other, of (A), say, at the expense of (B), or vice versa" (66).

We refrain from addressing such normative claims about what one ought to do in an age of authenticity; again, this is not our topic. The point we are

interested in here is that the very same debates about sincerity in role and relational ethics and its counterpart, an individualist ethics of authenticity, can be
found in contemporary discussions of ancient Chinese philosophy. When
Roger Ames and Henry Rosemont Jr. described ancient Confucianism as a role
ethics in line with a morality based on sincerity, they were, by proxy, confronted with the same criticisms that an ethics of sincerity has faced in modern intellectual history: If we look at Confucianism as a role ethics, do we not
thereby ascribe to it a lack of authenticity by tying the self completely to its
roles? Do we not thereby imply that Confucianism lags behind our age of
authenticity? Don't we therefore have an intellectual obligation to do our best
to find something corresponding to authenticity in Confucianism—some
notion of the individual *independent* of its roles? Isn't it our duty to accordingly
modernize Confucianism?

Criticisms of Confucian ethics seeking to move it beyond "mere" sincerity come from various positions. One that is dominated by contemporary
scholars working mainly in English and represented, for example, by Steve
Angle, maintains that Confucianism represents a type of virtue ethics.
According to Angle social roles on their own cannot provide suitable criteria
for either establishing or judging moral behavior. Angle (2012, 106) suggests
that the way to remedy this problem is to accept the idea of moral character or
agency outside roles and embraces what he calls agent-centered virtue ethics. May Sim (2007, 135) also wants to identify a Confucian self beyond its mere
role identity because "the Confucian self, if entirely relationistic, cannot function as a locus of choice and agency." In other words, there must be a self that
is not entirely tied to or lived through social roles.

Another line of critique is found in the work of some contemporary Chinese scholars who are seeking to modernize and universalize Confucian
ethics. While there is general agreement about the importance of understanding the person (and morality) through roles and relations,[3] there is hesitation
over what is often seen as a complete reduction to social determinations. With
regard to moral theory, Chinese academics often simply shrug their shoulders
(even though Chinese rarely shrug their shoulders and often do not know what
doing so signifies) at the apparent redundancy of the Mandarin translation of
the term "role ethics" (*juese lunli* 角色倫理), simply because, from their perspective, ethics are by definition role based: lunli 倫理, or "ethics," literally
means "patterns" or "coherence" (li 理) of relationships (lun 倫). At the same
time many thinkers, such as Tu Weiming (see Tu, forthcoming), point out that

the self should not be entirely accounted for by its social roles. Yang Guorong 楊國榮 argues that the self is "a bearer of universal duties" that are "constrained by legal and social contracts" but not limited therein (Yang Guorong 2011, 272). Li Zehou 李澤厚 (2011) and Chen Lai 陳來 (2014, 2015) place an emphasis on social roles and their related virtues as instruments for cultivating the self but not as exclusively binding for self-identification.[4] Liu Qingping 劉清平 (2009, 173) suggests that multiple roles are integrated in the person but differentiates between a person's individual and social dimensions (2003).

On the other hand, Ames and Rosemont (as well as many others) defend a traditional Confucian role ethics of sincerity by pointing to how it counters the "illegitimate" vices of our age of authenticity (as described in part by Taylor in the foregoing); or they imply that it can become a resource for what Kelly (2010) has called a postauthentic New Sincerity. In other words, a Confucian ethics, precisely because of its focus on sincerity, can be recommended as a much-needed antidote to the overly individualistic excesses of authenticity. Henry Rosemont Jr. has been particularly vocal in this area. In his most recent book, informatively and provocatively titled *Against Individualism: A Confucian Rethinking of the Foundation of Morality, Politics, Family, and Religion*, Rosemont (2015) argues that many contemporary sociopolitical problems can be addressed by understanding oneself and others through roles and relations. Otherwise, Rosemont contends, it is difficult to establish new visions of social justice. By sincerely identifying with social roles, people are able to take on their duties to others as part of the process of self-making; or, in more familiar terms, as becoming who they are. Individualist notions of "being who you are" only threaten to further deteriorate today's already thin moral fabric. Rosemont states very clearly that an emphasis on the importance of roles need not entail the adoption of an altogether different set of values but rather "having different orderings of values" (21). Modern Western value orderings tend to portray the individual as isolated from social contexts, which implies that responsibilities toward others are mainly negative—that is, they are rooted in noninterference, which implies that one has little obligation to actively help others. Rosemont stresses this: "*To whatever extent we may be seen to be morally and thus politically responsible for assisting others in the creation and obtaining of those goods which accrue to them by virtue of having social and economic rights, to just that extent we cannot be altogether autonomous individuals, enjoying full civil and political rights, free to rationally decide upon and pursue our own projects rather than having to assist the less fortunate with theirs*" (66; emphasis in the original).

Insofar as authenticity fosters a strong sense of an independent individuality, it may give rise to a malignant ethics that ignores the relationships that contribute to our identity and through which we must form binding moral commitments. However, if Confucianism indeed represents an ethics of sincerity and, for better or worse, resists transformation into an ethics of authenticity, can we not perhaps detect an early Chinese tradition outside Confucianism that complemented it historically by coming up with such an ethics of authenticity? Can we perhaps identify a constellation in ancient China that mirrors the structures of contemporary debates in moral philosophy? And if we identify such a philosophy, don't we have to criticize its "illegitimate branches" too, just as Taylor criticized aspects of the current age of authenticity? As it turns out, this is very much what happened in recent scholarship on early Chinese philosophy. The ethics of authenticity in ancient Chinese philosophy has often been identified with Daoism, and as one might expect, a rich literature on how to understand texts such as the *Zhuangzi* as representatives of a philosophy of authenticity—along with potential lines of critical evaluations or apologetics—has sprung up in recent decades.

AUTHENTICITY, IRONY, AND DAOISM

In order to understand how the *Zhuangzi* could be interpreted as an "authentic" alternative to Confucian sincerity, it is prudent to first provide a brief account of the current semantics of authenticity and, in particular, of its relation to the notion or attitude of irony. In his insightful essay on the "Dialectic of Sincerity," Adam Kelly (2014) addresses in detail the complex relation between authenticity and irony as contemporary counterparts of an ethics of sincerity. Irony, as Kelly rightfully criticizes, "is only a very minor player in the grand dialectical opposition Trilling constructs between sincerity and authenticity"; but he immediately—and rightfully—excuses Trilling for this inevitable oversight, since in the early 1970s "Trilling could not at that historical moment anticipate the extent to which irony would emerge as postmodernism's dominant mode."

The emergence of modern Western irony as distinct from ancient forms of irony (such as, perhaps most important, Socratic irony) predates the advent of postmodernity and is usually associated with the Romantic age and its so-called Romantic irony. As a result, "irony may well be tied up with the long history of Western subjectivism: the idea that behind language, actions, difference and communication there is a ground or subject to be expressed" (Colebrook 2004, 20; quoted in Kelly 2014). In Romantic irony, the subject is confronted with a world that essentially transcends and escapes its attempts to rationalize it. The subject thereby experiences its own contingency and limitations through this dissonance and copes with it by creatively express-ing itself through literature, art, and philosophy. It develops its own subjectiv-ity in the continuous ironic undertaking to express and grasp the ineffable. Therefore, Romantic irony can be understood in apophatic terms (see Franke 2014) as a philosophy that realizes, or brings to consciousness, the limits of its own "sayability" and that through this very process makes "aesthetics become the measure of metaphysics" (Weinrich 1976, 579).

With this conception of irony in mind, Rameau, the mimic, could once more in hindsight also be understood "in a third intention." It is possible to also conceive of him as an early Romantic ironist whose aesthetic perfor-mance reflects an infinite aesthetic exercise of expressing and thereby creating oneself in experiencing the infinite possibilities of an ever-changing subjec-tivity. In this sense, Rameau would foreshadow a postmodernist irony and be an early instantiation of Richard Rorty's (1989) ironist who "employs irony as a tool of self-fashioning" (Kelly 2014). The Romantic ironist, as well as Rorty's postmodernist variation of the ironist, withdraws from social con-straints and moral obligations that surround them and see through their con-tingency. They distance themselves from contingent social norms and roles and no longer take seriously the obligation to be sincere. They doubt the ulti-mate validity of anything in particular. The Romantic as well as Rorty's ironist becomes an aesthete who retreats from the social into the private and experi-ments with and engages in continuous self-transformation and self-creation.

As can be concluded from both Kelly's (2014) and Magill's (2012) analyses, the ironic attitude, the playful distancing from a sincere engagement with social roles and norms for the sake of independent self-creation and self-transformation, represents a more recent evolution of the authenticity paradigm. It has become the new antithesis of sincerity. In today's popular culture, it consists in an often slightly humorous and paradoxical engagement with politics, fashion, or art, where one aims at proving one's uniqueness and individuality by being creative, special, and different. Magill (2014) writes, "Irony, or the ironic attitude . . . takes nothing very seriously—especially superficial things—inverts or changes meanings and symbols, and prides itself on aristocratic remove from the world. It believes in the power of dis-tance. It is an absolutely integral and necessary part of modern culture and of a mature, educated democratic population. It is what allows for skepticism and mental remove from everyday life, and what helps safeguard against the effects of propaganda and ideology." Irony defined in this manner can be seen as the younger brother of authenticity. It is, so to speak, an authenticity-related irony, and in conjunction with the authenticity paradigm it, too, has exerted a considerable influence on the semantics of contemporary interpretations of Daoism (see Youru Wang 2003 and Ziporyn 2012).

At first sight, both the Romantic and the postmodern ironist share much in common with the Daoist genuine pretender. Rorty (1989, 73–74) lists three central characteristics of the ironist:

(1) She has radical and continuing doubts about the final vocabulary she currently uses, because she has been impressed by other vocabularies, vocabularies taken as final by people or books she has encountered; (2) she realizes that arguments phrased in her present vocabulary can neither underwrite nor dissolve these doubts; (3) insofar as she philosophizes about her situation, she does not think that her vocabulary is closer to reality than others, that it is in touch with a power not herself. Ironists who are inclined to philosophize see the choice between vocabularies as made neither within a neutral and universal meta-vocabulary nor by an attempt to fight one's way past appearances to the real, but simply by playing the new off the old.

Rorty further explains what an ironist is: "I call people of this sort 'ironists' because their realization that anything can be made to look good or bad by being redescribed, and their renunciation of the attempt to formulate criteria of choice between final vocabularies, puts them in the position which Sartre called 'meta-stable': never quite able to take themselves seriously because they are always aware that the terms in which they describe themselves are subject to change, always aware of the contingency and fragility of their final vocabularies, and thus of their selves" (74).

These words betray some rather striking similarities between the ironist and the genuine pretender: a realization of contingence, an appreciation of humor, and an emphasis on distancing. At the same time, however, there are some differences that should warn us away from conflating Rorty's ironist and the genuine pretender. And these differences lie in their respective relation to autonomy and authenticity. As the historical successor of the authentic self, the ironist represents an effort toward self-creation and the aspiration toward unique individuality. This becomes clear in the following statement by Rorty (1989, 97):

> The last thing the ironist theorist wants or needs is a theory of ironism. He is not in the business of supplying himself and his fellow ironists with a method, a platform, or a rationale. He is just doing the same thing which all ironists do—attempting autonomy. He is trying to get out from under inherited contingencies and make his own contingencies, get out from under an old final vocabulary and fashion one which will be all his own. The generic trait of ironists is that they do not hope to have their doubts about their final vocabularies settled by something larger than themselves. This means that that their criterion for resolving doubts, their criterion of private perfection, is autonomy rather than affiliation to a power other than themselves. All any ironist can measure success against is the past—not by living up to it, but by redescribing it in his terms, thereby becoming able to say, "Thus I willed it."

Given Trilling's and Taylor's broader concept of authenticity, we suggest that it is fair to classify the autonomy Rorty ascribes to the ironist as a variation of authenticity. But we think that the genuine pretender of the *Zhuangzi* is better understood independently of the notions of authenticity and autonomy and thus also in part independently—namely, with respect to these two ingredients—of Rorty's ironist. The genuine pretender signals a different endeavor that leads historically not to modern Western existentialism and postmodernism but to the philosophies and practices of the so-called neo-Daoism of the Wei-Jin 魏晉 period and of Chinese forms of Buddhism such as, in particular, Tiantai 天台 and Chan 禪.

Expanding on our earlier (rhetorical) question, if one finds strong notions of authenticity in Daoism or the *Zhuangzi*, then should one not also expect that the age of authenticity would be similar to neo-Daoism and Chinese Buddhism? In other words, if the *Zhuangzi* did in fact promote authenticity, at least as Trilling and Taylor describe it, wouldn't contemporary Western society be rehashing intellectual and cultural issues of China's past? The trajectory that Chinese culture did in fact take shows, we believe, that the genuine pretender represents not a quest for self-creation but a quest for self-dissolution. As opposed to some later Buddhist and Daoist traditions, in early Daoism this quest takes place in an entirely mundane and intrasocial context (see Wang Bo 2014 and Jia 2015). No "mental remove from everyday life" is pursued.

Rather than being concerned with becoming special and unique, a genuine pretender hopes to maintain health and sanity, to survive in difficult times, and, as much as possible, to become a smooth operator cultivating excellence and experiencing pleasure while rambling through life. There is humor and irony, too, to be found in the genuine pretender, for sure; but this humor and irony is neither fully Romantic nor Rortian; instead, one may call it a form of "idiotic irony" (Moeller 2008).

The Daoist answer to a Confucian ethics and its dialectic of sincerity, we suggest, thus differs from both modern and postmodern solutions to this dialectic. This does not mean that there are no parallels at all. One could easily construct a bridge between the postmodernist ironist envisioned by Rorty and the genuine pretender, especially insofar as both recognize contingencies and refuse to prioritize their own views and vocabularies over and above others. This bridge would perhaps lead the modern ironist away from self-creation and the genuine pretender away from selflessness, such that they would meet somewhere in the middle; but for now we are not sure where exactly that meeting point would be. If they ever were to meet, though, they would probably read *Rameau's Nephew* in such a way that the titular character would be seen as a synthesis of a modern Western ironist and an ancient Daoist genuine pretender. But be that as it may, it is not our purpose here to speculate on such matters any further.

Before we move on to read the *Zhuangzi* from the perspective of genuine pretending beyond sincerity and authenticity, we take a closer look at the authenticity-oriented interpretations of the *Zhuangzi*, which serve as a backdrop for our approach and supply it with a hermeneutic contrast.

ON THE ASCRIPTION OF AUTHENTICITY
TO THE ZHUANGZI

Many contemporary interpretations of the *Zhuangzi*, especially those ascribing particular importance to the notion of *zhen* 真 (authentic, true, or genuine) and the related terms *zhenren* 真人 (authentic/true/genuine person) and *zhenzhi* 真知 (authentic/true/genuine knowledge), rely upon a modern understanding of authenticity and thus reflect the general semantics of Taylor's "age of authenticity." While it is not our intention to assess the accuracy of comparisons between existentialism and Daoism, we do want to point out that the notion of authenticity ascribed to Daoist texts, and especially the *Zhuangzi*, is generally imported from ideas found in the writings of thinkers such as Martin Heidegger, Friedrich Nietzsche, or Søren Kierkegaard (see D'Ambrosio 2015). Heidegger's concept of authenticity (*Eigentlichkeit*) is perhaps the frontrunner in these discussions and has provided a widely used conceptual and terminological framework for interpreting a variety of Daoist texts.

In his *Being and Time*, Heidegger famously develops what Theodor W. Adorno has critically labeled a *Jargon der Eigentlichkeit* (jargon of authenticity; Adorno 1964). *Eigen*, the first part of the German word *Eigentlichkeit*, means "own," or "specific." *Eigentlich* is a common word meaning "specifically," "actually," or "originally." It is turned into a noun by adding the nominalizing suffix *keit*. We can thus understand *Eigentlichkeit*/authenticity as a kind of "originalness" or "ownness." For Heidegger, *Eigentlichkeit*/authenticity is achieved largely through consciously taking into account aspects of one's own historicity, including the disposition to moods and commitments, and one's social context. Awareness of these concrete conditions allows one to "own" actions, thoughts, and feelings. This enables the individual to avoid simply falling (*verfallen*) into the average everydayness of the "they" (*das Man*). An individual who becomes conscious of "being-with" (*Mitsein*) others or the "they" understands that this simultaneously constrains and constitutes authenticity. One's potential is limited by this being-with if one allows oneself to simply live in modes of being that only mirror others or the they. Such an unreflective being-with is averageness or inauthenticity that simply follows the they and "falls away from itself as an authentic potentiality for Being its self" (Heidegger 1962, 220). The individual thereby gives up ownness. Heidegger explains,

> In utilizing public means of transport and in making use of information services such as the newspaper, every Other is like the next. This Being-with-one-another dissolves one's own Dasein [i.e., the individual] completely into a kind of Being of "the Others," in such a way, indeed, that the Others, as distinguishable and explicit, vanish more and more. In this inconspicuousness and unascertainability, the real dictatorship of the "they" is unfolded. We take pleasure and enjoy ourselves as *they* take pleasure; we read, see, and judge about literature and art as *they* see and judge; likewise we shrink back from the "great mass" as *they* shrink back; we find "shocking" what *they* find shocking. The "they," which is nothing definite, and which all are, though not as the sum, prescribes the kind of Being of everydayness.
>
> (164)

Heidegger's argument here is that people are often in an inauthentic mode of being-with where they do not own their behavior. Being-with-others can easily deteriorate into simply living up to, or sincerely subscribing to, social expectations, values, and roles. To be authentic, which includes owning one's actions, is defined largely in contrast to being-with, "being of everydayness," and the they. Heidegger's description of ownness has informed the ways in which many contemporary commentators have analyzed the *Zhuangzi*, especially where the latter seems to highlight or extol the unique thinking and behavior of its protagonists, characteristics that set them apart from common social or role expectations. The ancient Daoist text is thus often read as commending individual or authentic expression and creativity in contrast to the mere performance of socially prescribed practices.

Reflecting the popularity of Heidegger's philosophy along with the popularity of authenticity-based values such as uniqueness and creativity, the term *zhen* is often translated as or associated with authenticity. Relatedly, the age of authenticity mantra "being true to oneself" is also commonly used to explain what *zhen* means in the *Zhuangzi*. For Steve Coutinho, *zhen* represents a synthesis of sincerity and authenticity. He writes, " 'Zhen' can refer to what a thing is in its innermost nature, and also has connotations of truth: being true to oneself, or authenticity, and being true to others, or sincerity" (2013, 35). Coutinho's teacher, Roger Ames, offers a similar understanding in his description of *zhenren* as the "authentic person" who is "being true to oneself" with a "primacy given to the creative contribution of the particular person" (Ames 1998, 2). Others are more explicit in referencing thinkers taken to be existentialist; for example, Daniel Coyle (1998, 199) writes, "*zhen*, as implemented in the *Zhuangzi*, denotes 'authenticity' within a transforming world, genuineness in the Nietzschean sense of being true to oneself."

In contemporary Chinese scholarship on the *Zhuangzi*, the term *benzhen* 本真 is typically used to signify the notion of authenticity in a Heideggerian sense. It is often used along with another, more common word, *zhenzheng* 真正, meaning "genuine," to render *zhen*. This clearly shows how *zhen* in the *Zhuangzi* tends to be understood in terms of authenticity. Ren Fuxin 任付新 (2013, 50), for instance, says that the philosophies of both Heidegger and the *Zhuangzi* express "the way of *benzhen*." Luo Linhui 羅琳會 (2003, 14) remarks that both Heidegger and Chinese Daoism are "strongly concerned with the authentic self [*benwo* 本我] and authenticity [*benzhen*]." Na Wei 那微 (2003, 115) contends that the *Zhuangzi* is concerned with the same type of "authentic existence" (*benzhen cunzai* 本真存在) found in Heidegger. Na distinguishes, on the one hand, the "*zhen* person," and the essentially identical "utmost person" (zhiren 至人), "spiritual person" (shenren 神人), and the "sage" (shengren 聖人) from, on the other hand, "common people" (changren 常人), saying that the former are "authentic" (benzhen), while the latter are not. Additionally, Na borrows the Heideggerian notion of "openness" (changkai 敞開) to the world that defines Dasein to describe the zhen person.

Authenticity and *benzhen* are not only introduced as equivalents or translations of *zhen* but also provide, with important philosophical repercussions, interpretative models for explaining various other aspects of the *Zhuangzi*. Chris Fraser (2011, 115), for example, identifies the relationship between nature and the human as "perhaps the fundamental problematic of Daoist philosophy" and argues that negotiating this relationship well means living an "authentic human life" (112). Accordingly, the terms "wandering" (you 遊) and "virtuosity" (de 德) in the *Zhuangzi*, which refer to the effective interaction between humans and nature, are understood in conjunction with Heidegger's notion of authenticity (112).

Fraser (2014, 551) also sets out to resolve a potential conflict between the conceptions of wandering and virtuosity in the *Zhuangzi* and the capacity for human agency and rich emotional experience by relying on a Heideggerian framework. Insofar as wandering may preclude any fixed or predetermined goals or norms in its "continual adaption to change," it may be seen as posing a challenge to the concept of intentional agency. Emotional experiences may be denied to a person when the *Zhuangzi* calls for "not injuring one's body internally by means of likes and dislikes, constantly going by what is self-so without adding to life" (Zhuangzi 5.6; quoted in Fraser 2014, 560). However, for Fraser (2011, 100), authentic Daoist virtuosos are by no means "utterly emotionless." Instead, Fraser supplies the ideal, authentic Daoist individual—or, as he calls it, the "Zhuangzist Virtuoso View"—with agency and emotions by importing Heidegger's concept of *Sorge*, or "care." Care is, Heidegger argues, an essential feature of the ontological structure of being. According to Fraser, the sage or virtuoso in the *Zhuangzi* shows "care"-like emotional commitments. Fraser classifies both the *Zhuangzi* and Heidegger as proponents of an "authentic exercise of agency" on the basis of a care that allows one to own one's conditional endeavors and create a self (120). Fraser illustrates this with his own writing process as an example of the interrelatedness of care and cultivating authenticity: "This project is meaningful to me. My commitment to it and related projects forms part of my self-identity" (111).

For Katrin Froese (2007, 58–59), the *Zhuangzi* "encourage[s] the reader to look at things from his or her own perspective, and therefore help[s] to create an authentic, lived relationship with the world." While she acknowledges important differences between existentialist thinkers and Daoism—for instance by noting that the *Laozi* and *Zhuangzi* do not "share [Heidegger's] preoccupation with 'ownness' and maintaining the self" (72)—this does not prohibit her from using Heideggerian terminology in her expositions of Daoist philosophy. In particular, she finds a common denominator between Daoism and Heidegger in a fundamental ontological authenticity: "Laozi and Zhuangzi . . . maintain that authenticity necessitates attunement to the Dao, just as Heidegger insists that authenticity be grounded in Being" (72).

Contemporary Chinese scholars have drawn similar conclusions regarding the parallels between Dao in the *Zhuangzi* and Heidegger's Being. A search in the academic section of the search engine Baidu 百度 reveals more than three hundred peer-reviewed articles that include both "Zhuangzi" and "Heidegger" in their titles or subtitles. Many of these articles have keywords such as *dao* 道, "Being" (*cunzai* 存在), "wandering" (*xiao yao you* 逍遙遊), "authenticity" (*benzhen*), and "authentic self" (*benwo* 本我). Typically, these publications compare the notion of Dao in the *Zhuangzi* with Heidegger's Being and explain Daoist wandering and *zhen* with reference to an existentialist authenticity, or *benzhen*.

The trend to supplement Daoist philosophy with existentialist concepts like "freedom" (*ziyou* 自由 [see, e.g., Chen Guying 2008 and Bao 2004]), "unique mode of human existence" (*dute de rensheng cunzai fangshi* 獨特的人生存在方式 [see, e.g., Wang Limei 2002, 66]), and "creating one's self" (*cheng qi zishen* 成其自身 [see, e.g., Na 2005, 27]), all of which are related to authenticity, can be traced back to Chen Guying's annotated versions of the *Laozi* and *Zhuangzi* (1983a and 1983b, respectively), which have been required reading in numerous Chinese higher education programs for many years. According to Chen, Daoists and existentialists alike critically reflect on social norms and values to make room for the individual to develop and find inspiration outside the limits of cultural conscriptions. In recent lectures, Chen has identified parallels between the writings of the *Zhuangzi* and Nietzsche's negative attitude toward the "herd mentality," arguing that both philosophies encourage one to develop a sense of individual identity that transcends social roles and thus traditional forms of sincerity. Therefore, the *Zhuangzi* is seen as challenging Confucian sincerity with a call for authenticity in a way reminiscent of Nietzsche's own challenge against Christianity. Chen claims that his approach to the *Zhuangzi* continues the work of a previous generation of Chinese scholars, including Chen Duxiu 陳獨秀, Lu Xun 魯迅, and Li Dazhao 李大釗, all of whom, according to Chen, were heavily influenced by existentialist ideas of "liberation of personality" (*gexing jiefang* 個性解放) and "spiritual freedom" (*jingshen ziyou* 精神自由 [Chen Guying 2008, 434]). As Chen sees it, the *Zhuangzi* in particular emphasizes the importance of individual liberty and spiritual freedom in its criticisms of Confucian (sincerity) values (481–82).

Following in the footsteps of Chen Guying, Ge Ling Shang (2007, 130) argues that the *zhen* person in the *Zhuangzi* represents an even more radical idea of selfhood than does Nietzsche's *Übermensch*. Shang defines self-overcoming as a self-creation enticing one "to be yourself and a creator of yourself" (130). According to Shang, such aspirations toward authenticity can already be found in the ancient Daoist classic—but in purer form than even that found in Nietzsche.

Chen Xunwu (2004) paints with a wider brush than Shang but makes essentially the same claim about self-creation as a central idea in the *Zhuangzi*. He finds evidence for notions of authenticity not only in the *Zhuangzi* but even in Confucianism. Chen thinks that, for Confucians, authenticity has to do with "self-identity and self-creation," whereas for Daoists it is "an issue of how to live with the *dao*, not with culture, and how to have individual freedom and happiness" (33). Living in accordance with Dao not only leads to authenticity but, as Chen says, even to "universal truth": "For Zhuangzi, authenticity means living in truth. Living in truth means living in the universal truth" (82).

Eske Møllgaard's interpretation of the *Zhuangzi* also incorporates a Nietzschean conception of authenticity. In *An Introduction to Daoist Thought*, Møllgaard discusses the famous story of the master swimmer who is able to dive into a waterfall that even fish and turtles avoid (*Zhuangzi* 19.12). In his comments on the philosophical significance of the swimmer's explanation of his marvelous skill, Møllgaard (2011, 62) points to Nietzsche, saying that "when the swimmer says that he 'comes to completion in the destined' (*cheng hu ming* 成乎命), then this should be understood in something like the sense of Nietzsche's injunction to 'become who you are.'" Clearly, this remark itself reflects the values and language of the age of authenticity.

In sum, we contend that the predominance of associating authenticity with the *Zhuangzi*—either as a translation of the central term *zhen* or as a general interpretative framework representing the spirit of the text—occurs in the context of the age of authenticity as described by Taylor and Trilling. Against the background of this zeitgeist, it seems only natural to assume that Confucianism represents a philosophy of sincerity and Daoism, as its counterpart, a move toward authenticity. In this book we explore other alternatives. We thereby question whether the dialectic of sincerity must necessarily lead to authenticity, or if other possible reactions to the problems inherent in an ethics of sincerity exist.

By searching for an alternative to authenticity in the notion of genuine pretending, we'd like to reiterate that we do not wish to discuss the extent to which various existentialist or Heideggerian readings of the *Zhuangzi* are warranted. *By no means do we intend to claim that Daoism and existentialism are essentially incompatible or that comparisons between, for instance, Heidegger and Daoism are fruitless or invalid.* However, in our view, a shift of direction may be in order: one suggestion would be to try to read more *Zhuangzi* into Nietzsche and Heidegger rather than vice versa and thus to "reorient" (Maraldo 2012) the two German thinkers a bit. With respect to Nietzsche, the scholars who have ventured the furthest in this direction are, among others, Graham Parkes (2013) and Günter Wohlfart (1999) (see van der Braak 2011 and Moeller 2004b) and, with respect to Heidegger, Shi Ying Zhang (1992), Eric Nelson (2004), John Maraldo (2012) and Graham Parkes (1987). Through such readings, one may end up not only with a *zhen* person without authenticity but also with an *Übermensch* and even a Dasein without authenticity—but it is for others to judge if such projects may be worthwhile.

In this book, we present an alternative view of the *Zhuangzi* and conceive of *zhen* as a form of genuine pretending that permeates its philosophy. Unlike authenticity, genuine pretending neither engages in essentialist self-constructions nor emphasizes the uniqueness of the person (although it also does not reject uniqueness). As we intend to show, a genuine pretender realizes that his or her *zhen* is devoid of personality. It is neither constituted through the process of living particular social roles (radical sincerity) nor does it consist in the affirmation of certain essential qualities (being true to one's self) or in the creation of an original self (authenticity). Instead, a genuine pretender develops a capacity to playfully and skillfully enact social personae by looking at things, including oneself, from a "zero perspective."

2. THE CONFUCIAN REGIME OF SINCERITY

A man then, as it seems, who is able by his wisdom to assume every kind of character and imitate every sort of thing, if he came into our city wishing to show himself off along with his poems—we would bow down before him as before a sweet and holy wonder, but we would also say that there is no such man among us in our city, nor is it lawful. We would anoint his head with myrrh, crown him with fillets of wool, and send him to another city.

—Plato, *The Republic*

No man engaged in a work he does not like can preserve many saving illusions about himself. The distaste, the absence of glamour, extend from the occupation to the personality. It is only when our appointed activities seem by a lucky accident to obey the particular earnestness of our temperament that we can taste the comfort of complete self-deception.

—Joseph Conrad, *The Secret Agent*

THE RECTIFICATION OF NAMES, "DUAL CORRESPONDENCE," AND ROLE MODEL ETHICS

In the previous chapter we showed how the contemporary age of authenticity has colored readings of the *Zhuangzi*. By extension, assumptions about the importance of authorship, creativity, and a unique self that produces a sense of ownness have also impacted interpretations of the relationship between the Daoist and the Confucian traditions. Echoing what Trilling called the move from sincerity to authenticity, some scholars read Daoism as an attempt to overcome the Confucian reliance on social roles and relationships in defining the self. As an example, we referred to Chen Guying's analogy between the reaction to the Confucian tradition in the *Zhuangzi* and Nietzsche's criticism of the Christian "herd mentality." Consequently, Confucianism is often understood as advocating a type of sincerity while the *Zhuangzi* is believed to promote a type of authenticity.

While we find the ascription of authenticity to the *Zhuangzi* unsatisfying and suggest the philosophy of genuine pretending as an alternative, we do agree that Daoism criticizes the Confucian conception of the self as significantly shaped by (living out) social conscriptions. Given that it is difficult to construct any valid interpretation of the perspective on the self in the *Zhuangzi* without first understanding the Confucian views that inform it,[1] we propose that it is first necessary to discuss some of the debates concerning the self in Confucianism. From a historical perspective, the philosophy of genuine pretending in the *Zhuangzi* emerges as a critical counterpart to the early Confucian tradition and its notions of achieving selfhood.

We generally agree with an impressive array of Chinese interpreters, including, to name just a few, Li Zehou (2008a), Yang Guorong (2009a), Chen Lai (2014, 2015), and Chen Guying (1983a), as well as with Roger Ames (2011) and Henry Rosemont (2015), who, in one way or another, take the Confucian view of personhood to be tied to a moral project that requires cultivation in accordance with social roles, relationships, and (relationality-based) virtues. This project requires that the person develop, maintain, and live through particular roles and relationships. In short, Confucianism asks for a sincere (*cheng* 誠) commitment to moral demands pertaining to an external social life that is achieved through internal and external self-cultivation (*xiu shen* 修身).

In early Confucianism—namely, in the *Analects*, the *Mencius*, and the *Doctrine of the Mean* (*Zhongyong* 中庸)—self-cultivation is often described with reference to the ancient Chinese debate on the relation between names (*ming* 名) and actualities (*shi* 實). Names can refer to titles, assignments, reputations, social roles, proclaimed virtues, achievements, functions, and the like. Actualities may include the performances, activities, and moral or emotional qualities of humans, personal character, or the shapes of living beings such as plants and animals or of inanimate objects deployed in rituals. The proper match between names and actualities was a hotly debated issue in pre-Qin Chinese thought (see Xu Yinchun 2006; Liu Liangjian 2015; and Cai 2013).[2] Virtually all major schools of thought, including Confucianism, Daoism, Mohism, Legalism, and the School of Names, contested the way names and actualities are supposed to correspond to one another. A passage in the *Hou Han shu* 後漢書 ("Huang Qiong zhuan" 黃瓊傳) has given rise to an idiomatic expression often found in contemporary Chinese scholarship on this subject: *ming shi nan fu* 名實難副 (it is difficult to get names and actualities to

correspond).[3] In the following chapter we provide a more detailed account of
the perspective on names and actualities presented in the Zhuangzi, but for
now we want to show how the discussion of this correspondence is important for what we like to call the Confucian pursuit of sincerity. We intend to
demonstrate that in early Confucianism, even the simplest examples of relating names and actualities can have both descriptive and prescriptive over-
tones. For example, when Confucius says in Analects 6.25, "[A] gu ritual drinking
vessel that is not a gu ritual drinking vessel—a gu indeed! A gu indeed!"
(Ames and Rosemont 1998, 109), he is lamenting that when the name gu 觚—
which signifies a particular type of ritual vessel—is applied to other objects,
or "non-gu," a misunderstanding arises about the object itself, as well as the
rituals it is used in. Thus, the lack of descriptive accuracy has moral repercussions. If something is named gu, it should also be or "live up to" what the
name indicates. Even more so than to ritual vessels, this "logic" relates to
human beings. Applying Trilling's terminology to the Confucian take on the
proper correspondence between names and actualities—or, in other words, to
the Confucian aspiration of a rectification of names—we understand "names"
as representing an "external power of society" and relate "actuality," then, to
the performance of a self (or Me) that is burdened with the task of sincerely
living up to the roles that society provides.

   That the proper correspondence between names and actualities is central
to the Confucian project is made clear by Confucius's famous response, in
Analects 13.3, upon being asked what he would do first if given political power:
"Without question it would be to ensure that names are used properly" (Ames
and Rosemont 1998, 162). In terms of social order, the rectification of names
(zheng ming 正名) essentially means "to make people fulfill their prescribed
roles." But the thrust of Confucius's argument—and his real contribution to
the debate on names and actualities—lies in his demand that the rectification
of names be grounded in a process of self-cultivation by which the Me develops
sincerity. In other words, for Confucius, simply acting or playing one's roles is
not enough. A person's heart-mind (xin 心) must be involved in one's adherence to external conscriptions or in one's enactment of virtues if one's self
is to be truly refined. If one's thoughts and feelings are not in line with one's
behavior, then this behavior is morally empty since it is devoid of personal
commitment. Along these lines Confucius distinguishes his understanding
of the proper match between names and actualities from that of his contem-
poraries by expounding on what it means to be filial (xiao 孝). Analects 2.7 says,
"Those today who are filial are considered so because they are able to provide

for their parents. But even dogs and horses are given that much care. If you do not respect your parents, what is the difference?" (77).

The act of providing can carry moral significance and become actual filial piety only if it is accompanied by the appropriate mentality. Farm animals are afforded many of the same comforts given to elderly parents, but the moral distinction between the ways they are cared for is found in how their care-givers feel toward them. The moral weight of taking care of one's parents cannot be measured in material terms alone.

This perspective can be contrasted with the one-dimensional Legalist approach to the matter as represented by the *Hanfeizi* 韓非子. The *Hanfeizi* argues that only a person's actual behavior should be taken into consideration when conferring or checking the correspondence with names, whereas personal intentions, desires, or other psychological aspects should be dis-regarded (see Jiang 2010, 62–71; Bai 2012). It illustrates this idea with a well-known anecdote: When a lord gets drunk and falls asleep, the royal hat keeper protects him from the wind by covering him with the royal robe. Once the lord awakens and discovers that the keeper of the royal hat has placed the robe on him, he promptly punishes not only the keeper of the royal robe for failing to live up to his title but also the keeper of the royal hat for overstepping the boundaries of his role. The lord may well have been aware that the keeper of the hat had only good intentions, but he disciplines him all the same (*Hanfeizi* 7.2).

This story shows how the emotional commitment to enacting one's role that Confucius regards so highly falls outside the equation for a Legalist like Hanfeizi. To highlight this difference, we suggest distinguishing between a single and a dual correspondence between names and actualities. The method (represented by the *Hanfeizi*) of measuring the correspondence to names by assessing observable behaviors alone while ignoring any psychological states we call single correspondence. Here, only external actions matter. Requiring that one's mental and emotional states are in line with one's name or role con-stitutes a call for an additional layer of correspondence. By suggesting the term "dual correspondence" for the Confucian approach to role commitment, we are admittedly not adding anything substantial to standard readings of Confucianism. But we hope that this term can emblematically summarize a basic conception of sincerity that is not only embraced by many Confucian authors and texts but also serves as the background against which the *Zhuangzi* develops its philosophy of genuine pretending.

Some interpreters of Confucianism have specifically highlighted the superior importance of the second level of the demand for dual correspondence. Fei Xiaotong 費孝通 (1992), for instance, contends that Confucian morality is all about establishing proper emotional connections and states. For him, filial piety means to have the right attitude when providing for one's parents in order to ensure that harmony or "peace of mind" prevails in the kinship group. He writes, "Sons and daughters should become thoroughly familiar with their parents' personalities in the course of daily contact, and then should try to please them in order to achieve peace of mind" (12). Roger Ames and Henry Rosemont (2009, 61), too, describe the adherence to moral prescriptions in Confucianism as a matter of "personalization." They write, "What makes these [Confucian] ritualized roles and relationships fundamentally different from rules or laws is the fact that they must be personalized, and moreover, that the quality of the particular person invested in these li [rituals and roles] is the ultimate criterion of their efficacy."

Li Zehou (2008a, 64–65) similarly prioritizes the personal touch in moral interaction. Commenting on the passage on filial piety in Analects 2.7, Li argues that "Confucius's notion of respect should be differentiated from Kant's categorical imperative." Li argues that respecting one's parents does not mean just recognizing respect as a Kantian duty; it means that sons and daughters need to develop a natural (emotional) inclination to be respectful. He stresses that, for Confucians, being moral is a matter of doing something not for the right reasons but rather from the right "emotional-rational psychological structures" (14).

Echoing Li's assessment, Bryan Van Norden (2011, 28) also emphasizes the psychological dimension of a Confucian ethics: "[Confucius] thought there were certain emotions a person ought to have, and that someone could be praised or blamed not only for their actions, and not just for their intentions in acting, but also for how they feel." To stress the role of feelings in Confucian moral cultivation, Hans-Georg Moeller (2011) has used the expression "emotional immediacy." The emotional personalization that accompanies the enactment of one's social roles and relationships produces moral sincerity. And it is this second level of correspondence—the correspondence between one's mind-set and one's roles—that counts the most. Here, no dissonance is tolerated. This becomes particularly clear in an often-cited dialogue in Analects 17.21, wherein Confucius accuses his student Zaiwo of being bu ren 不仁—that is, "not humane" or "perverse" (Ames and Rosemont 1998, 209)—for feeling comfortable enjoying fine food and wearing fancy clothing "only" one year after a parent's death, rather than the period of three years prescribed by the mourning rituals. Such a mind-set is, for Confucius, in blatant violation of what the role of a good son requires. Remarkably, Confucius nonetheless explicitly allows Zaiwo to indulge in these pleasures anyway since he already *feels* like doing them. From this we can infer that mere behavioral correspondence to role expectations without a corresponding emotional commitment would be pointless and worthless. Moral honesty must be anchored in dual correspondence; only then is it sincere. Names indicating social roles thereby become ethically prescriptive. *Analects* 12.11 is often read as a paradigmatic statement regarding this prescriptive aspect of the rectification of names:

> Duke Jing of Qi asked Confucius about governing effectively (*zheng* 政). Confucius replied, "The ruler must rule, the minister minister, the father father, and the son son."
> "Excellent!" exclaimed the Duke. "Indeed, if the ruler does not rule, the minister not minister, the father not father, and the son not son, even if there were grain, would I get to eat of it?"
>
> (Ames and Rosemont 1998, 156)

In his commentary to this section, Zhu Xi 朱熹 (d. 1200) trades on the fact that words in classical Chinese can take on various parts of speech and that the reader thus readily understands the repetition of the three role names (ruler, minister, or father) as verbal constructions in the sense conveyed in the translation here. Contextualizing the passage historically, he further explains, "At that time Duke Jing had lost [the proper way of] governing. . . . Rulers, ministers, fathers, and sons had lost the way" (Zhu 2011, 136). Zhu Xi thus implies that, although rulers, ministers, and fathers under Duke Jing were of course still technically rulers, ministers, and fathers, they no longer deserved these names because their practices were not in accordance with their social roles, and they did not adopt respective emotional attitudes and ways of living. In other words, in the Confucian understanding, a role name not only is a nominal designation but also, and more important, carries a prescriptive power demanding proper and sincere enactment and commitment.

The Confucian insistence on the prescriptive power of role names is tied to a moral methodology that operates via the establishment of role models that personify the sincere enactment of roles and serve as exemplars for emulation. This methodology is clearly manifested in the ubiquitous use of historical and legendary references to moral heroes and villains in texts such as the *Analects*, the *Mencius*, and many others. More generally, this methodology is already hinted at in Confucius's admonition that rulers ought to rule well, fathers ought to father well, and so forth, which is, at least implicitly, connected to role models in two ways. First, in order to become a good ruler or father, one can follow the examples of others before or around one; second, it is insinuated that by being a good ruler or father, one also becomes a moral model for others. Methodologically, *this results in a role model ethics*. The importance of learning from both positive and negative role models in order to cultivate one's own role enactment abilities is expressed very directly in *Analects* 7.22: "The Master said, 'In strolling in the company of just two other persons, I am bound to find a teacher. Identifying their strengths, I follow them, and identifying their weaknesses, I reform myself accordingly' " (Ames and Rosemont 1998, 116).

While the focus of this passage is on emulating exemplary others and avoiding the emulation of nonexemplary people, the passage also portrays everyday social life in terms of continuous role modeling, where people constantly observe one another—and consequently develop a sense of being under constant observation by others. One is, so to speak, put to a permanent moral test as soon as one is in company. This means that one is not only supposed to be continuously learning to be—or not to be—like others but also to make oneself someone that others can learn from. In *Analects* 2.11, Confucius concisely spells out this call to never cease working on becoming a role model—or a "teacher" (shi 師)—by following role models: "The Master said, 'Reviewing the old as a means of realizing the new—such a person can be considered a teacher' " (Ames and Rosemont 1998, 78).

The moral methodology of emulating models and setting up examples builds up a social context of peer pressure and peer scrutiny extending to others and simultaneously reverting back to oneself. One is not only forced to exist under the constant observation of others but also to engage in persistent introspection and reflection on how one appears in public. Everyone is a teacher and a student at all times, and a teacher is not only forced to continuously evaluate his or her students but also subject to continuous counterevaluations by them—not entirely unlike the way in which our contemporary universities operate, actually.

Given the strong and explicit emphasis on the primacy of the second layer of dual correspondence (the sincere commitment to one's social roles), the moral methodology of role modeling becomes significantly more onerous than the oft-maligned Legalist insistence on strict—but *merely*—behavioral accordance with role names. Given its emphasis on "emotional-rational psychological structures," the Confucian model is arguably even more "totalitarian" than its Legalist counterpart. Every individual is not only subject to continuous supervision by superiors but also made to engage in a never-ending self-examination of one's own progress in becoming a sincere role model. One is asked not only to identify with and thus affirm social roles but at the same time—and even more urgent—to develop one's own identity accordingly. It is not enough to simply "review the old" and adopt social patterns appropriately; one has to put this review of the old into the service of "realizing the new," which is to say one must "relive" the social order as it is manifested in role names by sincerely internalizing it. Thereby, one is supposed to develop and improve it, if necessary, and to pass it on to future generations, who will have to engage in the very same "biopolitical" exercise, if we are allowed to speak with Foucault here.

From such a biopolitical perspective, the Confucian ethics of sincerity represents an early call for a complete psychophysiological embodiment of a social order imposed by role names. From this perspective, the problem of the impossible *regime of sincerity* is that it is *too sincere* from the start. The main thrust of the anti-Confucian critique of the Zhuangzi is its "deconstruction" of Confucian sincerity and the role model ethics attached to it.[4] With humor as a major tool the *Zhuangzi* subverts and undermines the fixation on sincerity that the Confucian project attempts to proliferate throughout society by ridiculing not only its role models but also a role model ethics in general. As we argue, the *Zhuangzi* does not intend to replace Confucian sincerity with something ostensibly more "sincere"—namely, authenticity—but instead offers a way out of the regime of sincerity altogether via a philosophy of genuine pretending.

From a Confucian perspective, however, a different problem arises from the permanent occupation with the sincere internalization of social roles. One can never be sure if others and oneself are sincere enough. Thus, contrary to the Daoist line of criticism, the problem for the Confucians is that there is always suspicion of a *lack of sincerity*. Consequently, a major problem haunting Confucian authors and texts is the possibility of insincerity, pretense, lying, and deception. As its other side, this problem inevitably accompanies the Confucian regime of sincerity.

THE FEAR OF INSINCERITY AND THE MORAL ONTOLOGY OF SINCERITY

If one of the Confucians' major contributions to moral discourse in ancient China is the introduction of dual correspondence to debates on properly matching names and actualities, then naturally one of their biggest concerns should be falsity. While interpreters of Confucianism have always tended to stress the importance of having sincere moral thoughts and emotions, some of the more recent literature has turned the focus toward the corresponding problem of pretense (see Ames 1996; Puett 2002; Seligman et al. 2008; D'Ambrosio 2012a). As the *Analects* already profess, as much as Confucius was engaged with rectifying names through dual correspondence, he was worried about the flip side of sincerity: the misrepresentation or misappropriation of names by way of simple single correspondence. A complaint by Confucius in the *Analects* 17.13 summarizes this concern: "The Master said, 'The "village worthy" is excellence (*de* 德) under false pretense' " (Ames and Rosemont 1998, 207). These so-called village worthies are insincere in behavioral display of virtue. Confucius's lamentation is further explained in the *Mencius* (7B:37):

> Wang Zhang said: "If the village declares them worthy people, there is nowhere they will go where they will not be worthy people. So why did Confucius regard them as thieves of virtue?" Mencius replied, "If you try to condemn them, there is nothing you can point to. . . . They are in agreement with current customs; they are in harmony with the sordid era in which they live. They seem to dwell in devotion and faithfulness [*zhong* 忠 *xin* 信]; their actions seem to be blameless and pure. The multitude delight in them; they regard themselves as right [*zi yi wei shi* 自以為是]. But you cannot enter into the Way of Yao and Shun with them. Hence, Confucius said they are 'thieves of virtue.' "
>
> (Van Norden 2008, 195; translation modified)

Here the *Mencius* relies on the logic of dual correspondence to clarify Confucius's remark. Confucius's worry over "thieves of virtue" is that they are people who only seem to be in "agreement with current customs" or "in harmony with the sordid era in which they live." Mencius is implying that the village worthies in fact lack the proper thoughts and feelings and are thus insincere. They illustrate virtuousness only in terms of a Hanfeizian type of single correspondence; only their actions are "blameless and pure."

As opposed to one who is merely in agreement with common practices or laws, only the person who cultivates a moral psychology is also able to truly impress others and serve as a model for the proliferation of a sincere moral order in contemporary and future society.[5] Having the proper emotions allows the person to apply what he or she has learned from role models—provided either in classical texts or by personal experience—and to pass it on in a creative and perhaps even innovative way. The motto for such proactive sincerity is found in Analects 15.29: "It is the person who is able to broaden the way, not the way that broadens the person" (Ames and Rosemont 1998, 190). As Geir Sigurðsson (2015) has suggested, the way (dao) as a moral force and tradition is created, maintained, and evolves through human undertakings. Someone who simply imitates what others do may appear to always be correct but, lacking personal involvement cannot "enter the way of Yao and Shun with them." By imitating what was previously done by others without any sincere commitment makes no new tread marks and leaves the way or tradition lifeless. Insincerity and pretense therefore become major obstacles for the passing on of Confucian morality to future generations—and so they are great dangers to the regime of sincerity, which, like the Confucian tradition in general, tends to be very much concerned with continuity, posterity, and procreation.

An emblematic expression of the great dangers associated with imitation, falsity, and pretense is found in the writings of the Later Han–dynasty thinker Xu Gan 徐幹, who warned that the potential threat of "false names" (wei ming 偽名) is often all too easily overlooked: "People only know about the good that names do and are ignorant of the bad that false names do. It can be catastrophic! Nowadays, is it only the 'village worthies' who throw virtue (luan de 亂德) into disorder by making false names? The myriad affairs are complex and interwoven; when 'aberrant numbers' (bian shu 變數) proliferate, it is certain that the path leading to the disordering of virtue has more than one starting point" (Makeham 1994, 14; translation modified).

Xu Gan's pessimistic account mirrors a Confucian moral and sociopolitical concern with insincerity on the basis of a lack of dual correspondence. Granting titles and reputations to village worthies who perform only what society asks them to do is considered especially dangerous in a political environment where supposed inner virtue is used as a predictive measure of one's goodness and employability. Insincerity thus emerges as a menace to social order and stability.

In addition to allowing a person to act properly in everyday situations, the commitment to sincerity is supposed to ensure that people will become reliable and orderly—or "disciplined," one might say—in increasingly complex sociopolitical frameworks. Ideally, each person first cultivates their sincerity in family relationships. This begins when the child starts to observe their most immediate role models: their parents. Seeing how parents treat family members—and especially the way they act toward their own parents—provides foundational examples for how to behave morally both within the family and in larger social spheres. Children are also exposed to other forms of education, including narratives and music, that provide additional models for emulation.

Hence, becoming moral starts with becoming filial—that is, acting and feeling appropriately toward one's parents. The next step involves behaving appropriately toward one's siblings, and this behavior, too, must be coupled with the right psychology. From there, people develop their character so that they can better follow the role models they have seen and learn to interact well with people outside their family. Similarly, a filial attitude toward one's parents sets one up for being deferential to all other elders. Confucius imagines that sincere behavior reverberates in concentric circles throughout society. A well-ordered state begins with a well-ordered family, and all this is due to a concern with the prevention of insincerity "from the start"—or, more concretely, from birth—by insisting on dual correspondence. *Analects* 1.2 provides a succinct description of this: "Master You said, 'It is a rare thing for someone who has a sense of filial and fraternal responsibility (*xiaoti* 孝悌) to have a taste for defying authority. And it is unheard of for those who have no taste for defying authority to be keen on initiating rebellion. Exemplary persons (*junzi* 君子) concentrate their effort on the root, for the root having taken hold, the way (*dao* 道) will grow therefrom. As for filial and fraternal responsibility, it is, I suspect, the root of authoritative conduct (*ren* 仁)'" (Ames and Rosemont 1998, 71).

Through a morality based on the doctrine of the rectification of names— for example, of truly "soning" and "brothering"—a sincere commitment to social roles is shaped in the self; and as this passage clearly emphasizes, this has the primary sociopolitical purpose of avoiding social conflict, disorder, and rebellion.[6] Vice versa, it has to be concluded, insincerity can be identified as the root cause of all social and political calamities. As Ames and

Rosemont rightly translate, it is precisely the embodied "sense" of, for instance, "filial responsibility" that is supposed to guarantee order. Therefore, its presumed absence must be perceived as potentially catastrophic and as an indication of the utmost personal and social "perversion" (bu ren 不仁) that should be avoided at all cost. The regime of sincerity that education needs to impose on all humans clearly betrays the construction of a most elementary and thoroughgoing social suspicion and fear of a lack of psychosomatic commitment to social roles that every member of society is expected to internalize.

According to the political philosophy of the Analects, persons who cultivate their character sincerely are the building blocks of a stable society. Earlier commentators such as Chen Shan 陳善 and Wang Shu 王恕, as well as contemporary philosophers such as Li Zehou 李澤厚 (2008a, 32–33), Yang Guorong (2011), and Chen Lai (2015), contend that this passage from Analects 1.2, besides its obvious political significance, also defines what it means to be human on a more ontological level. "Human" is—like "ruler" or "father" in Confucius's paradigmatic remark in Analects 1.2—not simply a biological label. Being human implies a certain degree of cultivation; it is a matter of being civilized. As such, it is simultaneously an ontological and ethical designation. Li Zehou (2008a, 30) in particular focuses on this conjunction and argues forcefully that one must xue 學—that is, "study" (or "emulate" role models)—in order to "become a person" (zuo ren 做人; emphasis added). Relying on the common argument that the word for moral virtue, ren 仁, or "humaneness," is pronounced in the same way as the word ren 人, for "human" or "person," Li maintains that "filial and fraternal responsibility" (xiaoti 孝悌) are, in effect, also the root of being human. Establishing just such a moral ontology, Li writes, "Humaneness is part of natural human determinacies ['ren' (ren xing) '仁' (人性)]" (346). Accordingly, only a fully moral person, or one who sincerely lives one's roles, can be accepted as a true human being.

Other Confucian texts, including the Mencius and the Zhongyong, also define what it means to be human on the basis of a sincere moral commitment. One of the most famous passages of the whole Chinese philosophical tradition, Mencius 2A:6 states very clearly that those who do not develop the proper "emotional-rational psychological structures" that inform their relationships with others are "not human" (fei ren 非人):

The reason why I say that all humans have hearts that are not unfeeling towards others is this. Suppose someone suddenly saw a child about to fall into a well: anyone in such a situation would have a feeling of alarm and compassion—not because one sought to get in good with the child's parents, not because one wanted fame among one's neighbors and friends, and not because one would dislike the sound of the child's cries. From this we can see that if one is without the feeling of compassion, one is not human. If one is without the feeling of disdain, one is not human. If one is without the feeling of deference, one is not human. If one is without the feeling of approval and disapproval, one is not human.

(Van Norden 2008, 46)

Only through a development of and sincere emotional commitment to the Confucian "sprouts" of humanity—for example, humaneness (ren 仁), righteousness (yi 義), propriety (li 禮), and wisdom (zhi 智)—is one human. Emphasizing the importance of constant practice, Roger Ames and Henry Rosemont (1998, 49) thus prefer to speak of "human becoming" rather than "human being" in the context of classical Confucianism.[7] Bryan Van Norden (2008, 151–52) makes a similar point and interprets the famous image from *Mencius* (6A:8) of the barren Ox Mountain that no longer sprouts because it has been overused for lumbering and herding as speaking to the human need for constant moral upkeep. Those who neglect the cultivation of their supposed moral nature cut away at their own humanity and are eventually in danger of becoming mere animals. Conversely, this means that one must cultivate one's moral sprouts by cultivating moral sincerity, or *cheng* 誠. As quoted earlier, *Zhongyong* (22) summarizes this onto-ethical demand for sincerity most concisely: "Sincerity is the way of heaven; to make it sincere is the way of the person." As a result, sincerity becomes at the same time an ontological condition of the human "way" and a moral prescription that is inevitably and incessantly tied to this condition.

ALTERNATIVE READINGS OF CONFUCIANISM AND A PRELIMINARY CONCLUSION

We believe that our critical understanding of early Confucianism as a kind of role model ethics focusing on sincerity corresponds to the view of Confucianism as presented in the *Zhuangzi*. Ours is therefore a historically adequate interpretation based not only on primary sources but also on their reception by rival contemporary schools of thought. In addition, we think that many of the contemporary scholars whom we have cited reflect a similar understanding of texts such as the *Analects* and the *Mencius*. However, we are well aware that our approach to Confucian philosophy is not without opposition. Here we would like to give a short account of contemporary readings of Confucian ethics by authors who do not tend to conceive of it as amounting to a "regime of sincerity."

There is an alternative line of interpretations of Confucian philosophy that is somewhat in disagreement with the Confucian sincerity project as presented in the preceding. This rather "modernist" line of argumentation assumes that early Confucian ethics does not require moral sincerity in one's commitment to one's social personae. For example, one may please one's parents by praising and eating the food they have prepared but is not required to actually enjoy it. However, from the perspective of a regime of sincerity, any such dissociation feeds the suspicion of hypocrisy that the Confucian texts tend to dread so much. We therefore do not think that such a view of early Confucianism coheres with certain passages (such as *Analects* 1.2) that identify a dissonance between one's feelings and actions toward one's family members as the root cause of any sociopolitical disorder. At the very least, we think that the *Zhuangzi* had good reason to understand early Confucian ethics as devoted to achieving ever more intense moral sincerity.

One example of an interpretation of Confucian ethics that dissociates the self from its social performances is found in May Sim's (2007) comparative study *Remastering Morals with Aristotle and Confucius*. Here, Sim first insists that morally approvable action in early Confucianism is possible even when one's social roles are played rather than lived. Commenting on *Analects* 12.11, she writes, "Confucius goes so far as to assert that just playing one's roles will bring about effective government" (152). Even (or perhaps especially) as a moral agent, a Confucian person may well be entitled to internally distance themselves from their outward actions. For instance, one can—and normally should—be loyal to one's parents, even if one is not in perfect agreement with them. It is usually expected, Sim points out, that in case of a disagreement with one's parents, one performatively submits to them, but at the same time one remains free to think or feel otherwise. She explains, "The individual must put his or her desires and thoughts inside—even to the point of setting aside thoughts of what is better. One strives to play a role of a good son instead of asserting what he (as an individual) thinks of a situation" (152).

According to this view, single correspondence can often suffice in Confucianism, and there is no general requirement for dual correspondence. The
release of the individual from the demand for sincerity frees it from its immediate social context. The self then is no longer entirely relationistic, as it is
often portrayed by Ames and Rosemont. Sim thus goes further than Tu Weiming (forthcoming) and other modernizers of Confucianism by allowing for
not only the autonomous agency of the Confucian self but also insincerity and
pretense. We wonder, therefore, if Confucius, having to face a person with
such a self, would not lament allegorically, "A *gu* ritual drinking vessel that is
not a *gu* ritual drinking vessel—a *gu* indeed! A *gu* indeed!"

One of the most radical and explicit dismissals of what we have described
as the sincerity interpretation of Confucianism can be found in *Ritual and Its
Consequences: An Essay on the Limits of Sincerity*, coauthored by Michael Puett (see
Seligman et al. 2008). Puett assumes that early Confucianism operates on the
basis of an even stronger underlying "true self" than that posited by Sim.
Puett's is a self that ought to be radically separated from one's social persona.
In a unique reading of the paradigmatic passage *Analects* 12.11, Puett suggests
that one should take Confucius there to be advocating that "kings, fathers,
and wives should *stop acting from their true self* and align themselves with their
proper roles" (135; emphasis added), Apparently, Puett takes Confucius to be
saying that people possess and usually "act from" a true self, and that they
ought to suspend this true self when in office or in social interaction with
others.[8] To underscore his point, Puett further explains that, for Confucius,
good kings are supposed to only act "*as if* they were kings" (135; emphasis in
the original). We cannot but read this to say that, for Puett, Confucius is paradoxically demanding here that kings ought to dissociate their personalities
from their roles and cease to "really" be kings. Consequently, Puett denies that
the "famous rectification of names (*zheng ming*) movement" represents "the
move of sincerity" (135). Puett then defines (from our perspective, somewhat
confusingly) the "move of sincerity" as the demand "to make the names properly reflect the true nature of the thing," while the goal of the rectification of
names is, on the contrary, "to make the nature of a thing correspond to its
name" (135). For us, this latter goal is precisely the goal of sincerity and not its
opposite as it seems to be for Puett—but then we may have just failed to properly reconstruct the logic of Puett's argumentation.

As a preliminary conclusion, we want to point out that we think that, at
least when looked at through the lens of the *Zhuangzi*, one finds in early

Confucianism a moral prescription that humans ought to take heed of culti-vating their nature in correspondence with the social identities that their names indicate. This prescription makes Confucian ethics an ethics of sincerity and establishes a sociopolitical regime of sincerity. In effect, the Confucian regime of sincerity stems from the emphasis on what we call dual correspondence with respect to the doctrine of the rectification of names. The simple demand to make one's behavior correspond to one's social roles and relationships is psychologically charged by the early Confucians with the demand for a full internal commitment to them. This brings about a Confu-cian role model ethics that employs a moral methodology based on the emu-lation of role models. This emulation has to be wholeheartedly and creatively adopted—that is, it must be internalized through a sincere commitment to the models one embraces and presents to others. At the same time a suspicion of insincerity emerges, since true sincerity is hard, or rather impossible, to prove. How can one be totally sure about even one's own internal mind-set when only one's outward actions are clearly observable? Along with the fear of insincerity, a moral ontology is constructed that declares being human to be an open process of gradually *becoming* human. This process burdens every-one with constantly having to prove their true humanity by confirming a sin-cere identification with their social personae. This is, in sum, what we call the Confucian regime of sincerity, and we argue that it constitutes the background against which the *Zhuangzi* develops its philosophy of genuine pretending.

In the following pages, we discuss how the *Zhuangzi* casts doubt on the very possibility, and moreover the desirability, of achieving Confucian sincerity or dual correspondence. By establishing an impossible ideal, the regime of sincerity creates more problems than it solves. However, the Daoist perspective should be distinguished from the criticism of dual correspondence found in the *Hanfeizi*. While Legalists generally worry that establishing a moral politics prioritizing intentions and emotions produces a potential for manipulation and deception, the point made in the *Zhuangzi* is much less antagonistic. The *Zhuangzi* deemphasizes the importance of names, asking, can the self really be molded by social expectations? Shouldn't we be open to identifying with a variety of perspectives outside our roles and relationships? And, even more radically, why should we develop a sense of identity or self at all?

While these are the sort of questions that stimulated modern Western thinkers into overcoming sincerity and provided the impetus for developing notions of authenticity as a creative process whereby one "owns" one's self, we will show how the *Zhuangzi* reacts to philosophical sincerity in a dramatically different manner. Daoist genuine pretending is not another kind of authenticity. It is not about authoring or creating a self, a sense of ownness, or transcending social norms. Strong attachments to any type of self are rejected outright in genuine pretending, as is an individual, isolated sense of self. The genuine pretender does not cultivate an identity according to authenticity or individualism nor according to a socially constructed relational self.

From the Confucian perspective, the genuine pretender may simply make light of social roles or be a cynic. It is true enough that genuine pretenders do not take themselves as seriously as Confucians. There are sobering precautions about the Confucian cultivation project in the *Zhuangzi*, but many jokes about it as well. (And with a little imagination one could perhaps extend these precautions and jokes and direct them against a contemporary obsession with developing authenticity.) Therefore, we will now take a serious look at the *Zhuangzi*'s humor and how it deconstructs the regime of sincerity by playfully illustrating, welcoming, and aesthetically employing the incongruity of names and forms.

3. PHILOSOPHICAL HUMOR AND INCONGRUITY IN THE *ZHUANGZI*

"What art thou, friend, who dost stop a traveler in this manner upon his most gracious Majesty's highway?" said the Knight.

"Marry," quoth Robin, "that is a question hard to answer. One man calleth me kind, another calleth me cruel; this one calleth me good honest fellow, and that one, vile thief. Truly, the world hath as many eyes to look upon a man withal as there are spots on a toad; so, with what pair of eyes thou regardest me leith entirely with thine own self. My name is Robin Hood."

—Howard Pyle, *The Merry Adventures of Robin Hood*

IN THE PRECEDING PAGES, WE HAVE OUTLINED AN INTER-pretation of early Confucian philosophical theory and practice focused on a regime of sincerity. We hold that, from the perspective of the *Zhuangzi*, the Confucian ethics of sincerity sets up impossible stipulations for individuals and collectives and thereby produces not only contrivance, hypocrisy, and lies but also, a fortiori, pathological states of ineffectiveness and unhappiness. The first and foremost reaction of the *Zhuangzi* to an ethics of sincerity is not to promote insincerity instead, or to aim at transforming it into a truer ethics of authenticity; rather, it is to counter, disarm, and subvert the ethics of sincerity through humor. In this chapter we intend to show concretely how this is done.

Our account of the philosophy of humor in the *Zhuangzi* finds completion with an analysis of the general philosophical framework that supports the objections brought forth against a Confucian demand for a sincere match between roles or names and shapes or forms. This analysis in turn provides the background for our exposition of a Daoist alternative to the regime of sincerity found in the Zhuangzi—namely, the paradoxical art of genuine pretending. While the Zhuangzi's humoristic stories and witty allegories mocking Confucian sages of sincerity may be taken as mere ornamentations of a deeper theoretical message to be found in more straightforward argumentation, we believe that with perhaps more justification—and by recognizing their more immediate effects on the reader—they can be seen as constituting the most basic and powerful dimension of the philosophy of the Zhuangzi. Sigmund Freud (1922, 204) was quite right when he wrote, "Where the argument seeks to draw the hearer's reason to its side, wit strives to push aside his reason. There is no doubt that wit has chosen the way which is psychologically more efficacious."

Our approach toward humor in the Zhuangzi is philosophically motivated; this means that we do not intend to add to the rich psychological, biological, or anthropological research on humor or to the research on humor in linguistics or literary criticism. We also restrict ourselves to an analysis of humor in early Daoist philosophy and hope thereby to complement other studies on humor in Confucianism (Harbsmeier 1990; Weihe Xu 2004) and on the cultural, historical, and comparative aspects of humor in China (Harbsmeier 1989; Chey and Davis 2011; Davis and Chey 2013; Trauzettel 1999).

TOWARD A DAOIST THEORY OF HUMOR

PHILOSOPHICAL THEORIES OF HUMOR

It may be prudent to present a brief overview and critical analysis of some of the major tenets in the philosophy of humor before we identify humorous dimensions in the philosophy of the Zhuangzi. This task is not overly onerous since, as John Morreall, one of the most prolific contemporary humor philosophers, hastens to point out in his extensive entry on this subject in the Stanford Encyclopedia of Philosophy, one of the most surprising aspects of the philosophy of humor is how little interest it has sparked overall. Morreall (2013) adds that not only have philosophers tended not to speak about humor in the first place but also, when they have, they have tended to express their disapproval of it in various ways and degrees. Notwithstanding this generally negative philosophical attitude (to which Bergson 1924 is a notable exception), more recent decades have seen a number of attempts, particularly by North American scholars, to produce critical classifications of existing theories of humor following the publication of D. H. Monro's *Argument of Laughter* in 1963. As stated by Smuts (2015), "according to the standard analysis, humor theories can be classified into three neatly identifiable groups: incongruity, superiority, and relief theories."

Historically, the superiority theory of humor has been dominant in Western philosophy. According to Morreall (2009, 6), "before the Enlightenment, Plato and Hobbes's idea that laughter is an expression of feelings of superiority was the only widely circulated understanding of laughter." In line with this explanation of the origin of laughter as "laughing *at*," humor was understood as arising from the alleged "good" or "amusing" feelings evoked by the perception of the shortcomings of others. The relief theory is associated primarily with the works of Sigmund Freud and Herbert Spencer. Generally speaking, relief theorists have assumed that laughter releases physiological and mental energies. The function of humor would thus be to dissolve psychosomatic tensions and to set excess energies free. Today, both superiority and relief theories have been partly discredited and "the incongruity theory is the reigning theory of humor" (Smuts 2015). The incongruity theory can be traced back to a remark by Aristotle in his *Rhetoric* (III, 2), where he expresses the idea that "the best way to get an audience to laugh is to set up an expectation and deliver something 'that gives a twist'" (Smuts 2015). A formulation often identified as a classic representative of the incongruity theory is found in Kant's (1911) *Critique of Judgment*. In section 54, Kant states that "laughter is an affection arising from the sudden transformation of a strained expectation into nothing." In Morreall's (2013) formulation, "the core meaning of 'incongruity' in various versions of the incongruity theory, then, is that some thing or event we perceive or think about violates our standard mental patterns and normal expectations."

By relating to and integrating a wide range of psychological and biological as well as anthropological and aesthetic studies, several other theories of humor have been suggested as modifications of or additions to the three standard models. Among these are "play theories" that "try to classify humor as a species of play" and see humor as "an extension of animal play" (Smuts 2015). In humorous play, otherwise serious situations, events, or forms of behavior are reenacted or perceived in a disinterested or disengaged way and can thus be experienced as pleasurable. In this context, laughter can be understood as having evolved "from play signals in pre-human apes" (Morreall 2013). It indicates, for instance, that no real aggression or threat is intended but rather a playful and friendly banter. By integrating elements of incongruity into a play theory, humor can be ascribed the function of helping us to safely deal with the unusual or surprising: "We experience, think about, or even create something that violates our understanding of how things are supposed to be. But we suspend the personal, practical concerns that lead to negative emotions, and enjoy the oddness of what is occurring" (Morreall 2013). In line with this definition of humor, Morreall (2009, 49) has outlined his own version of an integrated incongruity-play theory and identifies "the playful enjoyment of a cognitive shift" as "the basic pattern of humor."

Another more recent humor theorist, Robert Latta, has also modified elements of the relief and incongruity models and suggests a "relaxation theory" of humor. According to Latta (1999, 38), "every normal person" experiences what he calls an "initial-stage-unrelaxation" during "most or all his waking hours" by simply having to be attentive or making an effort to be engaged in "even such comparatively relaxed behavior as taking part in everyday conversation just for the sake of the talk, or doing easy reading." A humorous cognitive shift, however, momentarily leaves the "initial-stage unrelaxation without object, point, ground, or function" (44) and relaxes us. The relaxation provokes laughter and is experienced as pleasure—and this combination of pleasurable relaxation and laughter represents the phenomenon that is humor. Importantly, it is provoked through making the cause of the initial unrelaxation seem unnecessary and nonsensical (at least temporarily).

As both Morreall's and Latta's humor theories show, there are various elements of the three standard theories that are not incompatible with one another, and so "presenting these theories as rivals is misleading" (Smuts 2015). In fact, the various theories "focus on different problems" (Smuts 2015) related to humor, such as the objective or subjective reasons why something is funny, or on the physiological, social, or evolutionary functions of humor and laughter. Morreall (2009, 6) goes a step further in questioning the division between the three standard theories and points out (correctly) that none of them has been adopted by any "group of thinkers consciously participating in a tradition." They do not represent strict isms that are popular in today's philosophical discourse. Therefore, one should refrain from wholly identifying any one particular theorist of humor with one of the three standard constructs. If Kant's brief account of humor, as Morreall (6) points out, already contains "elements of the relief theory" despite its usual classification as a primary example of the incongruity theory, then it is even more problematic to compress an elaborate theory of humor (such as Freud's) within the narrow confines of the standard model.

Given their increasing modification and expansion and, perhaps more crucially, their tendency to prejudice or partially distort one's understanding of often more complex theoretical approaches to humor, we do not adopt here any of the older standard theories for our discussion of humor in the *Zhuangzi*. Instead, we refer to a number of specific insights formulated in newer "hybrid" theories of humor—namely, Latta's relaxation theory and Morreall's variation on play theory. In addition to these two theories, we rely on aspects taken from both Kant's and Freud's theories of humor. Though the standard theoretical models tend to dismiss these two thinkers, we find their accounts crucial for gaining an appreciation of the use of humor in the *Zhuangzi*. We also employ a theorist who is rarely mentioned in the current North American literature on humor—the Russian thinker Mikhail Bakhtin (1895–1975; see Morris 1994). On the basis of these sources, we list several features and aspects of humor that will help us to identify the philosophical use thereof in Daoist texts. These features are not meant to provide a comprehensive or universal definition of humor. Not all forms of humor exhibit all these characteristics, but we think that each of them can be important for understanding the philosophical significance of humor in the *Zhuangzi* and, by extension, in Daoism.

SIX FEATURES AND THREE PHILOSOPHICALLY RELEVANT ASPECTS OF HUMOR

As sketched in the preceding, Latta's relaxation theory of laughter presumes that, as adults, we are normally engaged in tasks of varying degrees of seriousness and that these impose a certain stress on us such that we are in a state of unrelaxation. Morreall highlights that, in humor, as in play, we disengage from an activity or an idea by performing a cognitive shift that deprives a situation of its seriousness. This disengaging shift is experienced as pleasurable.

A joke discussed in detail by Freud can illustrate the relaxation process of a humorous intervention that, often through paradoxical means, undermines the earnestness of a situation and therefore provides pleasure. Freud (1922, 372) cites a literal case of *Galgenhumor*, or "gallows humor": "The rogue, on being led to execution on Monday, remarked: 'Yes, this week is beginning well.'" A widely known, more contemporary variation of *Galgenhumor* is the famous scene in the *Life of Brian*, a film that parodies the New Testament, wherein the protagonist, while being crucified, sings and whistles a happy song with the refrain "always look on the bright side of life."

Both the man in front of the gallows and the parody of Jesus's crucifixion illustrate how the respective protagonists manage to distance themselves from one of the most serious and sad experiences imaginable to humans—one's own death—through humor, and how they thereby achieve a remarkable relaxation. The same process of relaxation also takes place in the listener of the joke or the viewer of the movie: an expectation of witnessing a scene of severe cruelty and horrific suffering is built up and, by experiencing a natural empathy and sympathy with the protagonist, mental stress and unrelaxation are provoked. The paradoxical reaction of the delinquents, however, undermines the seriousness and allows not only the fictional protagonists but also the listeners or viewers to disengage and relax. This relaxation is a pleasurable experience that will often stimulate laughter or at least a smile.

Freud explains the reasons for the relaxation experience in cases of *Galgenhumor* by pointing out that "economy of sympathy is one of the most frequent sources of humoristic pleasure." The word "sympathy" (*Mitleid*) is used here in the sense of "pity," and the word "economy" (*Ersparnis*) in the sense of "saving" or, more concretely, of not having to engage in an effort or not having to expend something (e.g., one's energy), contrary to what one expected. The narrative structure of *Galgenhumor* makes us invest some initial pity or fear—both very serious, strong, and potentially strenuous feelings—by proxy. But then a paradoxical or absurd twist *saves* us the expected expense of an *emotional effort*. Initially we are unrelaxed, but an ironic statement ("this week is beginning well") or turn of events (the singing Brian) distances us from the situation, deprives it of its seriousness, and relaxes us.

By combining Latta's and Morreall's models with Freud's theory, we can identify six characteristics of humoristic communication that will be important for the following analysis of humor in the *Zhuangzi*: (1) a disengaging effect that distances us from a serious situation or the serious protagonists of a narrative; (2) a narrative contradiction or *disappointment* of initially provoked expectations that is brought about by (3) instances of *incongruity* typically produced by paradoxical, ironic, or nonsensical statements; (4) a *relaxation* of strenuous or strong emotions; and (5) an experience of *pleasure* resulting from this relaxation as well as from (6) the saving of mental efforts or the experience of mental *effortlessness*.

Play theories of laughter, such as Morreall's, at least implicitly connect with an important element of Freud's theory of the humorous that is often neglected in the references to him in the standard classifications of humor theories. Just as in Freud's general psychological theory, childhood experiences are of crucial importance for his theory of wit. On the one hand, they can foundationally shape us psychologically and greatly inform our later psychological development. Certain experiences—of a sexual nature, for instance—can have traumatic effects that result in various pathologies as we grow up. However, the psychological experiences of children can also often be contrasted with the mind-set of adults who need to cope with what Freud (1930) famously called the discontents (das Unbehagen) of civilization. Very briefly put, Freud argued that the process of socialization forces us to inhibit drives, such as those related to sexuality, whose satisfaction would provide us with pleasure. This inhibition tends to make us unhappy and results in a contrast between the psychological state of "civilized" adults and that of children with a yet limited exposure to social or cultural restraints.

In Wit and Its Relation to the Unconscious Freud often compares the pleasure of experiencing something funny to pleasant experiences in childhood, which are often related to play. A thorough reading would therefore also justify a classification of Freud as a play theorist of humor. Be that as it may, Freud concludes his book on wit with a very short summary of his ideas and explains the "mechanism of humoristic pleasure" as resulting from saved mental efforts (Freud 1922, 383–84). He specifically postulates that (a) the pleasure of wit results from a saved inhibition effort (e.g., we do not have to restrain our enjoyment of the communication of sexuality), (b) the pleasure of the comic results from a saved intellectual effort (we find that we do not have to engage in strenuous thinking), and (c) the pleasure of humor results from a saved emotional effort (e.g., we are unexpectedly saved from having to engage in feelings of pity or fear). Interestingly enough, he then concludes that in all these cases of deriving pleasure from the humorous through saving ourselves psychological efforts, we "strive to bring back from our psychic activity a pleasure which has really been lost in the development of this activity. For the euphoria which we are thus striving to obtain is nothing but the state of a bygone time in which we were wont to defray our psychic work with slight expenditure. It is the state of our childhood in which we did not know the comic, were incapable of wit, and did not need humor to make us happy" (384).

Remarkably, Freud says here that the basic function of engaging in humorous communication and thoughts (which he subdivides into the categories of "wit," "the comic," and "humor" proper) is to return at least momentarily to a blissful childhood state that has been lost and now remains otherwise inaccessible to adults. As not-yet-socialized children we were often, to speak with Latta, in a state of relaxation ("we were wont to defray our psychic work with slight expenditure") and not pressured to make stressful psychological efforts. Or, we can identify the *Stimmung einer Lebenszeit* ("the state of a bygone time" in the quoted passage, or, more literally, "the mood of a period in life") that Freud refers to as the mode of play, to speak with Morreall. Freud's theory of the psychogenesis of wit suggests that wit "attempts to replace" the *Stimmung* (mood) that "was once contented with mere playing" (Freud 1922, 202). He says that wit "begins as play in order to obtain pleasure from the free use of words and thoughts. As soon as the growing reason forbids this senseless play with words and thoughts, it turns to the jest or joke" (211). Freud identifies play as the predecessor of wit, and wit as an evolved form or replacement of childhood play. As socialized adults, we increasingly lose the ability to reenact the childhood mood of play and attempt to return to it through humor. When making a joke, watching a comedian, or reading a satirical story, we simulate the relaxed play that we used to enjoy as children. On the other hand, as young children we were not yet able to understand jokes, comedians, or satirical stories because we were still enjoying a pleasurable and joyful *mental ease of play*.

For our purposes it is necessary to follow Freud one step further at this juncture. In his reflections on play, he also states that "imitation is the child's best art and is the impelling motive of most of its playing" (Freud 1922, 368). In other words, for children, an eminent way of (a) experiencing pleasure and (b) being "artful" or efficacious or feeling competent is to engage in playful *pretending*. A child derives pleasure and feels competent by imitating certain movements, gestures, or ways of speaking. Pretending play is, according to Freud, not yet comical but, as he says, "pure pleasure"—it is *genuine pretending* in its most immediate form. If humor, in the sense of being in a comical mood, makes us return to the state of mind of play, and if it is a psychogenetic successor of play, then humor allows a momentary return to a state of genuine pretending. It is a way for adults to be able to feel pleasure and to experience meaningless skillfulness at the same time.

Freud's relaxation and play-theoretical conclusions allow us to formulate a philosophically significant aspect of humor, particularly with respect to the use of humor in the *Zhuangzi*: humor is related to an experience of play and thereby also to an experience of genuine pretending. In this euphoric state, we are able to effortlessly and nonseriously enact any kind of behavior without being identified by our roles or taking on responsibility for what we do, because we are just playing. When we dressed up as cowboys and shot our friends, we were neither really cowboys nor did we really shoot anyone. We were only pretending; but at the same time, we were euphorically enjoying ourselves and our competence, and we most intensely interacted with others. We could be euphoric, competent, and capable of interacting intensely precisely because we were pretending and because we were not really who we pretended to be. The same "insincerity" is involved in telling a joke or making fun: we do not tell a real story and do not really identify with any message that we convey.

As Freud and many others after him have remarked, play shares another characteristic with humor: it is a social or communicative activity involving company. We cannot make a joke on our own. As Freud (1922, 288) explains, jokes involve at least three persons: the one telling the joke, the fictional persona(e) or character(s) in the joke, and the person to whom the joke is told. The function (highlighted by Morreall 2013) of laughter as a play signal clearly shows the social dimension of humor as well. As he puts it, humor "serves as social lubricant." He also points out that, similar to play and music, it "strengthens our social bonds."

The relation between play and humor can help us to interpret Kant's concise definition of laughter in a more subtle way than that offered by the usual incongruity classification of his theory referred to earlier. When Kant says that laughter arises "from the sudden transformation of a strained expectation into nothing," he not only already implies Latta's relaxation theory but also, upon closer inspection, hints at an aspect of humor as play. When we play, our roles and actions turn out to be *nothing* real or substantial. The shot from our toy gun does *nothing* to our friend whom we pretended to kill. Similarly, a joke or humorous story can function on this basis by emptying a narrative of a specific meaning or, in particular, a specific *moral*.

In his definition of laughter, Kant explicitly insists on the importance of the word "nothing" (*nichts*). He says that in the case of jokes, unlike in other stories, expectations are not transformed into their opposite but are instead completely dissolved. Unlike in a drama or murder mystery where a person whom we expected to be good may turn out to be actually bad, a joke deprives the story of a substantial final message altogether. Here, the whole expectation of a real meaning of the story, be it ethical, religious, or existential, is dismantled.

When, for instance, we are presented with a scene where we are prepared to hear the last words of a man walking to the gallows, we expect some meaningful words. If the scene appears in a drama, our expectations may well be contradicted and the meaning of the words that we hear will change our previous understanding of the narrative. Perhaps we will find out that the man whom we always expected to be innocent finally confesses his guilt. This contradiction of our expectation would not make us laugh, though, and we would not find it funny. In a joke, however, such as the one related by Freud, or a comedy such as the *Life of Brian*, our expectations are not exactly contradicted but indeed, as Kant says, "made to disappear into nothing." The humorous quip of the rogue and the absurdly happy song of Brian render impossible any serious message of the story. The point of a joke is often precisely that, contrary to previous expectations, it does not have a particular point. There is no deeper meaning behind the story. Instead, we realize, and enjoy, the absence of a deeper meaning.

Günter Wohlfart (2010) has convincingly shown how such a reading of Kant's definition of laughter can, contrary to what one may expect when reading Kant, be aligned with the function of laughter in Chan or Zen Buddhism.[1] When laughing about a joke, just as when achieving Chan Buddhist enlightenment, one may gain "the sudden insight that there is no such thing as 'enlightenment'" (Wohlfart 2010, 225). We can therefore conclude with Kant that humor can convey a playful *experience of emptiness of meaning*. Particularly in Daoist and Chan Buddhist contexts, this aspect of humor, too, can become philosophically relevant.

The frequent absence of a moral (ethical or otherwise) in jokes leads us toward another philosophically interesting characteristic of humor: it is often seen as suspending or violating morality and so as morally bad or evil. Morreall's account of the condemnation of humor in the history of Western thought begins with Plato and Aristotle, continues with quotations from the Bible as well as ancient and medieval Christian thinkers, and ends in early modernity with Hobbes and Descartes. Summarizing, he says that "from ancient Greece until the 20th century, the vast majority of philosophical comments on laughter and humor focused on scornful or mocking laughter" (Morreall 2013). What Morreall (2009, 1) says about the "traditional rejection of humor" seems to confirm much of what Nietzsche famously said in *On the Genealogy of Morality* about the "slave morality" in European thought: moral indignation against humor, particularly in Christian contexts, was often directed against its perceived unethical aggressiveness, hostility, and lack of restraint. Humor, it was feared, tended to be nihilistic and could easily become morally subversive and provoke deviance. Consequently, a maxim found in

Epictetus's *Enchiridion* 33 represents a widespread ethical attitude against humor: "Let not your laughter be loud, frequent, or unrestrained" (quoted in Morreall 2013).

Quite in line with the main idea of Freud's *Civilization and Its Discontents* (which suggests that civilization, in order to achieve social cohesion, needs to inhibit individual satisfaction of pleasure drives, which consequently produces general psychological discontent), humor as a tool for individual relaxation and nihilistic disengagement or as an occasional outlet for aggression and anger was prone to be considered a moral and cultural danger. It was therefore often restricted, censored, or outlawed. Morreall (2013) points to (in)famous prohibitions against laughter in early and medieval Christianity and to the ban on comedy in seventeenth-century Puritan England. Today, humor is confronted not only by religious fundamentalism (as exemplified by violent attacks against humorists perceived as mocking Islam) but also by various kinds of social sanctions against allegedly insensitive or offensive humor believed to undermine basic ethical principles. Contemporary efforts to morally cleanse humor have been supported by philosophical ethicists who outlined standards that aim at informing us "when it is wrong to laugh" (de Sousa 1987). Despite his generally descriptive attitude toward humor, Morreall (2009, 102–10), too, does not refrain from presenting a normative assessment of humor and appends his survey of the "negative ethics of humor" with a list of what harm humor may do, such as promoting irresponsibility, diminishing compassion, and spreading prejudice.

In order to at least temporarily relieve itself from the regulations and restrictions it has imposed on itself, society has created protected spaces where it allows itself to engage in forms of deviant or amoral humor that it otherwise disallows. Perhaps the most well-known examples from Western history for such social reservations of humor are the ancient Roman Saturnalia, where "sexual rules were openly violated, and religious rituals were lampooned" (Morreall 2009, 2), as well as the medieval European carnival, where the same was the case.

With reference to the medieval carnival, Mikhail Bakhtin has developed what may be called a carnivalesque theory of humor. According to Bakhtin, the medieval carnival functioned as a counterculture that briefly established a topsy-turvy world of behavior, values, and social roles. It provided space for relief and relaxation separate from a world of strict hierarchies and institutionalized oppression and, in particular, an opportunity to overcome "moral fear." For Bakhtin this fear includes, for instance, the fear of social exclusion resulting from violating moral norms, the fear of punishment for immoral behavior, or the fear of bodily desires that may be considered immoral. All these moral fears are suspended in carnivalesque humor. Bakhtin (1990, 35) writes, "The medieval person experienced in laughter the triumph over fear. And this triumph was not only experienced as a victory over mystical fear (the 'fear of God'), and over the fear of the forces of nature, but most of all as the victory over moral fear, which subdues human consciousness, and suppresses and numbs it."

It is important to stress here that, for Bakhtin, the point of taking a break from morality in times of carnival and of suspending ethical rules and allowing what is from a moral perspective licentiousness and mockery was a merely temporary "triumph over [moral] fear" and not the ultimate replacement of moral rules by "immoral" ones. Humor therefore does not promote a different morality or immorality. Instead, carnivalesque humor, although often considered immoral by moralists, has a thoroughly *amoral* function— the dissolution of moral fear by undermining a moral mind-set or moral behavior rather than advocating any counter- or antimorality. Carnivalesque mockeries of religion, such as the medieval customs mentioned by Morreall (2009, 2), which included cross-dressing clerics, mock prayers or rituals, and the comical impersonation of bishops, were not primarily expressions of antireligious aggression or atheism but rather a *playful diversion* from regular moral and religious pressure.

Bakhtin (1990, 40) therefore insists that it would be wrong to assume "that the distrust of the people in seriousness and their love of laughter as a different truth would have always taken on a conscious, critical, and clearly confrontational shape." Instead, medieval foolish laughter "never creates dogmas and does not establish any authority" (41). Carnivalesque laughter "unites negation (mockery) and affirmation (triumph)" (54). And "absolute negation is as alien to the carnival as is absolute affirmation" (54). Carnivalesque laughter is "ambivalent"; it does not affirm or negate specific values but playfully deconstructs any evaluative attitude or social form that establishes binding moral or other constricting values (53).

To be sure, the traditional rejection of laughter is due mostly to the fact that humor was often seen as expressing or promoting immorality. The "immorality" of humor, however, is an ascription from an ethical point of view, not an inherent characteristic of humor. From the perspective of a theory of humor such as Bakhtin's carnivalesque theory of laughter, humor is not immoral but profoundly amoral. Its function is to dissolve moral fear by producing moral ambivalence: in Kantian terms, the transformation of moral expectations into nothingness, or in Daoist and Buddhist language, the emptying of a moralist form of thinking and behaving—as performatively enacted in the aforementioned medieval carnivalesque diversions.

A rather old-fashioned German joke about two local characters from the city of Cologne named Tünnes and Schäl can help demonstrate the amoral function of humor. While walking across a bridge over the Rhine, Tünnes encounters Schäl crying and deeply upset. Asked by Tünnes what the matter is, Schäl replies that a stranger just threw his sandwich into the Rhine. Showing concern, Tünnes asks, "Was it on purpose?" Still devastated, Schäl answers, "No, it was on rye."[2]

The joke builds up and then dissolves moral feelings. First, we are confronted with Schäl's misery and encouraged to feel pity for him—not so different in kind, albeit in degree, from the joke related by Freud about the man to be executed. But when Tünnes asks Schäl if the stranger had thrown his sandwich "on purpose" into the Rhine, a moral scenario evoking connotations of conflict and expectations of revenge or retribution for an injustice are established. Schäl's "foolish" answer, however, disappoints these expectations and dissipates any moral rage or "fear." The joke thus becomes a carnivalesque tale that humorously dissolves morality. It illustrates a third aspect of humor that we find philosophically significant in the Zhuangzi. In addition to (1) being related to childhood play as a practical form of genuine pretending and (2) conveying an experience of emptiness of meaning, it (3) playfully engages in amoral thought and communication.

STUDIES ON HUMOR IN THE ZHUANGZI

In one of the now classic studies on humor in ancient China, David R. Knechtges (1970–1971, 80) summarizes what may have been at the time a widespread scholarly view about a relative lack of humor in ancient Chinese texts: "It has been observed more than once that humor does not occupy a prominent place in traditional Chinese literature." Toward the end of his essay, Knechtges concludes that, while indeed some humorous texts or passages can be identified in ancient China, "most of early Chinese humor is essentially didactic and moralistic" (95). In comparison with this rather unexciting estimation, Knechtges's view on the Zhuangzi is quite remarkable: he writes that this "entire work is made up of a series of incongruities strung together in the aimless manner of sustained humor" (97). It seems that Knechtges felt slightly uncomfortable with conceding such a dissonance between the strikingly humoristic features of the *Zhuangzi* and the "essentially didactic and moralistic" humor anywhere else in ancient China, so he thought it better to surmise cautiously that Zhuangzi was probably just a madman with a "fondness for the bizarre and unconventional," whose humor was "unintentional" and a mere "by-product" of a strange imagination (97).

Knechtges was by no means the first to ascribe exceptionality to the *Zhuangzi* as a humoristic work in ancient China. In 1932, Lin Yutang published an influential essay called "On Humor" (Lun youmo 論幽默) in which he commended the spiritual merits of humor in the world in general and China in particular. He identified various humorous traditions in ancient China and labeled Daoism (mostly referring to Laozi and Zhuangzi) as the "humorous faction" in the history of Chinese thought, as opposed to the "orthodox faction" of Confucianism (Sample 2011, 174; see also Liu Jianmei 2016, 106–11). Among the Daoists, he singled out Zhuangzi as "the father of Chinese humor" (Sample 2011, 173). He thereby seems to have set the tone for similar judgments, such as a more recent one by Xiao Dong Yue (2010, 403), who states that Zhuangzi "is recognized as the very first humorist in China." As a rule, most contemporary interpreters of the *Zhuangzi* grant that it is an often witty text that uses humor among many other literary tools. Eske Møllgard (2007, 6), for instance, affirms that the *Zhuangzi* "employs prose poems, fables, satire, song, fictitious dialogue, spiritual exercise, didactic verse, aphorisms, and a number of literary genres we have still not identified and understood."

While statements of this kind abound in the literature—both academic and popular—devoted to the *Zhuangzi*, in-depth studies on its use of humor as either a literary or a philosophical device are more difficult to find. Nonetheless, one attempt to assess the philosophical function of humor in the *Zhuangzi* was made by Erik Schwitzgebel (1996). According to Schwitzgebel, humor in the *Zhuangzi* has the therapeutic function of making its readers capable of taking truth claims or assertions of facts less seriously and thus allows them to adopt a more flexible attitude toward pronouncements in language. He says that Zhuangzi simply "would like to see us take what people have to say less seriously" so that we are "willing to play around with it in a disrespectful way for humorous or other ends" (70–71). We sympathize with this view, particularly since it echoes our point that its similarity to play is a philosophically relevant aspect of humor, but also because it resonates with our claim that humor dissolves moral seriousness and empties out meaning.

Perhaps the most comprehensive attempt to analyze humor in the *Zhuangzi* from a literary studies perspective has been presented by Youru Wang (2003). In *Linguistic Strategies in Daoist Zhuangzi and Chan Buddhism: The Other Way of Speaking*, Wang adopts a deconstructionist perspective and deals specifically with "denegation" (i.e., negating and self-negating language such as the "negation of all polarities and double negation" [153]), paradox, and irony in the *Zhuangzi*, all of which he ties to the *Zhuangzi*'s self-ascribed use of the much-discussed "goblet words" (zhi yan 卮言; for interesting discussions of this elusive term, see Wang Bo 2004; Fried 2007; Morrow 2016).[3] According to Youru Wang (2003, 153), "the Zhuangzian denegation disagrees with the Derridean interpretation of denegation. . . . This Derridean interpretation still falls into a negation privileged over affirmation. Zhuangzi does not privilege negativity over positivity." Instead, Wang believes that denegation as found in the *Zhuangzi* expresses a playful toying with the relation between language and the ineffable, while uses of paradox illustrate "the dynamic convergence of various opposites." He thus links humorous rhetorical techniques to philosophical interpretations of the indirect "strategies of communication" (see Kupperman 1989) and "antirationalism" (see Carr and Ivanhoe 2000) found in the *Zhuangzi*. Wang (2003, 158) concludes, "When the use of denegation or paradox brings about self-negation or self-contradiction in an unanticipated manner, especially when it occurs in a form of self-mockery or self-ridicule, it involves irony." In short, for Wang, irony emerges as the major humoristic device in the *Zhuangzi* and, philosophically speaking, it "calls into serious question any logocentric or metaphysical closure in a frivolous or humorous way" (159).

Lee Yearley (2005) has also presented some ideas on "Zhuangzi's kinds of language" and, like Youru Wang, combines a literary analysis with philosophically relevant conclusions. Unlike Wang, though, he does not use a deconstructionist conceptual framework. His intention is to interpret Zhuangzi as a religious ethicist who uses "literary devices like satire or parody" (516; another interpretation of Zhuangzi as a religious ethicist is presented in Lee 2014) to convey a spiritual message and to call for moral self-reflection. According to Yearley (2005, 516), these humorous devices in the *Zhuangzi* are intended to provoke "hermeneutical crises that have spiritual implications" for readers so that they will eventually be forced to "evaluate their own spiritual maturity."

From a different philosophical perspective, James D. Sellmann (1998, 165) ascribes a transformative "mystical" meaning to humorous language in the

Zhuangzi. He affirms that "storytelling, irony, jokes, even a simple pun—all of the elements that make up comedy, laughter, and forgetting . . . are the literary devices employed in the *Zhuangzi*." Influenced by Kuang-ming Wu's (1990) approach to the *Zhuangzi* and partially reminiscent of Robert E. Allinson's (1989) reading of the text as a guide for "spiritual transformation," Sellmann further argues that through such devices the *Zhuangzi* shows "how one must awaken to 'transformation' and 'humor' by beginning to live the life that affirms one's own personal mutation" (172).

With fewer philosophical (but more historical and philological) ambitions than Wang, Yearley, or Sellmann, Shirley Chan (2011) has made an attempt at "identifying Daoist humor." While her specific focus is on the *Liezi* 列子, much of what she says is also applicable to the *Zhuangzi*, since several of the textual examples she discusses appear in both texts. Chan, too, pays attention to specific literary devices and points to "metaphor, exaggeration, hyperbole and *reductio ad absurdum*" (87). Interestingly, she connects both the *Liezi* and the *Zhuangzi* with the ancient Chinese category of "huaji-ists," or "humorists," who, as Knechtges (1970–1971, 82) remarks, "were considered important enough for Sima Qian to compile a monograph on them in his *Records of the Historian* [*Shiji* 史記]." They were "jesters at the courts of the Warring States kings and Han emperors" (83) and spoke "wittily and relevantly to persuade their lords to accept their advice" (Shirley Chan 2011, 75). Knechtges (1970–1971, 83) states that huaji 滑稽 "in the early period meant something like a 'smooth talker.'" The term's connotations were not necessarily positive, and so it makes sense that Chan reads the expression huaji 猾稽 as huaji 滑稽, or "humorists," in an interesting statement made in the *Shiji*'s biography of Xunzi 荀子. In Chan's reading, this statement has Xunzi dismissing Zhuangzi as someone "who attacked Confucian social conventions by being a humorist" (huaji luan su 滑稽亂俗 [Chan 2011, 232n11; see *Shiji* 74.11]).

The anti-Confucian trajectory of many of the humoristic passages in the *Zhuangzi* is discussed in further detail in a more recent essay by Katrin Froese (2014). Froese notes that Confucius is not only sympathetically depicted as a spokesperson for Daoism at times but also ambiguously "at the receiving end of so much biting satire" in the *Zhuangzi* (310). Although Froese does not explicitly refer to Henri Bergson—whose interesting but unfortunately now-ignored theory of humor assumes that laughter results from perceiving something human as nonhuman, as mechanistic or lifeless (Bergson 1924)—she identifies the function of anti-Confucian humor in the *Zhuangzi* very much in Bergsonian terms. According to her, the *Zhuangzi* mocks the at times "mechanist" Confucian attitude to ritual. She writes, "For the Daoist, ritual, when held up against the spontaneous and yet harmonious movement of nature, will always be comic because it is mechanistic, artificial, and forced" (Froese 2014, 210).

In the context of a collaborative comparative study on Kierkegaard and Zhuangzi (Carr and Ivanhoe 2000), P. J. Ivanhoe has discussed humor in the Zhuangzi by testing the text against the humor theory of D. H. Monro (1963), which preceded the present standard accounts by Morreall and others. Ivanhoe "ticks all the boxes" and attests that the Zhuangzi contains forms of humor that are compatible with any theory tracing humor back to "feelings of superiority, incongruity, ambivalence, or relief from inhibition or restraint" (Carr and Ivanhoe 2000, 136). Besides proving the Zhuangzi's humorous versatility and its capacity to live up to contemporary humor theories, Ivanhoe is particularly keen on defending Zhuangzi against any accusations of using humor in a morally suspicious way. For this purpose he suggests a strict distinction between the good-humored, authentic Zhuangzi who speaks in the Inner Chapters and the inauthentic falsifiers of him present in the Outer Chapters. He believes that "it is not too strong a claim to say that sections of the text that criticize Kongzi [Confucius] himself in a severe and malicious way are immediately suspect as the work of late pretenders to Zhuangzi's mantle." He specifically points to "the 'Robber Zhi' chapter," which he takes to "have been confidently identified as of rather late origin" (11). In the same vein, he categorically states that "one does not find the mocking humor of the assassin in the authentic parts of the text" (138).

Ivanhoe establishes a stark moral contrast between the mild, ethically instructive, and restricted humor of the genuine Zhuangzi on the one hand and, on the other, the "malicious" "humor of the assassin" of the "pretenders to Zhuangzi's mantle." Apparently he assumes that there is a kind of "devil in disguise" hidden in some parts of the book and thinks that the conscientious reader should beware of it. Perhaps Ivanhoe's drastic good/evil and authentic/inauthentic distinction is due to an influence of the long history of the moralistic "traditional rejection of humor" documented by Morreall (2009). Ivanhoe's distinction between good and evil humor in the Zhuangzi echoes the "moral fear" that has haunted philosophical and religious condemnations of humor for centuries in both East and West. It is therefore not surprising that it resurfaces in some of the literature on humor, including literature on the humor of the Zhuangzi. Accordingly, Ivanhoe is not the only one to judge Zhuangzi's humor morally; other authors, too, make an effort to identify an ethically clean humor in the *Zhuangzi* that is free from immoral or harmful traits. Lee Yearley (2005, 516), for example, writes, "Zhuangzi's humor rarely, however, just distances in a way that allows us to feel superior." Youru Wang (2003, 158) finds (inoffensive) irony in the *Zhuangzi* but not (offensive) sarcasm, saying that irony "differs from sarcasm, because sarcasm laughs at the hearer." Lin Yutang points out that Daoists "could have become cynical and disgusted with the world, but by arriving at cynicism and disgust, they would have lost an essential element of true humor" (Sample 2011, 175).

Unlike some of the authors quoted in the preceding, but in line with newer humor theories, we reject the traditional superiority perspective on humor that tends to find unchecked laughter morally suspicious. In our opinion, the ascription of such ethically negative attributes to humor results from a moralistic prejudice against humor. We intend to argue instead from an amoral perspective beyond good and evil that looks at humor as being, among many other things, a way to escape moral fear and not as a dangerous rhetorical device that, if not properly reined in and cleansed, will serve to assert one's superiority over others. We have therefore made our preceding sketch of several characteristics of a Daoist theory of humor in response to a not uncommon impression among readers of the *Zhuangzi* addressed by Brook Ziporyn (2009, viii): "Profound comedians have always been hard to come by; funny philosophers perhaps even more so. To enter into this work attributed to Zhuangzi is to find oneself roused and enraptured by its intellectual and spiritual depth, but also by its provocative humor." What we intend to do is make sense of the provocative humor of the *Zhuangzi* within a philosophical framework. This framework looks at Daoist humor, on the one hand, as a subversive reaction to the impossible existential demands of an ethical regime of sincerity and, on the other hand, as a way of experiencing the playful pleasure, effortless skillfulness, and childlike sanity of a genuine pretender.

PARODIES AND TRICKSTERS IN THE ZHUANGZI

THE EQUALIZING JOKEBOOK

As our overview of the literature on the *Zhuangzi* shows, interpreters have frequently acknowledged the humorous nature of the text, noticed its use of multiple comic literary devices, and identified witty passages and puns. Our present purpose is somewhat more ambitious than merely adding to the emerging list of funny segments of the text; we endeavor to take Knechtges's (1970–1971, 97) remark that "the entire work is made up of a series of incongruities strung together in the aimless manner of sustained humor" seriously and assume that there is a comical undercurrent permeating the *Zhuangzi*. After all, if one follows Ziporyn (2009, 3), the *Zhuangzi* begins with a quote from the fictitious *Equalizing Jokebook* (Qi xie 齊諧), from which the first allegory about Kun 鯤 and Peng 鵬, the giant fish and bird, is said to be taken. In our reading, this is an invitation to try out an approach to the *Zhuangzi* that sees the text itself as an equalizing jokebook and to read it in a humorous key.

If so, one would not have to assume with Knechtges that the *Zhuangzi*'s humor is aimless and collateral. Instead, it can be taken as crucial for producing hermeneutic consistency. Consequently, we believe that it is possible to understand if not the *entire* work, then at least substantial portions of it from a humorous point of view. To put it more precisely, we assume that an interpretative strategy based on a humorous perspective is fruitful for a philosophical understanding of the text in general and of many of its constituents. We intend to support this claim by showing how humorous readings of core narratives that are not necessarily understood as comical in standard interpretations not only make sense but also help to establish an overall picture of a Daoist philosophy in terms of a philosophy of genuine pretending.

The overall picture of Daoist philosophy that our humor-centered reading is meant to defend is not meant to contradict or replace other readings such as, for instance, practice-centered, spiritual, religious, metaphysical, or political readings but to complement them and open up a further dimension of Daoism. In fact, we think that readings from *dao jiao* 道教 (practical/spiritual/religious), *dao jia* 道家 (metaphysical, political), and humorous perspectives are often equally possible. Therefore, we introduce our own humor-focused interpretations with brief surveys of different approaches to the passages in question. Our guiding hermeneutic assumption is that the *Zhuangzi* is a multidimensional text that can be made sense of both humorously and nonhumorously. The resulting understandings will be different, but they do not have to mutually exclude one another.

We believe that the *Zhuangzi* is not only multidimensional and open to readings in different keys but also a highly complex text made up of heterogeneous strata. However, we do not think that those strata neatly divide the book into clearly differentiable segments of precisely identifiable origins. We think that the strata interfere and intersect with one another. With respect to our present issue, we particularly disagree with Ivanhoe's suggestion that the textual evidence allows for a distinction between a morally good humor of the authentic Zhuangzi in the Inner Chapters and a morally bad humor of some pseudo-Daoist forgers in the Outer or Miscellaneous Chapters. We suggest instead that a Daoist type of humor, characterized by various mixtures of some or all the characteristics we have depicted, comes to the fore throughout the whole book as soon as a reader is willing and able to perceive it.

HUNDUN'S DEATH: A PARODY OF A MYTH

The narrative of the Death of Emperor Hundun 渾沌, who finally perishes from the seventh hole that his two fellow emperors have drilled into his formless body to do him the favor of supplying him with a face, famously concludes the seven Inner Chapters: "The Emperor of the South Sea was Fast [Shu 儵], the Emperor of the North Sea was Furious [Hu 忽], the emperor of the centre was Hundun. Fast and Furious met from time to time in the land of Hundun, who most kindly entertained them. Fast and Furious were discussing how to repay Hundun's virtue. 'All men have seven holes through which they look, listen, eat, breathe; he alone doesn't have any. Let's try boring them.' Every day they bored one hole, and on the seventh day Hundun was dead" (see Graham 2001, 98; translation modified).

Perhaps Wang Bo (2014, 162) is right and the number of holes drilled into Hundun is intentionally parallel to the number of the Inner Chapters. If so, the sudden demise of the story's protagonist could signal to the reader that he or she, too, has come to an end and reached a stage of no return. With the completion of the seventh chapter, seven deep holes have been drilled into one's head and have transformed one irredeemably. Zhuangzi, too, may have repaid the kindness of those who took him home with equal kindness and deprived them of their intellectual innocence, killed their childlike state, and initiated them into civilization. But such an interpretation exceeds the degree of adventurousness of our present project, and we will therefore limit ourselves to a humorous reading of the story as parody.

Interpretations of the Hundun story are dominated by mythology-based readings. In his elegant and erudite study on *hundun* as the "theme of chaos" in early Chinese thought, Norman J. Girardot (2008 [1983]) has discussed this story at great length and with great subtlety, showing its eminent significance for the Daoist worldview. He reads it as a variation of the myth of Hundun as documented in texts such as the *Zuozhuan* 左傳, the *Shanhaijing* 山海經, the

Huainanzi 淮南子, and the *Liezi* and takes it as reflecting "a cosmological metaphysics of the principium of creation as *creatio continua* or *natura perpetua et infinita*" (232). The Hundun of the *Zhuangzi* thereby corresponds to other mythical images of self-generating cosmic origination, such as a cosmic egg, a primal gourd, or a giant flood.[4]

Seen in this light, the story of Hundun's death in the Inner Chapters reflects a wider mythological and cosmological framework. The two emperors of the southern and northern seas, Shu 儵 and Hu 忽, "are equivalent to the dual principles (heaven and earth, yin [陰] and yang [陽]) or twin deities established as part of the process of creation, the initial passage from 'one' to 'two'" (Girardot 2008, 70). Accordingly, the setting of the story depicts an initial cosmological stage of the world consisting of a central oneness that is void of shape and surrounded by a periphery split in two. Hundun constitutes an *axis mundis* around which the world is organized (71). The narrative then depicts the destruction of this cosmic structure through human intervention. It is consequently for Girardot a variation of a mythic model that is "'paradigmatic' or 'archetypal' for the theory and practice of early Daoism" (8). It presents "multivalent symbolic images" forming a "mythological narration of the beginning (*arché*—creation of the world, man, and culture), middle-reversal-fall (*peripeteia*—the 'dis-ease' of civilizational existence), and end (*lysis*—an end that is a return to the beginning)" (8). Moreover, by showing how Hundun was killed, it implies a call for his restitution or, as Günter Wohlfart (2000) has outlined, a call to humans to regain their true presocial "nonface."

The fact that "the primordial condition of perfect unity was lost" with the killing of Emperor Hundun indicates for Girardot (2008, 42) "that the Daoist seeks to reverse that original event and re-attain the paradise condition of *hundun*." The story's mythological meaning thereby becomes religiously relevant. It becomes an inspiration for soteriological hopes and sets up a model for practical emulation. It turns into a foundational text for personal or spiritual cultivation. As Girardot has succinctly put it, "the thematic structure of the *hundun* cosmogony gives form and meaning to the overall soteriological mode of being a Daoist" (34). Hundun thereby becomes a personification of a lost state of perfection that one can regain by systematically engaging in mythologically grounded and religiously motivated practice.

Such an entirely plausible mythological understanding of the figure of Hundun in the *Zhuangzi* easily connects with a religious approach to it that has become manifest in centuries of *dao jiao* history. But it does not necessitate such an understanding. In fact, the mythological cosmology that the allegory alludes to can equally give rise to metaphysical speculations about an initial cosmic condition. And such speculations, in turn, can lead to a political reading of the text as an ancient Chinese "cultural critique." Such a trajectory was concisely summarized by Max Kaltenmark (1969) several decades ago, who quipped that Hundun's "myth is a perfect symbol of the Founding King's original sin" (101). Kaltenmark refers to a reading of the story that conceives of the state—in both senses of "state" as a condition and a sociopolitical entity—of Hundun as an image of a state of nature. This state of nature is destroyed, as the story seems to decry, through human activity as represented by the doings of the Emperors of the North and South. Along such lines, Nicholas F. Gier (2000, 212) has identified the core message of the allegory by further elaborating on Kaltenmark's remark: "Most importantly, the original sin in this story is anthropocentrism, a fault that Zhuangzi continually attempts to rectify by constant reference to the nonhuman realm and nonhuman values,"

The readings of the Hundun story presented here show how it allows for diverse appropriations and reconstructions of its meaning. All of them, however, deal with it as a depiction of a downfall and therefore as a *tragedy*; and none of them see it, at its core, as a parody of a cosmological tale and thus as a *comedy*. In order to appreciate the story's humor, one has to first accept that the tale of Hundun in the *Zhuangzi*, while centered on a mythological character, is *not* a myth, and much less a cosmogenic one—rather, it is a parody of a myth.

Formally speaking, the story parodies mythological tales. The Emperors of the North and South Seas bring to mind ancient Chinese mythological depictions of the North and South Seas—that is, regions at the end of the world as documented in *Xunzi* 9.17. But their "silly" names Shu and Hu (translated as "Fast" and "Furious" by Graham in resonance with the meaning of the expression *shuhu* 倏忽 in ancient Chinese) deprive them immediately of their reverent appearance as emperors. The humoristic use of speaking names is very common in the *Zhuangzi* and can be found, too, in the ancient Greek comedies of Aristophanes. Just as the story contrasts the reverent title "emperor" with banal personal names, it also contrasts the emperors' serious moralist-ritualist preoccupation with the easygoing and spontaneous politeness of Hundun, who simply treats guests nicely (*shan* 善). This, too, makes the emperors look goofy. Finally, a wise pronouncement about that which "all men have" (*ren jie you* 人皆有) is put into the emperors' mouths. It has the exact same form as similar statements in *Analects* (12.5) and in the *Mencius*, of which the most

famous ones occur in chapter 6A:6, where Mencius illustrates human goodness by saying that anyone would immediately save a child falling into a well
because "all men have a heart that cannot bear the suffering of others." However, the emperors' stunning insight into universal "human nature"—namely,
that we all have seven holes in our face—turns out to be not only banal but
also, once applied into action, deadly folly. Seen in this way, the story emerges
as a parody of tales about lofty "founding kings," their solemn compartment,
and their sagely words. Hu and Shu are no mythological characters but two
caricatures of such figures.

Hundun certainly was a known mythological character at the time, as others appearing in the Zhuangzi were as well. Likewise, the Zhuangzi includes—
as is common in ancient Chinese texts—a huge cast of historical and legendary figures. Yet the appearance of such protagonists in the Zhuangzi does not
make it a historical or mythological document. Just as many events formally
depicted therein as historical records are fictional, the story of Hundun is a
collage of elements, some of which are of mythological origin and others of
which are idiosyncratic inventions of the author's imagination. As opposed to
other narratives about Hundun found, for instance, in the Shanhaijing and the
Huainanzi (see Girardot 2008), the text is not a written representation of an
orally transmitted myth but a work of literature. It surrounds Hundun with the
two mythological caricatures and thereby establishes a comical context that
turns Hundun, too, into a comical character. The text mimics elements of the
language and structure of a myth, but by integrating these elements into a
humorous and irreverent frame, it produces an ancient Chinese form of what
Bertolt Brecht called Verfremdungseffekt, or "distancing effect" (Brecht 1961).
Unlike in a real myth, one cannot look up to the characters in this play and
regard them as exemplars; instead, one can laugh about their goofiness.

In content, the story disappoints and reverses the expectations of a cosmogenic myth. At the beginning it operates within a pseudomythological format, thereby building up the anticipation that it will illustrate the creation of
the world or something of that order. In the end, however, the story of Hundun
changes into the opposite of a tale about creation: it concludes with destruction and death. Rather than being left with an explanation of the origin of
everything, the reader is left with a story of the origin of nothing. The "big
bang" that one may have eagerly hoped for is eventually an implosion into
emptiness. The story is not only not a cosmogenic myth but also not even a
proper destruction myth about the end of all things. We do not know what
happens after Hundun's death. Presumably, the Emperors of the North and

South Seas will have survived their murder, and we are left to live on with these scoundrels ever after.

As a parody of a cosmogenic myth, one can view it as a narrative counterpart of a parody of cosmogenetic "arguments" famously appearing in chapter 2 of the *Zhuangzi*, a passage that has been identified as humorous (e.g., Schwitzgebel 1996): "There is a beginning. There is a not-yet-beginning-to-be-a-beginning. There is a not-yet-beginning-to-not-yet-begin-to-be-a-beginning.... Now I have said something. But I do not-yet know: has what I have said really said anything? Or has it not really said anything?" (Ziporyn 2009, 15).

Here Zhuangzi may well have been mocking the philosophical urge to go back to the beginning of all beginnings—or even behind it—which eventually reveals itself as an idle, pointless, and ultimately comical effort. The Hundun parody can accordingly be read as a deconstruction of the futility of any mythological, religious, or philosophical "grand narrative." Once one begins to assume that one is in a position to explain everything and inform others about the origin of the cosmos in a story, one is in danger of succumbing to hubris and delusions of grandeur. Rather than partaking in the telling and further proliferation of such myths, the Hundun parody counters them humorously and twists and turns them so that they take on the form of a farce.

The point of the death of Hundun would thus be to show the emptiness of grand mythological narratives about ultimate beginnings and to comically undermine their credibility and enthralling effects. Seen in this way, the Hundun allegory in the *Zhuangzi* is one of many examples of the "distancing effect" produced in this work. When Zhuangzi writes in a humorous style, which, to quote Brecht (1961, 130), "we find in the circus clown's manner of speech," then "the spectator is prevented from feeling his way into the characters." Thereby, a distance from the discourse that, for a moment, we were enticed into seriously entertaining, is produced. Because of this distance, we get out of a grand narrative not only alive but even unfazed and with a smile as well—unlike the imprudent Hundun, whom we see dying.

It is not difficult to recognize humorist characteristics in the *Zhuangzi*'s version of the Hundun story that turn a myth into a parody. Clearly, the narrative disappoints the initially provoked expectations of an etiological myth. Statements and descriptions in the story turn out to be incongruent: The Emperors of the North and South Seas are depicted as having the good intention to "repay Hundun's virtue [*de* 德]," but then, paradoxically, their explicit statement expresses a decision for a violent aggression: "Let's bore some holes into him!" Moreover, the story disengages readers from its protagonists by various means. Readers do not identify with these characters, do not look to them as exemplars, and are not admonished to emulate them. This disengagement spares the reader the emotional expense of feelings of pity or rage despite being exposed to witnessing a murder. It produces a relaxed and pleasurable experience of amusement rather than a strenuous emotional investment. At the same time, the disengagement effects combine with the unexpected twist in the story to relieve readers from moralist instructions.[5]

In effect, the tale of the death of Hundun in the *Zhuangzi* is a parody of three failed sages: two inept Confucians whose clumsy attempt to do the right thing results in a disaster, and one naive Daoist whose incautious behavior leads to his untimely death. If the Hundun story is indeed concerned about our health and wants to save us from a similar fate, then one must agree with Girardot's (2008, 33) verdict that the "best way to characterize the Daoist idea of salvation is to see it as being fundamentally 'medicinal' in intention and structure." There are many kinds of medicine, and according to a popular saying, laughter is actually the best. But a medicine must match the disease, and so it is better to diagnose the sickness that killed Hundun, the clueless Daoist.

As a medicinal allegory, the story of Hundun contrastingly and ironically mirrors a major theme in the *Daodejing*—the art of being "good at holding on to life," as chapter 50 says. The same chapter also provides a description of those who have perfected this art:

When they walk in the hills, they avoid neither rhinos nor tigers.
When they go into battle, they carry no armor or weapons.
The rhino has no spot to jab its horn. The tiger has no spot to put its claws.
For weapons there is no spot to lodge a blade.
And for what reason? Because they have no spots of death.

Unlike Hundun, those who are good at the art of holding on to life "have no spots of death"; their sanity consists in being immune to penetrations. Like Hundun, though, they find themselves in the midst of all kinds of creatures who want to pierce them, which in their case are not emperors of the peripheral regions of the world but wild animals and fierce warriors. However, the artists of life offer no place of entry to those who threaten them. Unperturbed, they move freely through jungles and battlefields. Remarkably, they do not even have to hide. They are out in the open, but they refrain from directly taking their enemies on; they do not have weapons and do not fight. Unlike

Hundun, they seem to be very careful not to invite trouble. The difference between Hundun and the survival artists of chapter 50 of the *Daodejing* is that the latter, although they partake most directly in the frenzy of the world, do not get involved. In this way, they take care not to be caught up in its disputes and struggles so that they do not become vulnerable and can thus remain intact.

An artist of life is capable of maintaining sanity within the humdrum of a contentious society. Hundun, on the other hand, is unable to protect his sanity and consequently acts insanely. The narrative presents him as unable to resist the efforts of his social environment to pierce him, and he falls prey to his impertinent fellow emperors, who succeed in dragging him into their game. In his defense, one should admit that the position he found himself in was more difficult than the positions of the *Daodejing*'s survival artists. His killers, rather than easily identifiable as hostile, appeared to him and even to themselves as well intentioned. The murder unfolded step-by-step, with neither perpetrators nor victim noticing—although it was by no means hidden but plain for anyone to see. The piercing of Hundun does not occur in the form of a vicious attack by a beast or an enemy soldier; he is killed softly by two perfect hypocrites who succeed in making not only Hundun but even themselves believe that they are genuinely good (see also Chen Guying 2008, 264–65).

Hundun is mortally pierced by the seemingly gracious procedure providing him with a face. The emperors thought this a good idea, and Hundun—who was not well versed in the art of life—did not disagree. Unlike a sudden death by a tiger's claw or a soldier's spear, Hundun died a protracted death by socialization: the imposition of a face illustrates, in Girardot's (2008, 202) words, "the Daoist 'perspective'" that "'face' and 'name' are the fatally deceptive characteristics of a fallen human nature that accepts the values of human culture as ontologically definitive and normative." Put more simply, the story illustrates how one perishes from accepting an identity. The emperors, Hundun's "friendly" social environment, form Hundun into another social persona. They wish to transform him from an evasive, shapeless, and impersonal entity into a sincere and honest member of society (one who has a designated social role and matching actuality)—which is how they see themselves. He dies because he lacks the art of avoiding social identification.[6] He not only does not avoid it but also makes the mistake of inviting it. At the moment when his identity is complete, he perishes. In other words, his error consists in his lack of immunity against and the ensuing verification of the social identity that is imposed on him.

The perfidy of Hundun's death, its insanity, and the ensuing difficulty to avoid it—a difficulty that turns out to be harder to avoid than deadly stabs in the midst of rhinos or warriors—lay in the cloak of sincerity in which it is dressed. In a sociopolitical context, one is not in danger of being pierced and then eaten by a tiger. Here, one is penetrated by and then amalgamated into careers, positions, roles, functions. The art of being "good at holding on to life" in such circumstances, too, consists of being capable of moving freely around in an environment without getting attacked by and then devoured by such predators. And the most present danger is to fall prey to the sweet pretense of sincerity that follows the call for identification with one's social face and the corresponding beliefs and values.

Hundun is described as most kindly entertaining the Emperors of the North and South. But as soon as one invites social rank home, as soon as one commits to it or "treats it as a guest" (dai 待), one also creates an attachment (also dai) that diminishes one's capacity to move around lightly and unbiased in one's (social) environment. The Hundun allegory uses the term dai (which is of particular philosophical significance in the Zhuangzi) to connote all these meanings. Brook Ziporyn (2009, 214) explains, "Zhuangzi regards dependence [dai] as an undesirable condition to be overcome"; but at the same time, "freedom from dependence is attained not by withdrawal from interaction with things, but by emptying oneself of a fixed identity so that one can depend on—follow along with, 'go by'—the intrinsic self-posited value of anything that comes along [dai]." By receiving a face, or a "fixed identity," Hundun, the one who was too fond of hosting (dai), created a "dependence" (dai) and finally lost his goodness at "following along with" (dai).

As a failed Daoist sage, Hundun is not a model to be emulated but a character one should distance oneself from. He made the fatal mistake of falling into the trap of sincerity and allowed society to impose an identity upon him. As soon as this identity became his, as soon as he verified it with his face, he was destroyed. Read as a parody, the story of Hundun makes fun of an impossible personal verification of social roles and values. It distances us from the very attempt of such a verification and thus implicitly encourages genuine pretending—a playful approach to one's role or roles in society.

HUZI, THE FACE CHANGER: A PARODY OF A DIDACTIC TALE

The comically inverted myth of Hundun's death in the last of the Inner Chapters is preceded by a much longer story that is usually read as a didactic tale about how to become a true Daoist sage, or as an illustration of attaining spiritual perfection. In our view, however, this story, too, can be read as a humorous parody and, at the same time, as an illustration of the benefits of a playful facelessness—that is, genuine pretending.

As in the case of the Hundun narrative, the "cast" of the story (a variation of which is found in Liezi 2.13) consists of three characters. First there is Liezi, who, next to Laozi and Zhuangzi, was and is considered the third major representative of ancient Daoism. He appears a number of times in the Zhuangzi, including in two sections of the Inner Chapters. In addition to the passage from the seventh chapter discussed here, he is mentioned in the first chapter, wherein he is famously characterized as "riding the wind" (see Ziporyn 2009, 5). It has been noted frequently that in both these appearances Liezi is depicted somewhat critically as "misled by the glamour of magic," to quote A. C. Graham (2001, 290). In the passage in question, the criticism of this ancient competitor of Zhuangzi's goes so far that he is actually ridiculed as another failed Daoist sage.

Second, there is a "Master Hu" (Huzi 壺子) or "Master Calabash," if his name is understood literally and as a poetic construct (Defoort 2012, 466). He is depicted, as in Liezi (1.1) and Huainanzi (10.19), as Liezi's spiritual teacher. Third, there is a shaman (wu 巫) named Jixian 季鹹 who specializes in the art of ancient Chinese physiognomy (xiangshu 相術), which involves predicting an individual's future on the basis of their physiological and, in particular, facial features (Raphals 2013, 142–46). Jixian, as the passage tells us, could tell someone's fortune with extreme temporal precision, and the common people were so shocked by his supernatural powers that, when they saw him, "they would turn and run" (Ziporyn 2009, 52).

The narrative begins with Liezi meeting Jixian. He is so impressed with the shaman that he tells his master, Huzi, that he, Huzi, is no match for Jixian. Huzi is not happy about this, so he expresses his dissatisfaction with Liezi's progress in studying the Dao and challenges him to bring Jixian over to test him. Jixian comes, checks Huzi over, and predicts that he will soon die. When Liezi relates the bad news tearfully to his master, Huzi explains in colorful language that he had displayed the countenance of "the patterns of the earth"

(Ziporyn 2009, 52) and asks that Jixian may come again. Jixian does so and now states that Huzi has totally recovered, adding that this is probably only so because Huzi was lucky enough to have seen him on the previous day. Huzi later explains (once more in colorful language) that this time he displayed a specific countenance of "Heaven's soil" and asks to have Jixian come again. When Jixian comes on the next day, he is confounded: Huzi's appearance has changed once more. Unable to make an assessment, he blames Huzi for his incoherent state. Huzi then explains to Liezi in even more mysterious terms than before that now he displayed the countenance of a "vast gushing surge," after which he asks that Jixian come yet again. When Jixian meets Huzi on the next day, he runs away at first sight and can no longer be found, even though Huzi asks Liezi to get him back. In the usual mysterious terms, Huzi explains that he displayed the countenance of the state prior to having "emerged from the source" (53). He adds that his final shape was "something empty . . . admitting of no understanding of who or what," and that this was the reason why Jixian fled (53). Then the story concludes: "Liezi realized he had not yet learned anything. He returned to his home and did not emerge for three years, cooking for his wife, feeding the pigs as if he were serving guests, remaining remote from all endeavors, carved back into unhewn blockishness. Solitary like a clump of soil, he planted his physical form there in its place, a mass of chaos and confusion. And that is how he remained to the end of his days" (53; translation modified).

Interpretations of the narrative that read it from a *dao jiao* perspective typically pay attention to the respective self-descriptions of Huzi's changed countenance. Karyn L. Lai (2015, 108), for example, regards them as expressing "elements of the Heavenly dao," which Huzi, the "calabash," was able to store and reproduce—namely, "earthly patterns, heavenly grounds, vital energies, and the origins prior to the rise of the ancestors." Quite similarly, Livia Kohn (2015) sees Huzi's performances in the story as paradigmatic illustrations of the "origins of Qigong." For her, he is an early master practitioner displaying his extraordinary skills and proving that he "is completely at one with the Dao." In the same vein, Michael Puett (2002, 130) takes the story to show how Huzi, "through cultivation of his qi, is able to reach a state . . . in which the very concerns of life and death become irrelevant." Thereby, Puett argues, Zhuangzi intends to exemplify how a Daoist practitioner "gains access to the state that nothing can overcome" (130). Read in this way, the story basically contrasts the inadequate practices of shamanism and physiognomy as represented by Jixian with the true Daoist cultivation of Huzi, which enables one to reach extraordinary states that need to be described in extraordinary language since they transcend the normal boundaries of experience.

There is no doubt, historically speaking, that interpreters such as Karyn Lai, Livia Kohn, and Michael Puett are justified in reading the narrative in a context of Daoist cultivation efforts and transformative ambitions. The passage has exerted a profound influence on later Daoist practices and has traditionally been taken most seriously in this regard. The variation found in the *Liezi* has Huzi describing some of his transformations in even more detail, and this directed the major focus of attention of earlier Chinese interpreters to these elements of the story. In the appendix to his edition of the *Zhuangzi*, Ziporyn (2009) presents translations of numerous traditional commentaries, which are concerned mostly with explaining Huzi's richly poetic depictions of his respective appearances. Terms and expressions such as (in Ziporyn's translation) the "reservoir," the "patterns of the earth," the "froth of the salamander's swirl" (which is alternatively understood as a "whale in the depth of the ocean" or "a "swarm of small guppies" [53n13 and 208]), "Heaven's soil," or the "incipient impulse of all that flourishes" are explored and rationalized (207–10). In short, reflections on the practical meaning and significance of Huzi's cryptic language have dominated the reception of this story. It has been approached as a cultivation riddle in need of deciphering.

Alternatively, and highlighting not so much the presumed outcome of Daoist cultivation as its methodology, both Wiebke Denecke and Carine Defoort have read the story more recently as a didactic tale. For them, it paradigmatically illustrates the master-student relationship in Daoism. According to Denecke (2010, 274), the narrative is about a "new pedagogics of instruction in the *Zhuangzi*" that is supposed to operate paradoxically and end with rendering "the instructor superfluous" (276), since, as she assumes, in the end "Liezi no longer needs any kind of instruction." Similarly, Defoort (2012, 459) argues that the story is an "instruction dialogue" showing how the "non-availability of the teacher and his unwillingness to teach, are paradoxically, at the core of the teaching." Accordingly, it is said to promote "a non-teaching, in which the learner learns while the teacher does not teach."

The reading of the story as a didactic tale provides an occasion to look at the story in a different light. While *dao jiao* interpretations focus more or less exclusively on Huzi, now Liezi becomes an at least equally important character. We, too, think that Liezi's role is quite crucial in the narrative and that the traditional *dao jiao* reading, because of its "obsession" with deciphering the presumed riddles, tends to neglect his importance. Upon closer inspection of the text, however, we cannot fully agree with Denecke and Defoort and feel that their reading is in need of a decisive modification. Both assume that Huzi and Liezi are exemplary figures representing a paradoxical Daoist educational philosophy: Huzi is a model Daoist teacher and Liezi a model Daoist learner. After all, for Denecke, Liezi ends up in an enlightened state where he has transcended the need of any instruction, and for Defoort the story is meant to illustrate how the "learner learns" a presumably important lesson from a nonteaching teacher. Literally, however, the story ends with Liezi's realizing that "he had not yet learned anything," or, more literally, "had not yet begun to learn" (wei shi xue 未始學; Ziporyn 2009, 53). It seems that the Daoist paradoxical didactics illustrated by this story are even more radical than those proposed by Denecke and Defoort: following this "new pedagogics of instruction," not only does the teacher not teach but also the learner does not learn! In our view, however, such a didactics is not merely paradoxical, it is absurd. We therefore believe that the story can in fact be read as a parody of a didactic tale.

We do not see much evidence, neither philologically in the text itself nor historically in its reception, that would justify reading the story (as it appears in the Zhuangzi) as a tribute to Liezi's learning success. Traditionally, commentators have instead read it as criticizing Liezi's limited success in Daoist cultivation. Wang Fuzhi 王夫之, for instance, said that "Liezi studied only the patterns of the earth and nothing more" (Ziporyn 2009, 210). Or, to quote Graham (2001, 290) again, he has been understood as "misled by the glamour of magic." Rather than being an exemplary learner benefiting spiritually from his teacher's mysterious and unconventional methods, Liezi seems to make no progress at all. His teacher's miraculous efforts are rather wasted on him. In fact, we fully agree with Wang Bo's (2014, 10) observation that Liezi "comes out like a little clown" in this story and is portrayed comically. He does not appear as a model Daoist learner but, on the contrary, is caricatured as a wannabe-Daoist dimwit.

At the beginning of the story, Liezi is depicted as someone who is easily impressed and eager to jump on the bandwagon: He mindlessly falls prey to, or, as the text says, "becomes intoxicated by" (xin zui 心醉) a popular "guru" who trades in physiognomy. He then rushes back to his teacher, Huzi, only to tell him impertinently that the fashionable physiognomist is so much better than him. Huzi returns the insult by laconically lamenting Liezi's stupidity with the saying that without a rooster even a whole lot of hens will not produce a chicken. At the outset of the narrative, this already indicates that Liezi is hopelessly immune to instruction, no matter how much attention he is given. Liezi's stupidity is highlighted right after the first meeting between Huzi and the physiognomist. Liezi uncritically and wrongly accepts the latter's diagnosis and is so shaken by it that he sobbingly reports it to his teacher. His emotional outbreak is, as the stoic master soon explains, entirely uncalled for. Liezi's misplaced emotionality cannot, as the reader thereby understands, be taken seriously. It only enhances his overall goofiness. This goofiness, along with Liezi's general incapability, is later underscored when he is asked to call back the fleeing physiognomist after the final meeting with Huzi. Once more inept and helpless, he cries out, "He's gone! I cannot catch him!" (Ziporyn 2009, 53).

The story then ends with a satirical depiction of Liezi's "retirement." Liezi's realization that he "had not yet begun to learn" ironically echoes the preceding statement made by Huzi, who claimed that in his final transformation he had presented himself as someone who "had not yet begun to emerge from our ancestor" (wei shi chu wu zong 未始出吾宗). Huzi's grandiose but unfathomable exercises only make Liezi despair. He gives up studying the Daoist arts altogether and turns into a caricature of a Confucian who is subdued by his wife and practices ritual propriety with his domestic animals: we see him "for three years, cooking for his wife, feeding the pigs as if he were serving guests" (Ziporyn 2009, 53). Liezi resigns from his Daoist pursuits and becomes a henpecked family man with comically inverted Confucian attributes.

The concluding lines of the narrative play with the vocabulary of the *Daodejing* and other Daoist texts and have Liezi eventually living out his years "carved back into unhewn blockishness [pu 樸]"[7] and "solitary [du 獨] like a clump of soil"[8] (Ziporyn 2009, 53). Applied to the hapless Liezi in his retirement, these expressions lend themselves to an ironic reading as well. Such irony is particularly evident with respect to the term *pu*, which, as Christian Schwermann (2011, 93) has shown, has negative connotations in other texts of the era, such as the *Shangjunshu* 商君書, where it means "stupid" and is applied to the uneducated rural population. As the ultimate simpleton, Liezi lives out his years in blissful ignorance and so happens to adopt a "primitivist" Daoist way of life. But ironically, he could do so only after he gave up trying what he could never learn. Liezi thus emerges from this story as a failed, frustrated, and foolish Daoist practitioner. Only in his retirement, and after distancing himself from Daoist cultivation ambitions and training efforts, is he able to coincidentally—or perhaps "naturally" (ziran 自然)—partake in a Daoist experience.

From a humorous perspective, Liezi is an important character in the story, which, as a parody of a didactic tale, portrays him as an inept and feeble practitioner. The story outlines his way into retirement from his Daoist aspirations—and how he thereby still became a Daoist, if only by default. Liezi's comical counterpart in the story is Jixian, the quack physiognomist. Jixian's unfounded arrogance—his incompetence matched by unwarranted self-esteem—becomes clear after the second meeting with Huzi. Huzi, as the reader knows, is toying with Jixian and deliberately puts on a healthy appearance that contrasts with his earlier display of sickness. Jixian not only falls into Huzi's trap by coming up with the diagnoses he was led to infer but also shows his conceitedness by ascribing Huzi's change to his own magic healing powers. Huzi has thereby revealed the hollowness of Jixian's professed knowledge and skills and exposed him as an impostor. When Jixian sees Huzi for the third time, his arrogance turns into irritation. He is dumbfounded by Huzi's changed complexion yet again and instead of admitting his own limitations, only vents his frustration. He, too, is now helpless, but unlike Liezi the simpleton, he reacts with aggression. He is portrayed as a sore loser. At the final meeting with Huzi, Jixian is immediately brought to the end of his wits, and we see him disappearing in a cloud of steam, apparently enraged by his total defeat. He is caricatured as the angry scoundrel who has finally been debunked and expelled.

Given the comical features of both Liezi and Jixian, it becomes possible to view the character of Huzi, too, in a humorous context. While he is not an object of ridicule like Liezi and Jixian, he can well be seen as a jester who, in Socratic fashion, toys with his interlocutors and has them making fools of themselves. We have already mentioned how he makes fun of Liezi at the beginning of the story when he compares Liezi's cluelessness to a hen lacking a rooster. The story basically revolves around Huzi's increasingly teasing out the stupidity and preposterousness of Liezi and Jixian. Rather than literally teaching them any truths or skills, he figuratively teaches them a lesson by chasing both away: the angry physiognomist flees discredited, and silly Liezi retires to serve his wife and his pigs. Huzi leaves both without any message other than that they failed to deceive or convince him.

If the story is read in a humorous key, Liezi and Jixian emerge as laughingstocks, and Huzi as a jesting trickster.[9] But if Huzi is understood in this way, then maybe his art is not limited to changing his appearances and thereby confounding those who think of themselves as wise or on the way to wisdom. Maybe we can presume that not only his changing faces lack ultimate meaning but the changing words by which he describes them do so as well. Maybe he is toying not only with Liezi and Jixian—who fail to understand him—but also with countless readers from later generations who have tried hard to figure out what is truly behind the "froth of the salamander's swirl" or the "incipient impulse of all that flourishes." Maybe the heart-minds of those readers, too, have been intoxicated by magical appearances and trapped by a jester who had them make fools of themselves. Be that as it may, Huzi explicitly states at the end that he was showing himself as "empty" and "admitting of no understanding," and that this made Jixian run away. He showed himself, in other words, as nothing in particular and thereby paradoxically transformed a strained expectation into nothing: there is simply nothing to see—no secret, no truth, no authentic self. Apparently, there is no riddle to decipher.

We can thus detect quite a few characteristics of humor in the narrative. The story disengages its readers from its protagonists. We do not sympathize with Liezi or Jixian, nor do we find them role models to emulate. We do not want to become a student like Liezi or a physiognomist like Jixian. And if the story is read humorously, we may admire Huzi, but only as a nonserious jester and not as an exemplary teacher. He is not a straightforward model sage but someone who performs a practical joke on false sages. The story therefore contradicts the expectation of a didactic tale. Liezi is, paradoxically, not taught anything by his teacher, and he leaves him without any success. Ironically, he finds his Daoist ways only after he has left Huzi and given up altogether on learning and following a master. Numerous incongruent statements and depictions are found in the narrative, such as Jixian's false claim to have cured Huzi or the evoked image of Liezi treating his pigs as honored guests. Repeatedly, strenuous emotions are relaxed: Liezi's anguish about his master's imminent death is unfounded, and we do not empathize with Jixian's anger. Rather than sharing Jixian's anger or Liezi's anguish, we smile about both and thereby feel pleasure. We are also freed from certain moral pressures: teachers do not have to be venerated, and figures of authority (the fake star physiognomist) are deprived of their reverence. Huzi's last transformation, we are eventually told, shows that there is nothing behind his changing faces, and we are no longer asked for an "understanding of who or what." We are consequently left with an emptiness of meaning and can experience mental effortlessness; we do not have to engage in difficult explorations of the significance of any riddle.

As a literary character Huzi, the jester, conversely corresponds with respect to a remarkable detail of Hundun, the failed Daoist who succeeds him as a protagonist in the final narrative of the seventh Inner Chapter: the stories of both are about their faces. Hundun was faceless but allowed others to impose a face on him. Huzi has a face, but it is one that he can change at will so that no expert in facial recognition can identify him by its features. The two characters negatively mirror each other: Hundun is defeated because he adopts a definite face of his own, and Huzi triumphs because he does not let his face define him.

Huzi engages in an ancient Chinese variation of the art of mask changing (bian lian 變臉).[10] This illusionist craft evolved out of the traditional Chinese opera and has performers change masks instantly and apparently magically by swiping a fan or by a quick gesture of the head or hands while they are moving to theatrical music. The alternating masks represent different characters and moods. The multimedia performance of mask changing thus combines the stunning effects of illusionist art with the aesthetics of music and dance and the dramatic elements of theater. It resembles a miniature opera where all the characters and the whole plot are compressed into one short performance by a single actor. This amplifies the distancing effect found in the standard form of traditional Chinese theater as described by Brecht. Because of the extreme degree of temporal condensation, no coherent narrative emerges and no stage character takes shape. The performance completely deprives the presented "roles" of any consistency. Instead, the audience is exposed to a frenzy of rapid transformations of faces, moods, and motions.

While Huzi does not change his faces with the astonishing speed of a mask-changing illusionist, his performance nonetheless produces a similar effect in those who watch it: it becomes impossible to identify him as a particular individual with essential characteristics. As a contemporary interpreter has remarked, Huzi thus defies "any possible categorization whatever" and so, philosophically speaking, "reflects the self-transformations of the Dao" (Gier 2000, 223). Chen Guying (2008, 263), in a decidedly genuine pretending sort of interpretation, highlights Huzi's "multiple changes" (cici de bianhua 次次的變化), "empty self" (xu ji 虛己), and ability to "change according to the situation" (sui shun ying bian 隨順應變). Guo Xiang drew in effect a very similar conclusion nearly two millennia earlier when he commented on the passage that Huzi was "following smoothly along with any circumstance without anywhere being brought to an end" (Ziporyn 2009, 208). Huzi changes faces so radically and drastically that no essential self can be ascribed to him—the whole spectrum of human behavior and appearance is at his disposal, and he is capable of taking on *any possible face*. Like a mask changer who condenses an entire tradition of plays into one short act, Huzi condenses the "self-transformations" of human experiences into his performance. And, like a mask-changing display that follows no particular narrative sequence, Huzi, too, is not "brought to an end" but enacts whatever fits the purpose—which, in his case, is simply to stun and eventually undermine the physiognomist (i.e., the presumed identification specialist).

Seen in this way, the story contrasts Jixian's pretence of genuineness with Huzi's genuine pretending. Jixian pretends to be able to read people's faces and Liezi pretends to be a Daoist practitioner. In fact, both are deceiving themselves and others: Jixian cannot really read people's faces, and Liezi is not a true Daoist. Huzi, on the other hand, acts as a mask changer. He adopts shifting roles with great skill yet without personally adopting any of them. He is a genuine pretender, engaging in pure play.

In the *Zhuangzi*, the two narratives of Liezi's retirement and Hundun's death are separated by only a short paragraph that is usually interpreted as a philosophical comment on the role of Huzi in the preceding story. This comment contains the famous statement that "the consummate person uses his mind like a mirror, rejecting nothing, welcoming nothing, responding but not storing. Thus he can handle all things without harm" (Ziporyn 2009, 54). We read this as a paradigmatic formula of genuine pretending, the pure playacting that is not based on hiding or suspending a true nature. Genuine pretenders "do not store" and do not adopt any of the roles they play; they neither welcome them so as to make them their own nor do they reject them as unfit for themselves. Like a mirror, Huzi reflects what Jixian wants to see in him back onto Jixian and therefore makes it impossible for Jixian to identify and thereby predict and "own" him.

Most important, Huzi's art allows him to remain *unharmed* (*bu shang* 不傷). This final conclusion clearly sets up a contrast with the immediately following story of Hundun. In the midst of the pretence of genuineness Huzi remains unharmed, but Hundun perishes. Huzi is surrounded by the insincere Liezi and Jixian but does not give in to their attempts to make him adopt a sincere identity. Hundun, too, is surrounded by two pretenders: the emperors Hu and Shu. He, however, "kindly invites" them and thereby submits to their call for an identification of himself, which fatally harms him.

HORSEHEAD HUMPBACK AND THE FREAKS:
PARODIES OF THE "IDEAL MAN"

Chapter 5 of the *Zhuangzi*, "Markers of Full Virtuosity" ("De chong fu" 德充符; Ziporyn 2009), deals mostly with apparently ailing people: cripples, men severely mutilated by physical punishment, and physical freaks. Nevertheless, all these people can be seen as examples of accomplished Daoists. Interestingly enough, the chapter title is the only one in the Inner Chapters—or for that matter, in the whole book—that includes the term *de* 德 for "virtuosity," "power," or more generally, "health." The very title already indicates a striking incongruity, which is a marker of humor: a chapter featuring a parade of cripples is presented as a chapter on extraordinary vitality.

A brief section at the end of the chapter introduces the characters of Hunchback Limpleg and Jarsized Goiter (Ziporyn 2009, 37), two "physically challenged" individuals who made great careers as highly venerated court officials. Of the two dukes who, respectively, employed the short-necked cripples, it is said that each of them was so delighted with their new adviser "that when he saw the unimpaired their necks looked freakishly long to him" (37). Both Hunchback Limpleg and Jarsized Goiter are portrayed as men of outstanding *de* in spite of their conspicuously sickly abnormalities. The dukes they serve do not follow common modes of perception and indeed see an extraordinary healthiness in them. This leads the dukes to a "twisted" perception of health and sickness in which the normal no longer appears normal and the odd no longer odd.

The cases of Hunchback Limpleg and Jarsized Goiter are preceded by a much longer story about another hunchback, Horsehead Humpback. We learn that "when men are with him they can think of nothing else and find themselves unable to depart. When women see him, they plead with their parents, saying they would rather be this man's concubine than any other man's wife—this has happened at least a dozen times already!" (Ziporyn 2009, 35–36). Although he had "no position of power" and "no stash of wealth" (36), the Duke of Lu made him his prime minister—only for Horsehead Humpback to step down soon after and leave the court altogether. The devastated duke then asks Confucius for consolation and an explanation of all that has happened. Confucius answers with several allegories, including that of "some piglets still nursing at the teats of their dead mother" and the example of "a footless man" who "has no love for shoes" (36). He explains the relation of these images to the duke's encounter with Horsehead Humpback: The sow still looks to the piglets like their feeding mother, but they soon realize that her nurturing power is gone and abandon her "empty" body. Likewise, the man without feet can abandon his shoes because there is nothing to fill them. The cases of a body or body part deprived of its health to the utmost degree are contrasted with the case of Horsehead Humpback, the deformed man whom everybody— including the duke—instinctively trusts and whose company and advice everyone yearns for. The dead sow and the shoes of the footless man have the "whole form" (*quan xing* 全形), but they totally lack *de*, or vital efficacy. Conversely, Horsehead Humpback is a man of "complete *de*": a man of "complete power" or "complete health" (*quan de zhi ren* 全德之人) who nonetheless does not have the corresponding form. What appears healthy therefore may in fact be absolutely sick—and, as in the cases of Hunchback Limpleg, Jarsized Goiter, and Horsehead Humpback, the opposite may be equally true.

Read in this manner, the entirely plausible standard interpretation of chapter 5 understands it as a variation on the popular admonishment to not judge a book by its cover and applies it to judgments about physical appearances. Accordingly, the cases of Hunchback Limpleg, Jarsized Goiter, and Horsehead Humpback are understood as pointing to a paradoxical understanding of health. Unlike some common assumptions, health cannot be equated with immaculate physical appearance or an absence of ailments and physical "handicaps." The common nonparadoxical conception of health as simply the opposite pole of an unambiguous sick/healthy distinction is wrong, and, most important, it obstructs one's capacities for perceiving the extraordinary vigor emanating from the cultivation of one's *de*. Often enough, an apparently healthy form obscures a sick *de*, just as an apparently sick form may well obscure a healthy *de*. The allegories of the cripples are thus seen as illustrating a more appropriate understanding of "complete health" (*quan de* 全德) and serve as an encouragement to sharpen one's capacities for perceiving and producing it.

Interpretations along this line have been suggested by, for example, Chris Fraser (2014) and Steve Coutinho (2015), who writes, "These then are people whose natural capacity (*de*) has been twisted somehow, redirected, so that it gives them a potency (*de*) that is beyond the normal human range. At any rate, this out of the ordinary appearance, this extraordinary physical form, is a sign of something deeper: a potency and a power (*de*) that connects them more closely to the ancestral source. These are the sages that Zhuangzi admires:

those whose virtue (*de*) is beyond the ordinary, and whose signs of virtue indicate that they have gone beyond."

Understood in this way, the chapter outlines a kind of profound health that contrasts inner health and outward appearance. The "extraordinary physical form" of the characters in this chapter indicates "something deeper," an inner "potency" and "power" whose vigor is made evident precisely by its capacity to not only outweigh conventional standards of beauty but also overcome the associated social stigmatization. The chapter thus depicts, in Coutinho's words, the capacity to attain a form of *de* "that is beyond the normal human range." This very idea—the prospect of increasing "normal" human capacities, of "going beyond"—has become central to efforts of the *dao jiao* tradition. The line of interpretation of the chapter represented here by Countinho's reading thus corresponds neatly to the approach toward the *Zhuangzi* and other texts developed by Daoist practitioners in their pursuit of the cultivation of an encompassing health. In short, this standard interpretation of chapter 5 of the *Zhuangzi* provides a philosophical foundation for the engagement in an "internal alchemy" (*neidan* 內丹) aimed at enhancing one's powers and potencies in order to be connected "more closely to the ancestral source," to once more quote Coutinho. Characters like Horsehead Humpback thereby become models for spiritual and physiological cultivation.

As we saw, however, the illustrations of the state of a "complete *de*" in chapter 5 of the *Zhuangzi* are very conspicuously incongruent: the characters described as having it display at the same time a blatant lack of healthiness. They suffer, as anyone can plainly see, from gross impediments. In other words, they resemble characters like Mengsun Cai in chapter 6 of the *Zhuangzi* whose "name" (*ming* 名) is not matched by their "form" (*xing* 形) or "actuality" (*shi* 實), as we outline in more detail in the following. Yet while these characters do not possess the form or actuality (*wu xing* 無形 or *wu shi* 無實), they are nevertheless renowned or successful.

In chapter 5 of the *Zhuangzi*, Confucius uses this paradoxical "logic" to describe Horsehead Humpback; he is called "someone whose *de* does not take on form" (*de bu xing zhe* 德不形者); that is, he is someone who has a lot of vitality yet no corresponding physical nature—in fact, he is a caricature of a healthy physical nature.[11] As on many other occasions in the *Zhuangzi*, Confucius is once again used to contradict standard Confucian teachings. Here he revolts against the expectation that someone who is renowned for his complete *de* and who occupies a most revered position matches it with his form or constitution (*shi*). While Mengsun Cai's *ming* and *shi* are not in alignment because he lacks *shi*, Horsehead Humpback's exalted social rank, power, and health (*de*) do not match his *shi* because his deformed form is not "informed" by any *de* at all.

Seen in this light, characters such as Horsehead Humpback appear as incongruent parodies of the Confucian expectation that a person of excellence is sincerely excellent, or that his name or reputation or role is matched by what he "really" is. Of recent commentators, P. J. Ivanhoe is one of the few[12] to have noted the use of such anti-Confucian parody in chapter 5 of the *Zhuangzi*, and he finds it already in its very title.[13] Ivanhoe (2002, 187–88; emphasis added) acutely observes,

> There is an important contrast between Mengzi's [Mencius's] ideal of moral and physical perfection and the ideal described by Zhuangzi. Zhuangzi's exemplars do not follow a set of conventional virtues or accept conventional standards of physical beauty. They reject the Confucian standards of a fully developed and intact physical body along with its related taboo against bodily mutilation or natural deformation. Zhuangzi's exemplars often are the lowly, the deformed, the ugly, criminals who have lost limbs or been otherwise mutilated by punishment, and yet these very people have perfected their personal "virtue" (*de*). For numerous examples, see chapter 5 of the *Zhuangzi*. The title of this chapter, "The Seal of Virtue Complete" (*de chong fu* 德充符), may be *a conscious parody of Mengzi's notion of the ideal man*. One of the characters in its title, "to complete" or "fill out" (*chong* 充), is an important term of art in the *Mengzi*. It describes the process of developing and completing the nascent moral sense.

Here, Ivanhoe opens up quite a different avenue for understanding chapter 5 of the *Zhuangzi*. In fact, such a different understanding was also hinted at by Albert Galvany (2009, 85), who maintains that this chapter is an unconventional piece of literature and that "the remarkable position of the *Zhuangzi* should be duly emphasized." Galvany goes on, "Unlike what occurs in the remainder of the period's written tradition, in the *Zhuangzi*, amputees have a radically opposite function, and this should be carefully analysed." Galvany also stipulates that "the appearance of these mutilated characters needs to be interpreted in philosophical terms. In the unfolding and development of the ideas expressed in the work, this category of exceptional beings has a clearly defined role to play in giving shape to a major philosophical, social and political critique" (86). We agree with Galvany that chapter 5 of the *Zhuangzi* is quite extraordinary and that an alternative understanding of the significance of its main protagonists may indeed "lead to an eventual reinterpretation of the value of these important characters" (86). Such a reinterpretation can look at them as humorous characters mocking mainstream sociopolitical values and expectations of the time.

Once one views the characters introduced in chapter 5 of the *Zhuangzi* as, to use Ivanhoe's words, "a conscious parody of Mengzi's notion of the ideal man," then one is led not toward a (*dao jiao*) reading that conceives of them as exemplars of spiritual perfection one should seek to emulate in order to be connected "more closely to the ancestral source" and attain some form of ultimate health, but rather as counterimages of vain cultivation ideals set up by the Confucian tradition and the social structures and semantics of the time that reflect them. The story's cripples and criminals, with their perfect *de*, then emerge as comical parodies of those who claim or are assumed to "complete" or "fill out" (*chong*) the forms and thus to personally verify any of the values that society constructs. As tricksters and jesters, they performatively contradict those worthies or sages whose fame is based on the pretence that their social rank is grounded in their superior personal worth and beauty.

Other than a model for spiritual cultivation, Horsehead Humpback now appears as an absurd gigolo whose grotesque charm no girl who comes near him can resist. And Hunchback Limpleg and Jarsized Goiter are bizarre political celebrities to whom the aristocrats in their vicinity inevitably fall prey. As successful private and political seducers, they are carnivalesque figures mirroring the thinly veiled sexual connotations that the Confucian and pre-Confucian tradition had already projected onto personal relationships between rulers and ministers (see Granet 1919) by supposing that subordinates are bound to their superiors by the natural "attractiveness" of the latter.

The superior efficacy, power, or "complete health" of the cripples and criminals in chapter 5 of the *Zhuangzi*, seen from this perspective, then appears to be based on—nothing. Precisely because their power is not claimed to be founded on sincerity, virtue, or commitment in the first place—because they let go of the impossible ambition of a true match between social constructions and personal identity—they also cannot be accused of being in violation of true sincerity, virtue, or commitment. Their power therefore becomes most powerful and efficacious. It is perfectly immune to any suspicion of falseness and insincerity. The characters of chapter 5 in the *Zhuangzi* can thus be understood as humorous illustrations of the "cryptic" first lines of chapter 38 of the *Daodejing*:

> Higher *de* is not *de*,
> Therefore it has efficacy [*de*].
> Lower *de* does not let go of *de*.
> Therefore it has no efficacy [*de*].

In accordance with these lines, the profound health displayed by the cripples and criminals of chapter 5 of the *Zhuangzi* does not have to be understood as a "potency (*de*) that is beyond the normal human range" and thus attainable only through special spiritual and physiological practices. Instead, it can be understood as a healthy form of social efficacy that effortlessly emerges once one lets go of all aspirations of truly matching social values with one's personal "virtue," or once one "lets go of *de*" (shi *de* 失德) and does not claim that one is beautiful, good, healthy, or really all that important at all. At the same time, the effortless and groundless social success of the cripples and criminals of chapter 5 of the *Zhuangzi* serves to poke fun at all those whose elevated positions in society make them believe that these indeed reflect their real goodness, beauty, or virtue. In other words, as carnivalesque parodies characters like Horsehead Humpback show that those who are venerated in society and believe that, therefore, they surely must actually be full of *de* may in fact only be full of . . .

Seen comically, the seductive cripples of chapter 5 correspond to Master Huzi in chapter 7: they are all tricksters performing practical jokes on those who believe themselves to be genuine or virtuous or powerful. Their triumphs, which are based on nothing, expose the hollowness of those around them. As a parody, the story of Horsehead Humpback is once more marked by characteristics of humor: The exaggerated and grotesque features of the characters produce a distancing effect. Narrative expectations are continuously overturned, such as Humpback's stepping down from his post with no reason; and surprising statements, such as the dukes' finding the necks of normal men too long or young women's preferring to be Humpback's concubine to being the regular wife of someone else, occur repeatedly. Our emotions are toyed with. We cannot take seriously the feelings of the devastated duke. The story clearly undermines the reverence one was supposed to show to a duke and thus it has amoral features. We are not given any complicated rationale for Humpback's success and don't need one—intellectual efforts are spared, and all that we learn is that he is void of form, or empty: he deflates others by not being inflated himself.

Like Liezi's master, Huzi, Horsehead Humpback is capable of making others see him as what he is not. But also like Huzi, he is no fraudster or hypocrite. He does not cover up a real nature or secret motives or his true character. Nothing is hidden, just as nothing is revealed. Neither Huzi nor Horsehead Humpback is deceptive like the body of a dead sow is to her piglets; they do not indicate any concealed treasure within, unlike a shoe that may falsely promise a foot inside.

Horsehead Humpback and his fellow cripples are carnivalesque versions of genuine pretenders. They satirically mirror the hollowness of their social superiors while making no effort to challenge them with a moral doctrine or a call for sincerity—or authenticity for that matter. They do not claim original-ity or creativity. To the contrary, Horsehead Humpback, we are told, has "never been heard to initiate anything of his own" and is always "just chim-ing in with whatever they're already doing" (Ziporyn 2009, 36). He goes along with whatever is opportune.[14] Still, as a personification of incongruity, he makes those around him look at the world in a topsy-turvy fashion and cele-brate the ugly as beautiful, the sick as healthy, and the criminal as virtuous. That is to say, he makes the mechanisms that society has imposed on itself to create values and ideals work in his favor without sincerely embracing or productively developing them, but also without directly challenging them. He is found attractive, although ugly, and his amputee fellows achieve social estimation, despite the fact that they are convicted criminals.

As smooth operators, the absurd gigolos and bizarre celebrities of chap-ter 5 do not confront the mainstream culture of their time but excel in a soci-ety that they do not identify with and whose values, precisely through their grotesque success, they undermine. Their achievements are paradoxically founded: because their "*de* does not take on form" it remains so powerful. The Confucian concern with a sincere match between inner virtue and social value is shown to be hollow, or an impossible obsession. The supposed virtues indicated by social rank are exposed as nonexistent, and, consequently, the social values that supposedly manifest some actual qualities are rendered arbitrary. Thus, these humorous characters simultaneously affirm and negate social values—they effortlessly thrive on the very social constructs that they reverse.

A carnivalesque interpretation of characters such as Horsehead Humpback as parodies of the Confucian ideal of a match between one's social persona (name) and one's actual identity (form) is supported by the first episode of the fifth chapter. Here, we are presented with another counterimage of Confucius. A fictitious master named Wang Tai with obvious Daoist features is said to have had almost as many followers in Confucius's home state of Lu as Confucius himself. However, this negative double of Confucius's is, once again, presented as a deformed criminal "whose foot had been chopped off" (Ziporyn 2009, 32). Similar to Horsehead Humpback, he is not a man of great words who would engage in great moral teachings or explicit social criticism; rather, it is said that "when he stands he offers no instruction, and when he sits he gives no opinions" (33). When questioned about Wang Tai, Confucius endorses him as a better role model than himself and thereby confirms that this man's heart-mind is indeed perfect (xin cheng 心成), and not despite, but *precisely because* it is not "backed up" by any actual disposition or character. As the text points out, Wang Tai's outstanding quality is, paradoxically, that he "has no form" (wu xing 無形).

Ironically, Wang Tai, a footless and formless criminal who has nothing to say, not only is as big a success in Confucius's society as Confucius himself but even manages to rise to the top and have the master submit to him and pay him his respects—just as Horsehead Humpback, Hunchback Limpleg, and Jarsized Goiter were able to effortlessly make women and rulers willingly submit themselves to them. Wang Tai, too, thus illustrates the superior efficacy of having no actual identity corresponding to one's social role, and as another trickster, he also succeeds in making Confucius look like a fool.

If one accepts an interpretation of the characters in chapter 5 of the *Zhuangzi* as parodies of Confucian ideals, one does not have to look at them as straightforward models for spiritual cultivation but can reinterpret them as carnivalesque subversions of the Confucian insistence on matching social constructs with a sincere commitment to them. The alternative to the falsity and inefficacy that Confucian moral teachings unintentionally produce is precisely not a call to replace false sincerity with true sincerity, or false virtue with true virtue, but one to abandon the ideal of forming an identity modeled on social constructs of value and worth. Characters like Wang Tai and Horsehead Humpback do not try to verify social constructs by "truthfully" internalizing them. On the contrary, by "letting go of de" they get rid of the obsession with adopting a face and a true form. In this way, a Daoist philosophy of genuine pretending, as comically illustrated by those characters—and not that different from the intentions of dao jiao—also intends to cultivate health. But rather than looking for it in the form of extraordinary spiritual or physiological capacities, it achieves an unperturbed ease that nonetheless allows one to thrive through a playful childlike adaptation in society without an intentional concern for sincerity or real greatness.

ROBBER ZHI, THE CARNIVALESQUE REBEL: A CONVERSION PARODY

The character of Robber Zhi 盗跖, a most prominent personification of crime and evildoings in ancient China, occurs several times in the Outer and Miscellaneous chapters of the *Zhuangzi*. In all cases he is paired with "Confucian paragons of virtue" such as Bo Yi 伯夷, who, as legend has it, "starved himself to death rather than eat the rice of the Zhou dynasty, of whose violent revolution he disapproved" (Ziporyn 2009, 59; chapter 8.3), and other ancient Chinese personifications of moral excellence such as Zeng Shen 曾参 and Shi Qiu 史鳅, chapter 11.1. The stark moral contrast that is evoked by making mention of these antithetic paradigmatic figures, however, is immediately undermined in the text. Section 8.3, for instance, poses the following question: "Why should one be praised and the other condemned?" (59). This question is then answered *not* by advancing a moral relativism (in the form of "one man's freedom fighter is another man's terrorist") but by an amoral critique of the initial moral "corruption" that breeds immorality: "So why must we say that Bo Yi was right and Robber Zhi was wrong? Everyone in the world is sacrificing himself for something or other. Those who do so for Humanity and Responsibility are praised by the vulgar as exemplary men, while those who do so for wealth are condemned as petty men. But they are all alike in sacrificing themselves" (59). In other words, moral values—such as those created by Confucianism—intoxicate people's heart-minds and lead to moral fanaticism, which, as far as its destructive effects are concerned, is eventually indistinguishable from immoral fanaticism (see Moeller 2009).

A variation of this "amoral relativism" (which holds that deeply moral or immoral positions are equally uncalled for) is found in section 10.2. This section remains one of the most widely known passages in China from the *Zhuangzi*. It is generally understood as humorous, particularly because of the modern Chinese homophony of "the Dao" (*dao* 道) and the "name" or designation "robber" (*dao* 盗).[15] In typical carnivalesque fashion it thus mixes and reverses the low and the high, or the (morally) venerated and (morally) condemned. Asked if "robbers" (*dao*) also have a *dao* (literally, *dao yi you dao* 盜亦有道, a popular saying in China today)—or, in this context, a "right way"—Robber Zhi says, "Where can one go without the right way? To guess where the treasure is hidden is Sagacity. To go in first is Courage. To be the last to leave is Responsibility. To judge whether a job can succeed or not is Wisdom. To distribute the loot equally is Humanity. No one can become a great robber without these five virtues!" (Ziporyn 2009, 63; translation modified).

This passage confirms the amoral "message" of the *Zhuangzi* that moral values, in this case the five cardinal virtues of Confucianism, are at the disposal of anyone's desire for self-righteousness and can be used to adorn and justify any kind of preposterous behavior (see also Scharfstein 1995, 29). More important, the text does so by comically inverting the robber into a "card-carrying" Confucian and thereby comically exposes the immoral "robbery" hidden in the Confucian *dao*, or its "right way." By extension, it thus generates suspicion of *any* claim to know or have "the right way," including the Daoist right way. Thus, Robber Zhi's answer not only counters expectations (immorality surprisingly turns into morality) but also produces the typical playful and amoral relief effects of many kinds of humor by depriving the Confucian vocabulary of its awe and the moral fear that it normally evokes.

The famous pun in this passage that turns a robber into a follower of the *dao* and, by conversion, Confucian and other moralists into robbers sets the tone for a much longer narrative about Robber Zhi in chapter 29 of the *Zhuangzi*, which bears his name as its title. In our view, this narrative expands and explores the humoristic critique of morality found in the famous passage about Robber Zhi in chapter 10 and corresponds in many ways to the humoristic sections of the Inner Chapters that we discussed earlier. Far from being evidence of an evil forgery by later impostors (as suggested in Carr and Ivanhoe 2000), we believe that the "Robber Zhi" chapter artistically and philosophically connects with other sections of the book, and particularly so with the Inner Chapters. We do not intend to speculate on exactly when and by whom it was written, but we perceive it as coherent with the humorous strand that permeates the *Zhuangzi* as a whole.

A. C. Graham (2001, 221–23) has classified the "Robber Zhi" chapter as belonging to the "Yangist Miscellany" on the basis of its correspondence with the concern for individual survival and physical well-being, which is associated with Yang Zhu. Liu Xiaogan 劉笑敢 (1995), on the other hand, sees it as connected with an "anarchist" stratum of the *Zhuangzi*. Both regard it therefore as philosophically and philologically distant from the Inner Chapters and the "authentic" core of the work. On the other hand, as Esther Klein (2010) has demonstrated quite meticulously, the underlying hypothesis that the Inner Chapters are earlier or more authentic than other parts of the Zhuangzi is by no means settled once and for all. By pointing to a number of Han and pre-Han texts, she stipulates that there is practically no evidence for the existence of an Inner Chapters unit in the Warring States period. Other textual segments, however, are already explicitly mentioned in Han and pre-Han texts. The "Robber Zhi" chapter, for instance, is specifically named in the Shiji as the work of Zhuang Zhou. From this perspective, one could even make the case that chapter 29 is more "original" than (some of the) Inner Chapters. We refrain from such conclusions, however, and do not wish to either dismiss as inauthentic or "authenticate" this or any other segment of the Zhuangzi.

The Robber Zhi narrative begins with Confucius meeting his friend Liuxia Ji 柳下季, the brother of Robber Zhi. He admonishes Liuxia Ji to set his younger brother straight, but Liuxia Ji replies that such an attempt would be not only futile but also dangerous. Notwithstanding this advice, Confucius visits Robber Zhi with the intention of correcting him. Robber Zhi reluctantly receives him, but only to express his contempt for Confucius as a duplicitous moralist. Confucius, however, behaves with utter reverence, flatters Robber Zhi, and offers him enfeoffment with a large territory if he officially becomes a feudal lord rather than an "unincorporated" gang leader. Robber Zhi briskly refuses the offer on the grounds that becoming a lord would eventually ruin him. He then engages in a lengthy "lecture" beginning with a tribute to the benefits of a primitivist or anarchic lifestyle that returns "back to nature" and that allegedly existed before the world was corrupted by the civilization efforts of the Confucian founding kings. This civilization process, according to the robber, brought about only violence, suffering, and Confucian hypocrisy. He then lists a number of cases of moral and political exemplars, including Confucius himself, whose attempts to do good brought only misery to themselves and others. He concludes with the "Yangist" remark that life is short and that it is difficult enough to live out one's years in a reasonably satisfying way. Once more chastising Confucius for his "obsessions," he chases him away. Confucius hurries off in a discombobulated manner and meets Liuxia Ji again. When Liuxia Ji asks him about the visit, Confucius replies, "I was in a hurry to pat the tiger's head, braid the tiger's whiskers, and very nearly didn't escape the tiger's mouth" (Graham 2001, 239).

The story is written in a very elegant and subtle style typical of many parts of the Zhuangzi, and it combines a wide variety of literary devices. But, despite being generally rather well known (at least in China), it has received relatively little philosophical attention. Contemporary interpretations have focused on the aforementioned clearly discernible Yangist (Graham 2001) and anarchist or primitivist (Liu 1995; Rapp 2012) elements of Robber Zhi's long speech, as well as its equally obvious amoral aspects (Scharfstein 1995; Moeller 2009). In combination, the stylistic and philosophical characteristics of the story amount to a very strong anti-Confucian message that was already noted by Sima Qian. Esther Klein (2010, 318) translates the relevant statement in Zhuangzi's biography in the *Shiji*: "[Zhuang Zhou] created the 'Old Fisherman,' 'Robber Zhi,' and 'Rifling Trunks' [texts] in order to defame and refute the disciples of Confucius." Of course, this message has also been acknowledged by contemporary interpreters, some of whom endorse it to a certain degree (Chen Guying 2008), and others of whom find its radicalism objectionable (Carr and Ivanhoe 2000), while still others simply register it. An example of the latter group of interpreters is Alan Berkowitz (2000, 42), who conceives of Robber Zhi as the "Anti-Sage" and thereby evokes Nietzschean connotations. A new height of anti-Confucian readings of the story was reached during the Cultural Revolution in Maoist China when, in accordance with the schematic dialectical materialism of the time, Robber Zhi was identified as the leader of a revolutionary slave revolt challenging the ancient feudal system as represented by Confucius. He was depicted in popular political materials as a handsome and strong ancient Chinese rebel and champion of the oppressed who triumphed over the Confucian class enemy (Sommer 2007).

In our view, all these approaches are warranted, including even the understanding of Robber Zhi as the representation of a historical leader of a rebellious group of outlaws who posed a military and political threat to the rulers of the time. Popular as well as literary transformations of such figures into idealized or romanticized characters are by no means rare—Robber Zhi, for instance, has recently appeared as a character in the Chinese animated TV series *The Legend of Qin* (*Qinshi mingyue* 秦時明月—literally, "Qin's moon"). As Deborah Sommer (2007, 8) has pointed out, it is striking that the story of his encounter with Confucius "was interpreted as a sober account of historic events" in the Cultural Revolution, while it "was of course understood as a fictive parody in its own day." It is not just the Maoist interpretation, however, but also many other contemporary readings that fail to approach the story as a parody. To be sure, its humoristic aspects are sometimes noted: G. E. R. Lloyd (2014, 26) refers to it in the context of saying that the *Zhuangzi* "mocks the pomposity of Confucius's insistence on the importance of ritual," and Kimchong Chong (2011, 330) accurately remarks that "the Confucian association of certain moral qualities with human nature" are "ridiculed" in the text. In none of these cases, however, is the humorous nature of the story discussed much further.

The story begins comically by countering the expected image of Confucius: it introduces him as a close friend of the evil Robber Zhi's older brother. In this way, it literally relates good with evil and echoes the philosophical point (made throughout the amoralist passages in the book) that morality begat immorality in the first place.[16] At the same time, it exposes the mean within the lofty and vice versa. The following description of Robber Zhi's viciousness comes across somewhat humorously, too, because it incongruently depicts his viciousness in strangely beautiful terms. Moreover, the robber is portrayed not only as a cruel gangster but also as an anti-Confucian deviant who makes a point of breaking with Confucian morality: he reportedly "gave nothing to his kin, ignored his father and mother and brothers, refused to sacrifice to his ancestors" (Graham 2001, 235). Robber Zhi is thus portrayed ambiguously right from the start, as is typical for humorous characters: he appears as a comical inversion of suspicious moral exemplars and challenges their authority—and by proxy relieves readers of their moral fear.

In the subsequent conversation between Confucius and Liuxia Ji, the former is portrayed as a moral pedant who is rather stupid and "would not listen" (Graham 2001, 235) to the latter's sound practical advice to beware of Robber Zhi. Rather than as a sage, Confucius appears here as a fool destined for defeat. And when, in stereotypical fashion, he is depicted leaving for the audience with Robber Zhi "with Yan Hui driving the carriage, Zi Gong on the right," this impression is only reinforced: in the context of the story, the reader is led to think something like, "What a conceited idiot!"

In contrast with the pedantic and effete Confucius sitting in his carriage accompanied by his servile adepts, Robber Zhi appears on the scene in a manly manner—"chillin'" with his boys on the sunny yang side (associated with masculinity) of Tai Shan, the holy mountain in Confucius's home state of Lu. With grotesque exaggeration he is said to be "taking an afternoon snack of human livers" (Graham 2001, 235) when Confucius arrives. The following descriptions show Confucius as stiff and absurdly concerned with protocol while interacting with someone who is out in nature obviously defying conventions. Confucius is satirically insulted by the robber for his pompous dress and manners and attacked as a sophistic moralist who sells ethical rhetoric to crooks in power. Robber Zhi's irreverent bluntness, however, has no effect on Confucius. Quite the contrary: hypocritically (and thereby involuntarily proving his unfavorable characterization by the robber), he praises Robber Zhi's extraordinary "virtues" (de 德)—physical strength, charisma, beauty, smartness, courage, and leadership. Invoking the name-actuality distinction, Confucius concludes that these virtues directly contradict the name "robber." Instead of being labeled a robber, Confucius suggests, Zhi should rather join the ranks of the aristocracy and become a conventional feudal lord.

Confucius's speech is intricately ironic. Confucius—who, as was made clear, actually abhors the robber—hypocritically flatters him by calling him a virtuous person and then offers him a lordship, thereby satirically exposing not only Confucius's own moral double standards but also the moral corruptness of the Confucian social structures that makes robbers lords.[17] On the other hand, Confucius's depiction of Robber Zhi's virtuous characteristics is actually correct—Robber Zhi is handsome, intelligent, and charismatic and therefore truly found attractive and well liked by people. However, these virtues are not the ones most embraced by Confucianism. The passage shows the perversion of a Confucian morality that has replaced real virtues with fake virtues. It expresses a false sense of attraction, because, according to standard Confucian teachings, one is supposed to be attracted by moral people like Confucius but not by the sensual and uncivilized physical handsomeness of Robber Zhi. In carnivalesque fashion, the story makes fun of Confucius not only as a false sage who betrays his hypocritical nature but also as someone who is unmasked as ugly, unmanly, and unattractive. After being lectured by Robber Zhi in some more or less Daoist ways (Yangist, anarchist, etc.), Confucius is finally caricatured as a stupefied loser, letting "the reins slip three times before he could hold them." Ironically, he is finally depicted in very Daoist terms: "his dazed eyes saw nothing, his face was like dead ashes" (Graham 2001, 239).

Its carnivalesque, ambiguous, grotesque, and paradoxical elements clearly identify the Robber Zhi narrative as humoristic. The initial expectation of a moral conflict or potential conversion story of Confucius and Robber Zhi is soon overturned. As in many other narratives in the Zhuangzi, Confucius's position is reversed from instructor to student. The amoral and humorous "message" of the story produces emotionally relaxing effects, particularly through the repeated ridicule of Confucius's ritualistic stiffness. The exaggeration of Robber Zhi's vicious behavior combined with tongue-in-cheek praise of his unconventional attitude take away any emotions of fear and angry condemnation that would normally be aroused by his character. Just as Confucius is deprived of his awe, Robber Zhi is deprived of his gruesomeness. He, too, is caricatured and appears almost cartoonish: When he hears that Confucius is coming, "his hair bristled up so high it tilted his cap" (Graham 2001, 235). When Confucius enters, he is "furious, with legs spread wide, hand on hilt, eyes glaring" and speaks up "in a voice like a nursing tigress" (236). The initial emotional apprehension is dissolved by hyperbole, so that the reader can follow the story with comical pleasure. The reader is disengaged and distanced from the protagonists by their incongruity. Confucius, the sage, does not act virtuously, while Robber Zhi, the archvillain, has a witty mind and a handsome appearance. Both are depicted in contradistinction to the characteristics commonly associated with their name and role, so that the story becomes a parody and presents no role models for emulation.

Once the story is read as a parody, one can no longer agree with a central aspect of its "sober" Maoist interpretation: the character of Robber Zhi is not an outright hero. While the story doubtlessly makes him appear attractive (with respect to both his physical features and free-spiritedness), he remains a carnivalesque figure, bizarrely mixing the abhorrent and evil with the endearing and good. He is a cannibal with an attitude, a fearless rebel without a cause, close to nature and full of vigor, funny and poetic, ruthless and hedonistic, charming and terrifying, a challenge to established social hierarchies, and an ironically reversed image of moralist hypocrisies.

As a humoristic character, Robber Zhi's function is not so much to put forth a serious, straightforward philosophical challenge to Confucianism. The long lecture he delivers should, from this perspective, perhaps not be subject to much scrutiny. As others have correctly observed, it clearly contains Yangist, anarchist, and primitivist elements well connected with similar positions expressed in other parts of the *Zhuangzi* and in other Daoist texts. Philosophically speaking, there is not much that is new or surprising in these passages. In fact, Robber Zhi's rather conventional (for Daoist standards) speech to Confucius is, as A. C. Graham (2001, 234) has remarked, "a little out of character" since it does not convey his usual "ferocity." It thus serves only to philosophically complement the challenge he poses to Confucianism, which is much more poignant and sharp in its narrative dimension. At least in our reading of the story, the doctrinal contents of Robber Zhi's address to Confucius are supplementary aspects of his overall performance as a virile, witty, and ambiguously exaggerated social outcast who is set up as a carnivalesque counterimage to the meek and hypocritical moralist Confucius. Altogether, the story's narrative features are so vivid that it unfolds before the eyes of today's readers in a cinematic manner. It is not at all difficult to imagine its being transposed to a contemporary context and to envision Robber Zhi as a shrewd and fearless mobster or gang leader who, at the same time, continuously makes fun of and satirically exposes the weaknesses, conceit, and corruption of those in power and in office.

From a Daoist perspective, Robber Zhi's comical nature is rooted in the dissonance between his form or actuality and his name. As mentioned, Confucius explicitly compliments Robber Zhi on his healthy and beautiful appearance, his sharp intelligence, and his social charisma. At the same time, his form is distinctively contradicted by the depreciative social role designation "robber." Throughout the entire story, incongruent mismatches between actuality and social representation reoccur. Robber Zhi's health is extraordinary, he is most vigorous and powerful, yet he expresses only disdain for the outward symbols of beauty and propriety, such as fine clothing or a solemn comportment. He professes that he is "tall and handsome" and that others "take pleasure in the sight of [him]" (Graham 2001, 234), but he scornfully ridicules Confucius's elaborate attire as a "branching tree of a cap on your head and the hide off a dead cow's ribs around your waist" (235). He is an intellectual who speaks eloquently and at length and knows his history and philosophy well, but he lives like a tramp and identifies with the primitive and uncultured lifestyle of the so-called Nester clan people (chao shi zhi min 巢氏之民) (236). He is rich and powerful but has nothing but contempt for titles, rank, and a whole array of persons who have laid claim to them. After a long speech, he finally responds to Confucius's offer to exchange his name "robber" for an aristocratic title: "There's no robber worse than you. Why doesn't the world call you Robber Confucius instead of calling me Robber Zhi?" (237).

Quite clearly, the incongruity informing the humor and along with it the social critique of the Robber Zhi narrative is that between form and name. The correspondence between the names and forms of all characters in the narrative is constantly undermined. The decisive difference between Confucius and Robber Zhi is that Confucius responds to this incongruity with his standard "rectification of names" (zheng ming 正名) project—he aspires to confirm his noble name by being noble and wants Robber Zhi to copy this attitude and to bring his name-actuality relation in balance. Robber Zhi, of course, fundamentally opposes the idea of such a rectification of names. His whole lecture points out from various perspectives—including a Yangist, an anarchist, and a primitivist one—the personal and social insanity of the Confucian congruity ideal. Both as a literary character and through the words put in his mouth, Robber Zhi attacks the Confucian demand to match social values and ranks with personal commitment. Consequently, he is portrayed as living proof of the possibility of an opposition against the personal verification of social roles.

Unlike the smooth operators of chapter 5 in the *Zhuangzi*, Robber Zhi does not defy the Confucian sincerity project as a conformist but as a rebel. However, it must be stressed that his rebellion is a comical, grotesque, and carnivalesque one. He is not trying to set things right by demanding true sincerity instead of hypocrisy. He, like the smooth operators of chapter 5, represents a mismatch between form and name and does not strive to correct it. While the smooth operators succeed in conformity with society by not following the sincerity norm, Robber Zhi thrives and lives happily as a deviant outside the law. This makes him a different genuine pretender, but a genuine pretender nevertheless. He plays the robber perfectly and with great grace and skill, but he is not internally a robber, and thus he does not verify the name "robber" with a robber's heart-mind. The cripples in chapter 5 of the *Zhuangzi* and the Robber Zhi character in chapter 29 are complementary humorous depictions of paradoxically healthy and efficacious genuine pretenders. The former are, to refer to Wang Bo's and Wang Deyou's respective characterizations of a (post-)Daoist attitude, grotesque intrasocial hermits, whereas the latter is a comically caricatured extrasocial rebel (Wang Bo 2004, 2014; Wang Deyou 2012).

THE INCONGRUITY OF SINCERITY

In his final words to Confucius, Robber Zhi chastises the sage and chases him away: "Everything you say I reject. Away with you, quick, run back home, not a word more about it. Your way is crazy obsession, a thing of deception, trickery, vanity, falsehood. It will not serve to keep the genuine in us intact, what is there to discuss?" (Graham 2001, 239). Here, Robber Zhi summarizes very directly and thus not so humorously the Daoist critique of the implicit and unavoidable hypocrisy of the Confucian cultivation ideal and its insanity—it is denounced as a "crazy obsession" (*kuangkuang jiji* 狂狂汲汲). If our interpretation is correct, for the *Zhuangzi* the core object of criticism addressed here is the Confucian demand to personally verify (or personify) social roles. This ideal is accused of producing falsehood and of making people crazy and obsessed. Such an interpretation is supported by Chong Kim-Chong's (2011, 330) previously mentioned observation that what the "Robber Zhi" chapter mockingly attacks is "the Confucian association of certain moral qualities with human nature," if we are allowed to identify "certain moral qualities" as the Confucian value system expressed in social designations of roles and functions (i.e., the names). If moral values and role designations do not reflect human nature, then of course the attempt to prove them with one's nature can produce only "crazy obsessions" as well as "deception, trickery, vanity, falsehood." But if so, what is the "genuine in us" that Robber Zhi apparently intends to "keep intact"? (Although it is worth noting that he does not actually say so; he claims only that Confucius is unable to achieve genuineness, not that he, Robber Zhi, is himself able to.) Translated more literally, Robber Zhi speaks here of "complete genuineness" (quan zhen 全真), and interpreters often take this to be a Daoist notion of a pure or true sincerity or authenticity as opposed to a supposed Confucian insincerity or inauthenticity. Is the Daoist notion of zhen 真 necessarily a concept of authenticity? Is the zhenren 真人 in the Zhuangzi the authentic person? We do not think so and return to these questions in more detail later. At this stage, however, it may suffice to probe a little further into Robber Zhi's character.

If our analysis is correct, Robber Zhi is not a good exemplification of any "complete authenticity." As we pointed out, everything about Robber Zhi is incongruous: he is an exaggerated comical figure pairing, quoting Chong (2011, 343), an "utterly rough and violent character" with smartness, wit, and rebellious appeal. Given the thoroughly ambiguous and humorous characteristics of Robber Zhi, we can only assume that if he is actually meant to illustrate "complete genuineness," then this very notion has to be understood as equally ambiguous or humorous. Robber Zhi is in fact anything but completely genuine—his form and name do not match—and thus "complete genuineness" may only mean here, ironically, a genuine rejection of any claim to sincerity. In a Socratically ironic fashion, only those who do not claim to be sincere can achieve some degree of genuineness: they can genuinely engage in pretending. Complete genuineness, then, is paradoxically synonymous with "genuine insincerity." Accordingly, a comical figure based on incongruity and play is most suitable to represent such an ironical notion.

Notably, a term that is very similar to "completely genuine" (quan zhen) is associated with Horsehead Humpback, Robber Zhi's humorous and incongruent counterpart in chapter 5. As we saw, Horsehead Humpback was identified as "someone whose de does not take on form" (de bu xing zhe 德不形者) but yet as someone renowned for his quan de 全德, or "complete de." Something similar could be said about Robber Zhi, whose extraordinary "virtues" (de) as ascribed to him by the flattering Confucius do not manifest themselves in his social designation. Horsehead Hunchback, the cripple in office and esteem, and Robber Zhi, the captivating outlaw, both personify an incongruent *quan de* and an incongruent *quan zhen*. In both cases, their comical incongruity is precisely what makes them paradoxically genuine. They both fail to fulfill the unwarranted expectations of a match between actuality (form) and name. By extension, a similar incongruity is found in Huzi, the ancient Chinese mask changer. His virtuosity consists in being capable of displaying total incongruity: he changes his forms completely and thus disproves any attempt at categorization. In A. C. Graham's (2001, 98) translation, he's "not a medium possessed by his name," or in Ziporyn's (2009, 53) translation "a corpse presiding over [his] good name." In his case, too, his genuineness consists in performatively deconstructing the quest for a sincere correspondence between name and form.

In sum, the character of Hundun is a caricature of a failed sage whose failure consists in giving in to the demand of becoming sincere. Hundun is contrasted with an array of tricksters who are all capable of withstanding an ethics of sincerity and who flourish as jesters and comic performers. We saw Huzi, the confounding mask changer, "admitting of no understanding of who or what" (Ziporyn 2009, 53); we met Horsehead Humpback in his company of freakishly smooth operators, who "says nothing and yet is trusted, achieves nothing, and yet is loved" (36); and we encountered Robber Zhi, the grizzly but charming rebel "with strength enough to defy reprimands, [and] eloquence enough to dress up wrong as right" (Graham 2001, 235). All of them are puzzling, incongruent humorists without a specific message or morality; resisting emulation, they do not ask us to become just like them. At the same time, they performatively engage as comical characters in genuine pretending and thereby show how delightful it can be to be a "player" (as opposed to a "player hater").

THE INCONGRUITY OF NAMES AND FORMS

NAMES THAT ARE GOING ONLY SO FAR

As indicated earlier, we think that the humorous critique of the Confucian moral demand of sincere double correspondence between social roles and names and mental and emotional states—or, more broadly, between roles and names and one's identity—does not stand on its own in the *Zhuangzi*. It is complemented by nonhumorous or merely slightly humorous expositions that, often enough, also employ allegories and narratives. As in the case of the humorous critiques, these expositions are not simply negative dismissals of Confucian ideals but at the same time illustrate a Daoist alternative to Confucian sincerity in the form of what we like to call genuine pretending. The notion of genuine pretending, we believe, thus also offers a framework for a consistent representation of the philosophical discussions of the relation between names (ming) and forms (xing) or actualities (shi) as found in the Zhuangzi.

According to Yang Guorong (2009b), the Zhuangzi's view on names and (forms or) actualities can be summarized with a proposition found in section 18.5, which can be translated as follows: "Names go only so far with respect to actualities" (ming zhi yu shi 名止於實). Yang couples this statement with a better-known metaphorical pronouncement in section 1.4: "Names are the guests of actualities" (ming zhe, shi zhi bin ye 名者，實之賓也) (137). In line with Yang's observation, we think that many passages in the Zhuangzi seek to diffuse the emphasis placed on the determining power ascribed to names in the Analects and early Confucianism. Names, which include designations of moral virtue, labels of reputation, definitions of social roles, and the like, are rejected as providers of fixed guidelines for understanding a person or indications of how to act rightly. This rejection, however, does not imply that genuine pretending would amount to an outright "revaluation of names" such that a genuine pretender would by default embrace, for instance, nonvirtuous designations or bad reputations. According to the philosophy of genuine pretending found in the Zhuangzi, social names may either be accorded with or not, but neither rejecting nor aligning oneself with names has any priority—and neither one is constitutive for building identity. A genuine pretender may have a good name or a bad name, but in either case, the name goes only so far and merely remains a guest that is not matched with a sincere commitment in substance and does not infiltrate the (non-)identity of its bearer.

Consequently, incongruent Daoists in the Zhuangzi are described in section 2.6 as "going along with what is so" (yin shi 因是) and in section 3.2 as "according with heavenly patterns" (yi hu tian li 依乎天理). In other words, they lack any personal presuppositions about how to act or about what is right or wrong (shi fei 是非). Although "going along with what is so" or "according with heavenly patterns" can and often does include making assertions or expressing negations, these are never internalized as, for example, categorical, nor are they, in a more Confucian sense, tied to a state of personal cultivation such that they would be brought about by emotional immediacy. Free of internalized behavioral commitment, genuine pretenders have no self in the Confucian sense of having cultivated determining impulses for how to act in particular situations or relationships. The actions of genuine pretenders therefore never essentially reflect their psychology or who they are since they have no such essential self.

Because Confucian dual correspondence requires a constant matching up of one's behavior and moral psychology, it allows for a degree of personal predictability. The Zhuangzi lacks similar projections of a stable self or of constancy in making decisions, and this is why the Zhuangzi sometimes (such as in section 2.4) disparagingly refers to a "completed heart-mind" (cheng xin 成心). From a Confucian perspective, this attitude and lack of behavioral predictability may easily seem suspicious and indicative of falsity and trickery. But from the perspective of genuine pretending, incongruity does not equal deception, malice, or pretense. Genuine pretenders do not hide or suspend their real emotions or beliefs for the sake of personal gain and have no personal agenda to follow. In chapter 49 of the Daodejing this position is summarized with regard to the ideal ruler: "The sage-ruler is constantly without a heart-mind; he takes the heart-mind of the common people as his own heart-mind" (Moeller 2007, 117; translation modified). In the Zhuangzi this idea is extended to the way one may react to one's environment by rejecting fixed notions of right and wrong and the like in favor of going along with what "is so" (shi 是 or yin shi 因是).

Some of the best-known passages in the Zhuangzi speak of "forgetting" or "lacking" a self. For example, in the first chapter (section 1.3) the "consummate person" is said to "have no self" (zhi ren wu ji 至人無己). Such expressions can be seen as not only pointing to a general "selflessness" but also, and more specifically, pertaining to the negation of a self that is in sincere correspondence with the social designations by names. If the self that is lost in the Zhuangzi is understood in the philosophical context of pre-Qin thought, it connotes the idea of a person that has been cast in the mold of names. According to Wang Bo (2004, 107), the advocacy of a no-self in the Zhuangzi is meant to encourage people to free themselves from the social constraints imposed onto them.[18] Yang Guorong (2009b, 180) describes the zhenren 真人, or "zhenuine person" (see the following chapter on this term), in the Zhuangzi as an "individual who should maintain a distance from rituals, appropriateness, and civilization's conscriptions in general." Accordingly, "having no self" can be understood at least in part as referring to a state that counters the Confucian regime of sincerity and its emphasis on double correspondence with names.

The claim that "the utmost person has no self" appears toward the end of a passage (1.3) that begins as follows: "And he whose knowledge is sufficient to fill some one post, whose deeds meet the needs of some one village, or whose

Virtuosity pleases some one ruler, thus winning him a country to preside over, sees himself in just the same way" (Ziporyn 2009, 5). This passage depicts the common phenomenon wherein people find themselves "winning" a post or recognition thanks to favorable circumstances fitting whatever abilities or qualities they may have. They thus find themselves making a career owing to a lucky but ultimately coincidental fit. The luck itself is not problematic, but problems begin once one ascribes one's success primarily to one's own merits and thus builds an according conception of self. Building such a conception of one's self through an internalization of one's social roles and an ascription of virtuousness or worthiness means to observe oneself in terms of how one is observed by society. To build an identity in this way mirrors as a kind of side effect the Confucian cultivation project that aims at sincerely identifying oneself through the social roles one lives, and can thus appear morally prudent and justified.

The mechanism whereby one forms a sense of self by seeing oneself in the way one is seen by society is ridiculed by proxy in the following line of the passage. The text continues with a succinct verdict about those who develop a sense of ego in response to their social esteem: "Even Song Rongzi would burst out laughing at such a man" (Ziporyn 2009, 5). Song Rongzi 宋榮子, otherwise better known as Song Xing 宋鈃, was a contemporary philosopher loosely associated with Daoist and Mohist ideas. He is mentioned, for instance, in chapter 33 of the Zhuangzi (section 33.3), where he is said to have been "unbound by conventions" (120). As A. C. Graham (2001, 45) points out, Song Xing represents the "refusal to feel devalued by other men's judgments" and was famous for the doctrine that "to be insulted is not disgraceful." Just as Song Xing would have encouraged those disesteemed by society not to internalize this in the form of low self-esteem, he would not have much admired the opposite, either: the internalization of fame and social success. If even a half Daoist such as Song Xing already figured out that much, then it can be concluded with Wang Fuzhi's commentary on the passage in question that "we don't need to wait for the consummate person [i.e., zhi ren 至人] to find this laughable" (Ziporyn 2009, 131). The text then goes on to acclaim Song Xing's personal immunity to any identification of social name with personal form: "If the whole world happened to praise Song Rongzi, he would not be goaded onward; if the whole world condemned him, he would not be deterred" (5). Although Song Xing is not yet accorded the status of full-fledged Daoist, he is credited with an important step toward becoming a "consummate person" by radically disjoining name and form and understanding "the split between the outer [name] and the inner [form]" (nei wai zhi fen 內外之分).

As the text proceeds, Liezi is introduced as another character representing an approximation of the consummate person. Liezi is here famously praised for "riding the wind," a metaphor that can easily be interpreted as indicating a Daoist ability to adapt to different circumstances, seemingly favorable or not, and to flourish in accordance with them (D'Ambrosio 2014). However, as it is somewhat enigmatically put, "there was still something that he depended upon" (*you suo dai zhe* 有所待者)—namely, the wind, as one is led to think. It seems that Liezi is here taken to be an accomplished smooth operator (see the following chapter) who, although not infatuated by any of his specific social roles, is nevertheless still infatuated with his versatility in enacting them. Since he is paired here with Song Xing, maybe he can be seen as an illustration of someone who does not internalize specific social conventions and can therefore skillfully go along with all but who retains a sort of attachment to and identification with this very skill.

The consummate person and his or her affiliates will eventually avoid any identification or self-infatuation. Translated rather literally, the passage ends with the following dictum: "The consummate person has no self; the spirit-like person has no achievements; the sage has no name" (*zhiren wu ji, shenren wu gong, shengren wu ming* 至人無己，神人無功，聖人無名). Apparently, all these figures are supposed to represent people who do not identify with how others see them, are not attached to their success in society, and do not identify with social designations. Brook Ziporyn's (2009, 6; emphasis added) translation conveys these connotations better than the more literal rendering: "The Consummate Person has no *fixed* identity, the Spirit Man has no *particular* merit, the Sage has no *one* name."

Borrowing Tao Wanglin's 陶望齡 commentary on the passage, the consummate person is a "wanderer" able to move between different names and the merits that may come along their way, so that "everything is his self" (Ziporyn 2009, 132). Wang Fuzhi also interprets the passage in terms of the name-actuality semantics that it employs. He writes, "When no one name is made manifest, all actualities are safe from loss" (Ziporyn 2009, 133; translation modified). A sage can affirm any actuality by refusing to internalize a specific name. Liu Xiaogan (2010, 156), too, reads the passage as referring to a sort of liberation of the heart-mind from socially induced reputation, likes, dislikes, and value judgments.

The total dissociation from one's social role—particularly a venerated one—is depicted emblematically in the narrative of the "genuinely pretending tree" (section 4.5 of the *Zhuangzi*), which we discuss in more detail in the following chapter. The story of this tree, which was used as a holy shrine but did not internalize the religious values that society ascribed to it, ends with the rhetorical question (in Ziporyn's [2009, 31] explanatory translation,[19] which we find appropriate), "Is it not absurd to judge it [the tree] by whether it does what is or is not called for by its position, by what role it happens to play?" The tree that is designated and acts as a shrine but does not see itself as essentially having religious value, along with the many other smooth operators appearing in the fourth chapter of the *Zhuangzi*, illustrates impressively how "names go only so far with respect to actualities" and how they are merely "the guests of actualities."

MENGSUN CAI AND THE RADICAL TRANSFORMATION OF ALL FORMS

We agree with Yang Guorong (2009b, 137) that one story in the *Zhuangzi* elucidates particularly well the central idea that "names are the guests of actualities"—namely, that of Mengsun Cai, the master mourner, which appears in section 6.7 of the Inner Chapters. This tale first and foremost portrays the incongruity of names and forms as a paradoxical Daoist ideal. It also thereby becomes a paradigmatic narrative for what we call genuine pretending. The story begins as follows: "Yan Hui asked Confucius: 'Mengsun Cai wailed when his mother died, but did not shed a tear. At the center, his heart did not mourn. Conducting the funeral, he did not grieve. In spite of this threefold incorrectness, he is renowned as the best of mourners throughout the state of Lu. Isn't this an obvious case of someone winning a name (*ming*) without possessing the actuality (*shi*)? I am utterly amazed at it!'" (Moeller 2004a, 90; translation modified).

Confucius's disciple Yan Hui is troubled by the fact that Mengsun Cai could earn the reputation (name) of a great mourner through actions that are not reflective of his inner emotional states, or the actuality of his heart-mind. Yan Hui's apprehension reflects the deep concern expressed by Confucius in a comparable situation described in *Analects* 17.21, as discussed by us earlier—the case of the no longer saddened Zaiwo, who complains about still having to obey the mourning rituals a year after the death of a parent. There, we saw how Confucius grudgingly advised Zaiwo to discontinue his ritual practices, given the fact that his emotions no longer corresponded to them. Clearly for Confucius, sincerity trumps social conformity even—or perhaps especially—in the case of the arguably most important ritual convention in ancient China, the mourning rituals. In order not to violate the correspondence between the name-role "mourner" and the form or actuality of the psychological state of the mourner, Confucius releases Zaiwo from the duty to mourn. Mengsun Cai, however, does exactly what Confucius deemed as "perverted" (bu ren 不仁) with respect to Zaiwo: enacting the role-name "mourner" without the corresponding commitment. While Mengsun Cai's performance should, from a consequential Confucian moral point of view, be considered completely wrong, he is nonetheless awarded the reputation of an exemplary mourner— and this, ironically, in Confucius's home state of Lu, which, one would like to think, should be a haven of sincere correspondence between name and form in ritual matters. With Mengsun Cai, it seems, a Daoist genuine pretender has infiltrated the heartland of Confucian ethics!

Of course, Mengsun Cai's emotional coolness at his mother's funeral demonstrates the well-known "stoic" indifference exhibited by Daoists toward death—in particular, the indifference toward the death of loved ones and one's own demise. This indifference is strikingly rendered not only in related narratives preceding Mengsun Cai's story in the fourth chapter of the *Zhuangzi* but also in the famous anecdote (in section 18.2 of the *Zhuangzi*) relating Zhuangzi's own cheerfulness after the death of his wife. The emotional indifference toward death displayed by all these Daoist masters reflects the metaphysical realization of the constant transformation of all things (wu hua 物化) and the corresponding existential affirmation of life and death as equally valid and real segments of sequential change—just like the four seasons or day and night (see Moeller 2004a, 82–94). In the case of the Mengsun Cai narrative, this metaphysical and existential insight into the equal validity of life and death is expounded at some length by Confucius when he explains to Yan Hui—in ironic contrast to "regular" Confucian teachings—why Mengsun Cai is indeed right about matters of life and death, and why his emotional indifference is therefore not only morally justified but also philosophically appropriate (or, as one might say, wise).

It must be stressed that the Daoist's emotional indifference toward death and life does not amount to a denial of the difference between these two stages. On the contrary, the affirmation of the radical change of all things is at the same time also an affirmation of radical diversity and multiplicity. What is "one" (yi 一) or "equal" (qi 齊) is the existential validity or ontological reality of all things, stages, or states of being, including life and death. This oneness does not cancel out but rather provides the foundation for difference. Chapter 6 of the *Zhuangzi* exemplifies the Daoist affirmation of radical variation with the famous acclamation by Ziyu 子輿, a disfigured cripple facing illness and death, of the physical change that mortality brings with it. Ziyu muses about his left arm being transformed into a rooster once he has perished while his right arm may become a crossbow pellet, his ass may turn into wheels, and his spirit into a horse (section 6.5; see Ziporyn 2009, 45). The most widely known image of radical transformation employed in the Zhuangzi is the butterfly— as it appears in the butterfly dream allegory, which also illustrates the equal validity of death and life as segments of change.

Radical change implies both radical difference and the equal ontological validity and existential reality of different forms and actualities. At the same time, it also implies the radical transitoriness and insubstantiality of all things: if everything is subject to radical change and transforms into something that is entirely different (but of equal validity and reality), then nothing has an essential self. The Daoist idea of radical transformation is simultaneously an idea of radical ontological and existential selflessness.

The story of Mengsun Cai connects the Daoist critique of the Confucian ideal of a sincere match between name and form with the Daoist metaphysics of radical transformation and its existential indifference toward death. It thereby represents not only a criticism of Confucian ethics but, at the same time, also of Confucian metaphysics—which does not affirm the transformation of all things with the same radicality—and of a Confucian existential philosophy of life that turns out to be incapable of cultivating equanimity toward death. In effect, Mengsun Cai's lack of the form or actuality of a mourner points to all three of these philosophical dimensions and integrates them into a complex whole: all forms, states, and things are subject to radical change and are therefore only temporary—and certainly without essence or substantiality. They can therefore be equally affirmed, and there is no need to devaluate any of them—death is as much a valid and real part of the transformation of all things as life. This insight constitutes Daoist emotional equanimity. This equanimity based on the affirmation of radical transformation naturally supports the view that all forms or actualities indicated by social role-names are, while real and valid, at the same time insubstantial and inessential. The Daoist ontological and existential insight into radical transformation corresponds to the Daoist denial of the Confucian demand to make social names sincere by grounding them in an essential self. The idea of radical transformation also implies that no form can sincerely match a name.

Just as Mengsun Cai can go along with life and death and affirm both equally while, or rather precisely because, he does not essentially identify with either of them, he can also adopt all social forms, including that of a mourner, with equal ease and perfection *precisely because* he does not essentially adopt them. As Confucius, the Daoist, explains, "To Mengsun Cai, there are forms (*xing*) which surprisingly alter, but this does not harm (*sun* 損) his heart. To him, there is a new construction of a hut at a new morning, but he is not emotionally stirred by death. Mengsun is very much awake. When the others wail, he wails, too" (Moeller 2004a, 91; translation modified).

Genuine pretending is the ability to genuinely wail when the others wail without "becoming" a wailer—that is, without adopting the identity of a wailer. Not only does this ability have its ontological grounding in the insight into radical transformation but also, it is healthy: it allows Mengsun Cai to prevent his heart from being harmed (*sun*). He can socially transform along with the transformations of society and "construct a new hut on every new morning," as the imagery of the text suggests. Mengsun Cai, too, is a face-changing artist, like Huzi. Mengsun Cai, Huzi, and the other incongruent Daoists violating the regime of sincerity are all genuine pretenders: they are the sociopolitical equivalent to an ontology of the transformation of all things, an existential philosophy of equanimity, and a "negative ethics" of amorality.

4. SMOOTH OPERATORS

THE ARTS OF GENUINE PRETENDING

"Why," he asked, "do you use a false name?"

"My name is not false. Inquire of the banker Carli, who paid me fifty thousand florins."

"I know that, but your name is Casanova; so why do you use the name Seingalt?"

"I assume it, or rather I assumed it, because it is mine. It belongs to me so legitimately that if someone dared to use it I should challenge his right to it by every means, public and private."

"And how does the name belong to you?"

"Because I created it; but that does not keep me from also being Casanova."

"Sir, either the one or the other. You cannot have two names at the same time."

"Spaniards often have half a dozen names, and so do the Portuguese."

"But you are neither Portuguese nor Spanish, you are Italian; and after all how can anyone create a name?"

"It is the simplest and easiest thing in the world."

"Explain yourself."

"The alphabet belongs to everyone; there's no denying that. I took eight letters, and I combined them in such a way as to produce the word Seingalt. The word thus formed pleased me, and I adopted it as my surname, in the firm conviction that, since no one ever bore it before me, no one has the right to deny it to me, still less to bear it without my permission."

"That is a very far-fetched idea; but you support it with an argument which is more specious than well grounded; for your name can only be your father's name."

"I think you are mistaken, for the name you bear yourself by right of inheritance did not exist from all eternity; it must have been invented by one of your ancestors who had not received it from his father, even if your name were Adam. Do you admit that, Your Worship?"

"I am obliged to; but it is something new."

"There you are mistaken. Far from being new, it is very old, and I undertake to bring you tomorrow any number of names all invented by perfectly respectable people who are still alive and who enjoy them in peace without anyone's taking it into his head to summon them to the Town Hall to account for them, unless they disavow them when and as they please, to the detriment of society."

"But you will admit that there are laws against false names?"

"Yes, against false names; but I repeat that nothing is more true than my name. Yours, which I respect without knowing it, cannot be truer than mine; for it is possible that you are not the son of the man whom you believed to be your father."

He smiled, rose, and escorted me to the door, saying that he would ask Signor Carli about me.

—Giacomo Casanova, *History of My Life*

FROM DISSONANT TO EMPTY ROLE MODELS

The primary object of the critiques of Confucianism found throughout the *Zhuangzi* is the impossible Confucian ideal of sincerity, of shaping one's self in accordance with social models. We hold that the intention of the *Zhuangzi* is neither to substitute a false Confucian sincerity with a supposedly correct Daoist one, nor to replace it with a Daoist authenticity. Instead, the *Zhuangzi* proposes a radically different and paradoxical role model. This paradoxical role model, unlike the one assumed by many interpreters in our age of authenticity, does not represent a unique individual who, withstanding external pressures, is true only to herself and focused on permanent self-exploration. In our view, the alternative and ironic role model proposed in the *Zhuangzi* is not a self-creating person, strong enough to shape an identity in the midst of a potentially alienating society. Instead, it is a skillful player of roles who is capable of performing tasks well and with pleasure while avoiding any identification with them, thus remaining selfless or, in our terminology, a genuine pretender.

In the preceding chapter we showed how genuine pretenders are frequently introduced in a humorous fashion. Humor operates according to exaggeration and incongruity, and the characters it portrays have to be taken with a grain of salt. Unlike exemplary sages, they are not objects of unambiguous veneration such as Yao and Shun, the founders of civilization in the Confucian tradition. Thus they are not straightforward but "crooked" and ambivalent role models who, like Robber Zhi or Horsehead Humpback, combine shocking and grotesque elements that distance readers from them with clearly extraordinary characteristics or achievements one may admire. These figures are *dissonant*; they are, at the same time, attractive and repulsive.

In some cases, as in the antimyth of Hundun or the story of the inept Liezi's retirement, the reader is confronted with failed sages and failing practitioners of Daoism who can be seen as the very opposite of role models. Perhaps more precisely, they can be understood as parodies of role models who demonstrate the very problem of orienting oneself according to role models to begin with. They, too, illustrate incongruity and dissonance, but on an even more dramatic level. Trickster figures like Robber Zhi or Horsehead Humpback present carnivalesque counterimages of Confucian exemplars and allow us to establish a distance from role models; they undermine our allegiance to them by not demanding full commitment. Of course, a negative figure like Hundun also does not invite commitment. But in addition to showing which model one ought not follow in order to survive, such a parody of a mythological hero also—and more radically—undermines master narratives altogether and thereby the very conception of establishing models. The parody of the utterly failed sage Hundun is complemented by the caricature of the utterly hopeless student Liezi. He, too, not only exemplifies a pointless devotion one would be better off avoiding but also can more radically be taken to ridicule the very mode of devotion to masters—after all, his paradoxical master doesn't teach.

In the *Zhuangzi*, portrayals of Daoist tricksters and failed masters and students alike humorously discourage emulation and disengage readers from standard role models (see Schumm and Stoltzfuss 2011). They thereby set up a roadblock on the Confucian way to sincerity by an honest enactment of roles. If one distrusts role models to begin with and does not take them seriously, then the invitation to become one's role will not be appealing. An alternative Daoist role model therefore cannot simply invite people to just identify with other or better roles than the Confucians, and one cannot just ask to pursue a true rather than false sincerity, or to engage in a self-exploring authenticity project instead. The Daoist alternative role model is a dissonant one that may well encourage one to play roles but not to identify with them or become them. Accordingly, the *Zhuangzi presents dissonant or incongruent role models who do not identify with their roles.* In this sense they are *pretenders.* However, one has to play roles in society, simply because society is constituted by roles. Thus, one can avoid a direct conflict between one's true self and one's roles—and thereby hypocrisy, lying, and, ultimately, insanity—only by avoiding the adoption of a true self in the first place. If there is no self, then there can be no conflict between a true self and one's social persona. If there is no such conflict, then the playing of one's role is *genuine.* If there is no self, there is no falsity involved in role-playing. Role play without falsity is genuine pretending.

Of course, genuine pretending is, from an authenticity-oriented perspective, paradoxical. Authenticity is tied to self-formation and self-creation. Genuine pretending, on the other hand, dissolves selfhood and creates "empty" role-playing. Its role models—once again paradoxically—cannot be emulated since there is nothing particular that would identify them. They have no essential characteristics, and the roles they play are contingent, often changing, and typically circumstantial. Such paradoxical role models are found just about as regularly in the *Zhuangzi* as their humorous relatives. While these comical cousins allow readers to disengage from them—and by extension from role models altogether—by means of humorous incongruity, the *Zhuangzi* also presents a whole array of not primarily humorous but paradoxically empty role models whom one cannot identify with because they have no identity. As is usually the case with cousins, though, one can detect many family resemblances among them. And just as funny types are not always funny, more sober ones can display an occasional sense of humor. The prototype of the more sober version of the genuine pretender in the *Zhuangzi* is, we propose, the so-called *zhenren* 真人.

ZHENREN: THE ZHENUINE PRETENDER IN THE ZHUANGZI

Reflecting a dominating authenticity-based understanding of the *Zhuangzi,* the term *zhenren* has variously been translated as "authentic person" (Ames 1998, 2; Shen 2003), "genuine person" (Coyle 1998), or "True Man" (Watson 1968). As we indicated earlier, the term has been considered a representation of a Daoist ideal of personhood that constitutes "perhaps the closest approximation in Chinese thought to the authentic self portrayed by Heidegger and Nietzsche." This is because it supposedly serves to "encourage the individual in a process of self-making" (Froese 2006, 97; see also Shen 2003 for a Heideggerian depiction of the *zhenren* as an exemplar of authenticity). Very much in the same vein, Daniel Coyle (1998, 199) has adopted a Nietzschean perspective and maintains rather categorically in one of the few in-depth English-language studies on the concept of the *zhenren* in the *Zhuangzi* that "*zhen*, as implemented in the *Zhuangzi*, denotes 'authenticity' within a transforming world, genuineness in the Nietzschean sense of being true to oneself." Accordingly, for Coyle the *zhenren* is basically an early Chinese version of Nietzsche's *Übermensch* (201). Typically, as evidenced in the preceding quote, authenticity-based Western interpreters of the *Zhuangzi* acknowledge the transformative qualities of the *zhenren* but still insist on the aspect of "being true to oneself" or, in other words, posit a "personal integrity and uniqueness" of the *zhenren* along with a "primacy given to the creative contribution of the particular person" (Ames 1998, 2). Such readings impose certain contemporary vocabularies on the *Zhuangzi*. We choose a different path here and try instead to read the *Zhuangzi* in its historical context as directly responding to and rejecting the Confucian sincerity project by promoting genuine pretending. This counter-Confucian reading applies in particular to our interpretation of the notions of *zhen* and *zhenren* in the *Zhuangzi* (see Chong 2011 for a similar approach).

Early philosophical usages of the term *zhen* 真 occur in the *Daodejing* (chapters 21, 41, and 54) but not in the *Analects* or the *Mencius*.[1] Perhaps under the influence of the *Daodejing*, the *Zhuangzi* seems to have coined the term *zhenren*. It does not appear in any texts known to predate the *Zhuangzi*. Given its more or less exclusive resonance with the *Daodejing*, the term *zhenren* can be understood as a Daoist neologism intended to present an alternative to Confucian designations for exemplary persons such as *shengren* 聖人 (sage) or *junzi* 君子 (gentleman). Its usage in the *Zhuangzi* had a great impact on the depictions of *zhenren* in later texts such as the *Huainanzi* 淮南子 and the *Liezi*, and as early as the Han dynasty the term takes on an ever-widening significance in *dao jiao* circles and beyond. It was eventually used in Buddhist contexts to translate the term *arhat* into Chinese.

While *zhen* certainly became a common word for "true" or "authentic," it seems to have been a rather novel and unusual word at the time the *Zhuangzi* was composed. It is noteworthy that one of the three occurrences in the *Daodejing* associates it with fluidity or differentiation. Chapter 41 says, "Thorough genuineness resembles variation" (*zhi zhen ruo yu* 質真若渝). This is an obviously paradoxical statement occurring in a sequence of similarly paradoxical pronouncements: the preceding lines read, "Vast efficacy resembles the insufficient; solid efficacy resembles the infirm." These paradoxes are typical of the style in the *Daodejing* and other Daoist texts, and it is quite conceivable that a correspondingly paradoxical meaning of *zhen*, which takes change and transformation as the basis for genuineness or realness, has informed the terminological creation of *zhenren* in the *Zhuangzi*. In the *Daodejing*, *zhen* links the idea of "genuineness" (as the opposite of falsehood or fakeness) with the idea of fluid alternation or shifting identities. Paradoxically, *zhen* genuineness, or *zhenuineness*, implies nonessentiality. *Zhenuineness* has no *real being* and, precisely therefore, lacks authenticity.

The ambiguous nature of *zhen* reoccurs in the "Robber Zhi" chapter of the *Zhuangzi*, where, as previously discussed, Robber Zhi is the spokesperson for *quan zhen*, or "complete genuineness." Of note, this is the only occurrence of this expression in all pre-Qin texts listed as Daoist at the Chinese Text Project website (http://ctext.org/). Aside from the "Robber Zhi" chapter, it is found only once in Yang Xiong's (53 B.C.E.–18 C.E.) *Tai xuan jing* 太玄經 (Canon of supreme mystery) and four times in the "Suwen" 素問 (Basic questions) section of the *Huangdi neijing* 皇帝內經 (Inner canon of the Yellow Emperor), the latter of which is commonly regarded as an early Han-dynasty text. It seems that the usage of the expression in these later texts has been an important factor in its subsequent (and highly successful) "career" in the *dao jiao* tradition. After all, *quan zhen* is now best known as the self-designation of "one of the most important Daoist movements in Chinese history," which "remains the dominant form of monastic Daoism" (Komjathy 2013, 1). As the name of this movement (founded in the twelfth century), the term has been variously translated as "Completion of Authenticity" (Goossaert 2008) or "The Way of Complete Perfection" (Komjathy 2013). To connect the practices of this movement with the context of the occurrence of the term in the *Zhuangzi*, however, seems to present quite a difficulty given, for example, the explicit dietary preferences of Robber Zhi for human livers. At least in our reading, Robber Zhi is far from a straightforward model Daoist whose ways one should seek to exercise daily and internalize spiritually. We therefore do not intend to read the *dao jiao* meaning of the term back into the *Zhuangzi*. In the *Zhuangzi*, as we have tried to show, it echoes the ironical depiction of Horsehead Hunchback as having *quan de* (complete virtue, complete power, or complete health). Similar to the usage of *zhen* in the *Daodejing*, we believe that *quan zhen* as it appears in the *Zhuangzi* points not so much in the direction of authenticity but, quite the opposite, in the direction of the *zhenuineness* of genuine pretending, which of course includes a paradoxical component. In line with the usages of the terms *zhen* in the *Daodejing* and *quan zhen* in the *Zhuangzi*, we find reason to assume that the *Zhuangzi*'s apparent neologism *zhenren*, too, contains paradoxical,

dissonant, or incongruent elements. More precisely, we think it is used to signal the ambiguity of the Daoist alternative to a sincerity-based Confucian role
model. We believe that it can be taken to refer to the empty role model of a
person without personhood—a person who can take on any role but becomes
none.

Chapter 6 of the *Zhuangzi* begins with a rather lengthy exposition of the
characteristics of a *zhenren*. The exposition itself is introduced with a short
reflection on how to distinguish between what is "from heaven" or natural
(*tian* 天) and what is "personal" or human (*ren* 人). It culminates in the question, "how can we know if what we call 'heavenly' is not personal, and if what
we call personal is not 'heavenly'?" This question is then followed up with the
remark that "there first has to be a *zhenren*, and only then will there be *zhen*
[genuine] knowledge [*zhenzhi* 真知]"—or knowledge of zhenuineness. While it
is stipulated that the preceding question will eventually be answered further
on—namely, once we have learned about the *zhenren*—this is not the case. We
are soon told about the *zhenren* but not about *zhenzhi*. The initial question
regarding what is really of a personal quality in what we take to be "from
heaven" or "naturally so" and what is really "from heaven" or naturally determining one's person seems almost forgotten as the text moves on.

But perhaps we can come—if not to an answer then in a Wittgensteinian
way—to a *solution* of the question with the help of a similarly phrased statement from the famous butterfly dream allegory: "One does not know whether
there is a Zhou becoming a butterfly in a dream or whether there is a butterfly becoming a Zhou in a dream." In the butterfly dream allegory, the butterfly
and Zhuang Zhou can fully enjoy the respective transitory stages of waking
and dreaming only as long as they do not know of each other: during the
dream, the butterfly has no knowledge of Zhou; when awake, Zhou has utterly
forgotten his dream. If we do not identify with either of these two but instead
adopt a zero -perspective, we can also see both experiences as equally genuine (Moeller 2004a, 48). Their respective genuineness depends on not posing
the question whether what they happen to be, by "natural" or "heavenly" coincidence, corresponds with what they are personally. They do not question
whether they are what they are by and as themselves. Ironically, the capacity to
genuinely pretend to be a butterfly in a dream depends on *not knowing who one truly is*
while dreaming; it depends on not asking while one is a butterfly if one is in
actuality Zhuang Zhou. From this we can infer that the paradoxical *zhenzhi*
(genuine knowledge) of the *zhenren* is the complete absence of self-knowledge.
The butterfly in the dream, we think, can well be seen as a poetic illustration

of a genuine pretender: a selfless or impersonal *zhenren* with the non-self-knowledge of *zhenzhi*. This paradoxical *zhenzhi* corresponds with what is said in the first line of chapter 71 in the *Daodejing*: "To know, or to master, non-knowledge is the best kind of knowledge" (*zhi bu zhi shang* 知不知上).

Returning to the open question that initiates the discussion about the *zhenren* in chapter 6 of the *Zhuangzi*, we can see that it operates with the same terminological distinction between "heaven" (*tian* 天) and "person" (*ren* 人) as *Zhongyong* 22 ("Sincerity is the way of heaven; to make it sincere is the way of the person"), which we have identified as a representative pronouncement of the Confucian ethics of sincerity. As we have maintained, the question is left unanswered for a reason: just as the butterfly dream allegory suggests, the very posing of the question introduces the irresolvable quest for sincerity. In other words, just as it is pointless to try to sincerely become the butterfly that we are in a dream, it is pointless to "make the way of heaven sincere." This seems to be confirmed a little further along in section 6.1, where it is said that *zhenren* "do not with their personality assist what is 'from heaven'" (*bu yi ren zhu tian* 不以人助天). With a little more clarity, section 24.13 in the Miscellaneous Chapters of the *Zhuangzi* reaffirms this: "The *zhenren* of old" (*gu zhi zhenren* 古之真人), we are told there, followed along with what is "from heaven" (*yi tian dai zhi* 以天待之) but would not "with their personality enter into what is 'from heaven'" (*bu yi ren ru tian* 不以人入天). This puts the *zhenren* very much in opposition to what the *Zhongyong* asks one to do: good Confucians are asked to verify the roles they naturally encounter with their person, and this is exactly what a *zhenren* avoids. The long section poetically describing the *zhenren* in chapter 6, we think, can be read as an extended exposition of that short pronouncement in section 24.13.

Just as in section 24.13, the depiction of the *zhenren* in chapter 6 claims to portray "the *zhenren* of old" (*gu zhi zhenren* 古之真人). This phrase clearly mirrors such expressions as "the wise men of old" (*gu zhi xianren* 古之賢人), which occurs, for instance, in *Analects* 7.15, or "the sages of old" (*gu zhi shengren* 古之聖人), which can also be found in the "Liqi" 禮器 chapter of the *Liji* 禮記. As a newly coined variation of an established phrase for introducing role models in Confucian texts, the expression indicates that it will present an alternative kind of role model. Following the conventional rhetoric of the Confucian texts, it presents this alternative model as "ancient." However, this imitation may well be understood as mockingly mimicking these earlier expressions. To come up with a new term for supposedly ancient worthies can be seen as a humorously incongruent gesture: the text invents a new kind of ancients and thereby satirically exposes the arbitrary creation and veneration of an invented past in Confucian contexts. In the Confucian texts, the "sages of old" are seriously presented as historical figures, while the newly "genuine persons of old" in the Zhuangzi can easily be understood as fictional figures. If so, the very phrase "zhenren of old" connotes playful insincerity.

The text goes on to describe the "the zhenren of old" in the Zhuangzi's typically idiosyncratic poetical style that leaves a lot of room for interpretation. Modifying Ziporyn's (2009, 40) translation with the help of Graham's (2001, 84), we read the first lines of the description as saying, "The zhenren of old did not revolt against their inadequacies, did not hero-worship completeness, did not plan their affairs in advance. In this way, they did not regret it when they missed the mark, and did not feel self-satisfaction when they hit it. And thus they could ascend the heights without fear, submerge into the depths without getting drenched, enter the flames without feeling hot." Unlike Confucian descriptions of ancient exemplars, the text does not make any effort to personalize a model figure through association with specific historic achievements, known narratives, or any particular character traits. Here, the exemplary persons emerge from a void and remain vague and shapeless. Most of the given characteristics are not only abstract and obscure but also, and more important, negative rather than positive. We are told more about what these exemplars were not like than about what they were like.[2] Moreover, these negative descriptions highlight incongruity: in direct contradistinction to what one would typically expect from an exemplar, these exemplars were not great. They did not overcome their shortcomings. They did not do anything to improve themselves or others, and they had no agenda and failed to plan ahead (mou 謀). Significantly, they also "did not hero-worship completeness" (bu xiong cheng 不雄成) or feel satisfaction with themselves when "hitting the mark." This description puts them squarely at odds with the exemplars of personhood found in the Analects. There, Confucius insists that the "gentleman" (junzi 君子) will "plan ahead in accordance with the Dao" (Analects 15.32), "hit the mark" (zhong 中 or dang 當), and in particular stresses repeatedly the importance of completion (cheng 成). "Completion" is not only linguistically close to "sincerity" (cheng 誠)—they are related philosophically. By "completing one's tasks" (cheng shi 成事; see Analects 13.3, 13.17, and 19.7), one completes one's name (cheng ming 成名; see Analects 4.5). The correspondence between one's actions and one's name, or between oneself and one's role, is connoted by both terms. Both terms belong to the core Confucian vocabulary of sincerity, and this is exactly the vocabulary that is not hero worshipped by the Daoist antihero *zhenren*. In short, the Daoist *zhenren* has no "completion-oriented heart-mind" (*cheng xin* 成心), to speak with the vocabulary of the *Zhuangzi* (see, e.g., section 2.4).

By being unconcerned with either missing (*guo* 過) or hitting the mark (*dang* 當), the *zhenren* ignores a further central aspect of the Confucian doctrine of the correspondence between form and name and the ethics of sincerity. Confucius's concern with avoiding faults, or, more specifically, missing what is proper (*guo* 過), is expressed repeatedly in the *Analects* (e.g., 1.8, 4.7, 7.17, and 9. 25). *Zhenren*, on the contrary, are simply not bothered by such a correspondence. They thus avoid emotional affliction and are capable of dealing with drastic change, as highlighted in the Mengsun Cai story discussed earlier. The text praises this capacity metaphorically by depicting the *zhenren* as capable of going through highs and lows—as well as through heat—unfazed. Given the Confucian connotations of the vocabulary in the immediate context, these metaphors can well be taken to refer to the ups and downs of social life. Accordingly, it can be assumed that *zhenren* can enter the social sphere and be enthralled by its flames of praise and condemnation without "feeling hot" about this, because they are not personally invested in social success of failure.

In our reading, the passage then concludes by defining *zhenren* as those who manage to "assume any appearance along with the Dao," or, a little more concisely, "assume any appearance on the way" (*deng jia yu dao* 登假於道).

While *deng jia* literally means "to climb upon the borrowed," it "is an official euphemism sometimes used to describe the death of an emperor," who is understood to have "ascended into the distance, over the clouds" (Ziporyn 2009, 34). Accordingly, both Graham (2001, 84) and Coyle (1998, 201) read *deng jia* in the sense of an "ascension" to some higher realm (Ziporyn 2009, 40). It is correct that the expression is used in this way in the *Liji* and even in section 5.1 of the *Zhuangzi* itself. So it can be read here, too, in this fashion. However, the whole phrase *deng jia yu dao* appears in *Huainanzi* 7.9 and, in the variation of *deng jia qian dao* 登假千道 (assume any appearance of the thousand ways), in a partly parallel passage in the "Shoupu" 守樸 (Maintaining original simplicity) section in *Wenzi* 文子 (Book of Master Wen) 3. In both sections the phrase is used to describe the *zhenren*, and both resonate strongly with the *Zhuangzi* as well as the *Daodejing*. In these texts, the phrase is embedded in long depictions of the shapelessness and formlessness of the *zhenren*; these depictions make ample use of the rich Daoist vocabulary to illustrate these nonqualities in the course of constant transformation. The *Huainanzi* passage, for instance, says, "At rest, they have no appearance. In place they have no location. In movement they have no form. In stillness they have no body. . . . They plunge into the Fathomless and enter the Nonexistent, in order that their different forms evolve into one another, ending and beginning like a circle of which no one can trace the outline" (Major et al. 2010, 250).

In the corresponding passage in the *Wenzi*, the expression *qian dao* 千道 (thousand ways) is paralleled by the expressions *qian bian* 千變 (thousand alternations) and *qian sheng* 千生 (thousand life-forms), which once again highlight the form-changing nature of the *zhenren*. In their translation of the *Huainanzi*, Major and his coauthors (2010, 84) translate *deng jia yu dao* somewhat indirectly as "verge upon the way." In line with the literal meaning of the phrase that Ziporyn mentions—namely, "to climb upon the borrowed"—we think that it expresses the capability of *zhenren* to "mount" (*deng* 登) every transformative challenge and "borrow" (*jia* 假), "pretend," or "play" any shape or form presented to them by the *dao*, or the thousand ways, or the changing course of nature. Therefore we suggest the translation "assume any appearance on the way" for *deng jia yu dao* in both the *Zhuangzi* and the *Huainanzi*, while reading *deng jia qian dao* in the *Wenzi* as "assume any appearance of the thousand ways."

For our purposes, it is crucial to note that the term corresponding to "borrow" (or "pretend" or "play") appears a few more times in chapter 6 of the *Zhuangzi*. It is always associated with the alteration of forms. In section 6.5 the four friends Ziji, Ziyu, Zili, and Zilai discuss mortality and joyfully welcome the possibility that their body parts may eventually become animal parts or parts of other things. Here, the phrase *jin jia er hua* 浸假而化 is used, and this could be translated literally as "dipping into the borrowings and transform" in the sense of picking one form out of all those that are possible. Correspondingly, section 6.6 uses the phrase *jia yu yi wu* 假於異物 in the sense of "borrowing among all different things." In these instances, "borrowing" quite clearly means to temporarily take on a different form or "identity." From a sincerity perspective, these are false or deceptive identities. As it happens, "false," "deceptive," or "fake" are other meanings of *jia* 假.

Zhenren are masters in taking on false or pretended forms and shapes that they do not essentially match. They are themselves void of form and merely borrow these temporarily. Like Master Huzi, they are face changers with no personal face. This is the central, paradoxical nonquality of the *Zhuangzi*'s *zhenren*, which distinguishes them from the Confucian role models who sincerely match form and name. *Mencius* 2A:3, for example, decries as rulers by force rather than by virtue all those who "fake" or "feign" or (in Legge's translation

as accessed at the Chinese Text Project, http://ctext.org/mengzi/gong-sun
-chou-i) "make a pretense to" (*jia*) humanity (*ren*). But for the *zhenren*, any form
is borrowed or pretended, and *zhenren* assume any appearance on the way, or, as
one can also translate, assume any pretense of the way. From a Daoist perspective, the "thousand *dao*" are all borrowings or pretenses,[3] and the *zhenren* is
the one who can *zhenuinely* borrow them or pretend without intending to verify them with his person. As genuine pretenders, the *zhenren*, as *Zhuangzi* 24.13
says, "do not with their personality enter into what is 'from heaven'" (*bu yi ren
ru tian* 不以人入天).

After defining *zhenren* as those who can assume any appearance on the
way, chapter 6 continues with a long "ode" to *zhenren* and their wonderful
powers. This passage has been repeatedly analyzed, in whole or in part, by
contemporary scholars (e.g., Coyle 1998 and Chong 2011; Ziporyn 2009 provides extended footnotes to his translation). With obvious justification, it has
been read in context with corresponding sections in texts such as the *Huainanzi*, the *Liezi*, and the *Wenzi*, which all describe spiritual and physiological
features as well as cultivation practices of the *zhenren* in similar or partly identical terms (Yang Rur-bin 2003). These descriptions of the *zhenren* gave rise to
explorations of the somatic dimension of the term (Chong 2011) and had a
deep impact on the further development of *dao jiao* traditions (Miura 2008b).
Famous characterizations of *zhenren* as sleeping without dreaming, breathing
from their heels rather than from their throats, and having broad and plain
foreheads all originate in this passage. Daoist practitioners have tended to
approach some of these characterizations rather literally and indeed engaged
in emulation efforts. Proclamations such as "their food was plain and their
breathing was deep" (Ziporyn 2009, 40) could be read as direct suggestions for
how to live and what to do, while others such as "they gulp down their words
and just as soon vomit them back up" (40) or "with punishments as their own
body, they could kill or be killed gracefully" (42) could be taken as more metaphorical advice. Pronouncements such as "the *zhenren* of old understood
nothing about delighting in being alive or hating death" (40; translation modified) match very well the many illustrations of equanimity toward death in
the Inner Chapters and other parts of the *Zhuangzi*, and they could serve to
philosophically round up a general picture of *zhenren* as Daoist ideal figures
with a specific lifestyle and a corresponding spiritual condition and intellectual mind-set.

Historically speaking, a *dao jiao* approach has without a doubt dominated
conceptions of the *zhenren* in China, and, long before the contemporary

authenticity-based reading, these conceptions were associated with the depiction of the *zhenren* in chapter 6 of the *Zhuangzi*. We do not intend to dispute the validity of such readings. Throughout this book, we highlight the multi-dimensionality of the text, which has triggered diverse receptions both culturally and, in more recent times, academically. From our perspective, however, the poetic descriptions of the *zhenren* can also be read as toying with the standard format of setting up ideal figures of the past to "sell" a philosophical or political message—a format that is found throughout ancient Chinese texts and particularly those of Confucian provenance. The descriptions of the *zhenren* presented here are not humorous or satirical outright, to be sure, but they are, in an almost Romanticist fashion, exaggerated in the direction of the fantastic and surreal. In this way, they do correspond to the grotesque and scurrilous hyperbole characterizing so many of the humorous passages in the *Zhuangzi*. Concise and vivid poetic images such as those of the dreamless sleep and the breathing from the heels later became paradigmatic expressions of Daoist cultivation efforts. But in the context of the *Zhuangzi*, they can be understood as producing a powerful poetical distancing effect that sets the Daoist models apart from the ordinary and identifies them as creations of the imagination rather than as supposedly real historical persons.

In our view, features of *zhenren* such as their dreamless sleep and their breathing from the heels can be understood as evoking a *depersonalization* rather than a personalization; they transpose *zhenren* not to a mystical or transcendent beyond but into the realm of the imagination. We therefore read beautiful depictions such as "they were cool like the autumn, warm like the spring; their joy and their anger intermingled with the four seasons" (Ziporyn 2009, 40) more as foreshadowing later variations on these motifs in Chinese arts and Wei-Jin-period neo-Daoism (*xuanxue* 玄學) than as foreshadowing their effects on diverse cultivation practices in *dao jiao* movements (although, of course, the histories of Chinese arts and *dao jiao* are closely intertwined). In any case, just as the notion of the *zhenren* that was coined in the *Zhuangzi* did produce "emulating" readings in the *dao jiao* tradition, it also produced—equally early in history—poetic resonances. After all, the *Chuci* 楚辭 contains two poems mentioning *zhenren*: "Far-Off Journey" (Yuan you 遠遊) and "Maintaining Resolution" (Shou zhi 守志). The latter says, in Hawkes's (1985, 318; modified) translation,

> I visited Fu Yue, bestriding a dragon,
> Joined up in marriage with the Weaving Maiden,

Lifted up Heaven's Net to capture evil,
Drew the Bow of Heaven to shoot at wickedness,
Followed the *zhenren* fluttering through the sky.

These lines are an exquisite example of the flying and wandering metaphors that figure so prominently in both the *Chuci* and the *Zhuangzi*. They connect the *zhenren* implicitly with instances of the very same metaphors in the *Zhuangzi*—for instance, in the butterfly allegory or in the many passages about *you* 遊 (roaming, rambling, or wandering), some of which we discuss later. For us, the poetic depictions of *zhenren* given in chapter 6 of the *Zhuangzi* complement the otherwise humorously and philosophically produced ambiguity of the Daoist paradoxical role model. It is a dissonant and empty role model that escapes identification. It flies away, it shifts shape, and it takes on all possible and impossible forms. Its *zhen*uineness is not self-sustaining or self-creating; on the contrary, it skillfully and artistically evades the patterns of personal characterizations, "visiting" and "borrowing" here and there and "fluttering through the sky."

The long poetic description of *zhenren* in chapter 6 of the *Zhuangzi* not only depersonalizes *zhenren* by poetically connecting them with the surreal and fantastic rather than the historical and social but also distances readers from them and makes them, through the employment of linguistic ambiguity and ambivalence, impossible to grasp. Memorable and vivid—though surreal—depictions such as "breathing from the heels" are mixed with cryptic and opaque ones that have stunned readers and sparked extremely divergent interpretations and translations. Is it conceivable that the text here toys with its readers and hopes to provoke as many irreconcilable interpretations as possible in order to obscure the identity of the unidentifiable *zhenren*? Is the text perhaps a riddle that cannot be solved? Or, even more speculatively, is it conceivable that the text hides a rather straightforward philosophical description of the *zhenren* as a genuine pretender behind surface readings that point in different directions? We are not sure about this, but when read on the basis of Ziporyn's (2009, 41; modified) translation and neo-Daoist interpretation, the text does contain some very direct illustrations of *zhenren* as genuine pretenders: "They take joy in following through with things, but are not 'sages.' They are intimate with others, but are not 'humane.' Their timeliness is in accord with nature, but they are not 'worthies.' Benefit and harm do not get through to them, but they are not 'gentlemen.' They do what their names [*ming* 名]

require while getting rid of a self, but they are not 'steadfast knights.' When they perish, they do not take it to be real[ly they who perish], but they are not 'servers of others.'"

Read in this way, the zhenren not only are capable of fulfilling social roles with ease and playfulness but also, in typical Daoist fashion, do not take success or failure—not even death—personally. Crucially, they do not accept the Confucian names and titles and do not confirm the standard designations of the paragons of virtue. By resisting the verification of role models, they also resist becoming role models that are to be emulated.

However, while it is certainly possible to read this passage in the same manner as Ziporyn, he himself points out that all commentators known to him have read it as saying more or less the *opposite*: "He who delights in clearing the way for things is not a sage. He who favors his intimates is not Humane. He who is beholden to the seasons of Heaven is not a worthy. He who does not open himself to and comprehend both benefit and harm is not an exemplary man. He who works for fame and thereby loses himself is not a true knight. He who loses his life in the inauthentic is not really being served by others" (Ziporyn 2009, 41n10).

Once read in this manner, it becomes very difficult to reconcile the passage with its context, however, and this is why it has sometimes been regarded as corrupted or as an interpolation and is accordingly simply left out in other translations, such as Graham's (2001). Philosophical and philological problems and questions do not decrease as the text goes on. On the contrary, the immediately "following few lines are among the most resolutely ambiguous in all world literature" (Ziporyn 2009, 41n13); and we refrain here from adding to the attempts by countless traditional commentators and modern translators to make sense of them.

Without a doubt, the locus classicus of the depiction of zhenren in chapter 6 of the Zhuangzi is a highly elusive piece of literature. It is probably impossible to determine how far the elusiveness of the text is intended to convey the elusiveness of the zhenren as an empty role model that may "assume any appearance on the way." Rather than engaging in further speculations about the poetical descriptions of the zhenren, we turn now away from the more fantastic and surreal and toward the more prosaic and concrete descriptions of what we understand as Daoist genuine pretending. These descriptions are found in the many allegories and narratives that present instances of the art of genuine pretending in mundane scenarios and in comparatively mundane language.

SOCIAL SURVIVAL

THE GENUINELY PRETENDING TREE: USELESS USEFULNESS

Chapter 4 of the *Zhuangzi* contains three dialogues about envoys or employees facing dangerous missions, two allegories about useless trees, one about an equally useless cripple, a short narrative about an encounter between Confucius and Jieyu 接輿, "the madman of Chu," and finally a paradigmatic and paradoxical pronouncement that reads as if it were taken right out of the *Daodejing* but that actually has no direct parallel there: "Everyone knows how useful usefulness is, but no one seems to know how useful uselessness is" (Ziporyn 2009, 32). This final sentence can be taken as a conclusion of the whole chapter. Just like some trees whose wood grew too strangely to serve as lumber, or the cripple who cannot be called up for military service, or the madman of Chu, "the recluse who feigns madness" (Schneider 1980, 17) and thereby escapes the perils of politics, the three dialogues about the dangers of being on an official mission can be read, in a rather Yangist way, as recommending the benefits of withdrawing to the fringes of society. Only the hermits can live out their days in peace; otherwise, if found useful and employable, one will eventually be cut down and destroyed in a relentlessly competing and destructive society.

The great Daoist theme of survival permeates the whole of chapter 4, and the topos of being useless so that one can save one's skin plays a significant part in it. Given the strong presence of the survival theme, it is entirely plausible to read the chapter as a collection of short texts praising the paradoxical advantage of being disadvantaged, or, if one is not blessed with being disadvantaged, the art of successfully pretending to be. One particularly effective way of proving one's social uselessness (as in the case of the madman of Chu) is to be mad, or, alternatively, stupid. The wisdom of stupidity has been a perennial issue in Daoism; it figures prominently in the *Daodejing* not only in the form of the praise of "nonknowledge (*bu zhi* 不知; see chapters 71 and 81) but also in the image of "the heart of an idiot" (*yuren zhi xin* 愚人之心) that characterizes a Daoist sage (chapter 20). As Christian Schwermann (2011) has shown in a most meticulous study, stupidity became an important issue in Chinese intellectual, political, and cultural history. A Daoist aspect of the Chinese art of stupidity is emblematically expressed in Zheng Banqiao's 鄭板橋 (d. 1765) famous calligraphy *Nan de hutu* 難得糊塗 (It is difficult to be muddled). Zheng's dictum points to a paradox within the paradox: not only is it useful to be useless (and in particular to be socially useless because of, for example, intellectual deficits) but also it is *difficult to be simple*. One question that interests us here is, if it is difficult to be simpleminded and useful to be useless, is then stupidity or uselessness merely a matter of "feigning it," as suggested, for instance, by Schneider (1980, 17)? Or is the matter more complex? Can we perhaps say that being useless or idiotic is simple enough but that *pretending* usefulness and smartness while at the same time remaining *genuinely* useless and idiotic is difficult?

Before we get to the issue of *zhen*uinely pretending usefulness and cleverness, we have to address another point that is tightly bound to it. A standard reading conceives of the madman of Chu, who shows up in chapter 4 and in other passages in the *Zhuangzi* as well as in *Analects* 18.5 (which, according to Ziporyn [2009, 32n16], the *Zhuangzi* parodies), as a "recluse," in the words of Schneider. He is thereby associated with many characters in the *Zhuangzi* (including Zhuang Zhou himself) who clearly prefer a primitivist life over any form of participation in politics or regular social integration. However, just as the issues of uselessness and stupidity can become complex and paradoxical in a Daoist context, the issue of reclusion can become tricky and subtle.

In an appended essay on "The Recluse Phenomenon" in his book on the Inner Chapters of the *Zhuangzi*, Wang Bo (2014) discusses three kinds of Daoist hermits. Wang identifies the first as an escapist who flees society and avoids it altogether. Fictional characters transcending the mundane world as depicted in the *Chuci*, or the legendary *xian* 仙 immortals (revered in *dao jiao* traditions) living in the faraway mountains on a diet of air and dew, are idealized variations of such extrasocial recluses. However, the madman of Chu and his many fellow hermits in the *Zhuangzi* are not that far removed from society and remain within its boundaries, albeit in its furthest corners. According to Wang they are inner-worldly recluses living on their own in proximity with nature or in very small groups while avoiding sociopolitical integration as much as possible. In the popular imagination this type of hermit is commonly associated with Daoism, as, for example, in the form of a single man walking through the mountains depicted in a painting or a small group of friends enjoying a bucolic setting described in a poem. According to Wang, however, there is also a third form of reclusion that, if not directly found in texts such as the *Zhuangzi*, nonetheless corresponds with its philosophy. Hermits of this third kind do take on social roles and positions and thereby integrate themselves into society, but in Wang's (2014, 202) terms, they practice an "inner emigration" and go along with society while not getting mentally or spiritually involved in it (205; see also Jia 2015). We think that such hermits can be found in chapter 4 of the *Zhuangzi*, too, and we submit that they represent an art of inner-social reclusion exercised by genuine pretenders. In Wang Deyou's 王德有 (2012) terms, these socially integrated recluses are "social hermits."

Chapter 4 of the *Zhuangzi* includes the allegory of the "genuinely pretending tree," who accepts its role of a revered shrine without sharing the religious values of the society that worships it (D'Ambrosio 2012b). The allegory nicely combines the inner emigration of the social hermit with the pretense of usefulness that manages to maintain genuine uselessness. This giant tree could grow big and old only because it was found useless by humans—carpenters in particular—for their purposes, just as a second tree described later in the same chapter. It was blessed with the same deficiencies as "crippled" trees or humans who can therefore escape utilization by society. To speak in Marxist terms, they are lucky enough not to be considered a "commodity." Their uselessness is not natural but socially constructed—they are useless not in themselves but for specific social purposes (or in terms of specific social roles). It is a contingent uselessness that is neither essential nor original nature, and it is not something intentionally produced. Thus, these trees or humans cultivated nothing, and so their useful uselessness was most easy to attain; they did not do anything to achieve it. The useless tree in the genuinely pretending tree story, however, was eventually declared to be a shrine—and, as the carpenter's apprentice rightly remarks at one point in the narrative, was thus no longer useless. It was given a social role that it could not reject. After all, as a tree it would have been impossible for it to run away to another world or to some remote forest to escape its assignment.

The recluse options outside or at the fringes of society were not open to the genuinely pretending tree when he was turned into a shrine, and, we can conclude, they are not actually open to most of us either. With few exceptions, we are rooted in society as well, and it is not in ours but in society's hands to ascribe or not ascribe usefulness to us. Once declared useful, the only option that remained for the tree was an inner emigration—and, as a Daoist might ask, how is that different for humans? The genuinely pretending tree reacted to the social inclusion it could not avoid by playing its role without identifying with it. It did not personally commit to its socially ascribed usefulness. It did not affirm the value that society eventually foisted on it, and it withstood the pressure to acknowledge and recognize this value. At the same time, of course, it performed the role associated with the value. And here lies the difficulty of pretending usefulness while remaining genuinely useless: one has to manage (as the genuinely pretending tree did) to maintain "a difference from the people" (yu zhong yi 與眾異) while in their midst and, unlike them, refuse to pretend that such a thing as a shrine has any intrinsic usefulness. It thereby resisted the temptation to adopt its socially ascribed usefulness as its own identity and to conceive of itself as especially valuable.

THE VISIT TO WEI: FACING EVIL

The allegory of the genuinely pretending tree connects nicely not only with the immediately following stories of another useless tree and of the cripple Shu the Discombobulated (Ziporyn 2009, 31), who escapes war and labor conscriptions, but also with the preceding three dialogues between civil servants daunted by their tasks and a Daoist interlocutor who, in the first two instances, is played by Confucius. The stories of the second useless tree and Shu the Discombobulated illustrate the paradoxical usefulness of being found useless by society and suggest that those who are deemed worthless and crippled may actually consider themselves lucky rather than unlucky. The stories thereby correspond with the popular tale of "the old man at the fort" (sai weng shi ma 塞翁失馬) in Huainanzi 18.9, a tale that proverbially stands for the wise foolishness not to engage in judgments about good and bad luck. The case of Shu the Discombobulated shares a significant detail with the story of the old man at the fort: in both narratives a person is saved from potentially lethal military service because of a disability. But more important for us, the story of the genuinely pretending tree also connects with the three dialogues involving men who are unlucky enough to be physically fit for employment and who therefore have to face various social assignments.

In the first, longest, and most complicated of these three stories, Yan Hui, Confucius's beloved student, approaches his master with a plan to visit the vicious ruler of the state of Wei in order to turn him into a good person. Yan Hui is an idealistic young man, keen on changing the world. Unlike the protagonists in the other two stories, Yan Hui volunteers for his job rather than having it imposed on him by higher authorities. From a Daoist perspective, this makes his situation most problematic. He is already on the Confucian path toward actively embracing and affirming his social roles by pursuing virtuous actions. Thus, he has already been blinded to the dangers and hypocrisies of social life. He therefore needs to be de-Confucianized before he can be instructed as a Daoist—and this probably necessitates a longer narrative than in the following two cases, where the two prospective employees are more perceptive of the potential problems attached to social roles. Ironically, the task of de-Confucianizing Yan Hui is given to Confucius himself.

From the outset, the story of Yan Hui's visit to Wei resembles the story of Confucius's mission to convert Robber Zhi. In both cases, a moralist who "knows better" sets out to reform an evildoer, and this endeavor is portrayed as naive and conceited rather than courageous. But whereas Confucius actually does confront Robber Zhi—if only to face embarrassment and humiliation—Yan Hui is "set straight" before he commences his trip; or rather, we are not even told if he still wants to go after receiving Confucius's Daoist lesson. In any case, Confucius prepares him well to face such a mission in the spirit of a Daoist genuine pretender.

When Yan Hui tells Confucius that he intends to go to Wei to right the local ruler's wrongs, Confucius reacts in a comical fashion against Yan Hui's (and a reader's) presumed expectations. Surprisingly, Confucius does not laud his student's cultivation progress and the moral knowledge that is about to show itself in his actions; instead, he immediately scolds him for his moral delusion by saying, "Ah! You will most likely get yourself executed" (Ziporyn 2009, 24). Then, Confucius explains to Yan Hui at length the twisted nature of his (i.e., Yan Hui's) intentions. Confucius begins his exhortation with an ironical proclamation: "One has to first establish it [the *dao*] in oneself before one establishes it in others" (*xian cun zhu ji, er hou cun zhu ren* 先存諸己, 而後存諸人) (Zhuangzi 4.1). This statement is ironic because, on the surface, it seems to be very much in line with the orthodox Confucian idea that one first has to internalize social values (or the Confucian *dao*) before one can spread them across society. However, as will become clear at the end of the long dialogue, the *dao* that one has to establish in oneself is the Daoist *dao* of selflessness, which empties the self by the "fasting of the heart-mind" (*xin zhai* 心齋), as the text famously says. In other words, Confucius lays out a Daoist program of *de-Confucianization as deinternalization* for Yan Hui (Zhuangzi 4.2). Yet despite its anti-Confucian tendencies, the Daoist message shares an important concern with the Confucian approach to dealing with brutal tyrants: before interacting with them, one's motivations and strategies have to be clarified.

In his attempt to prepare Yan Hui for a dangerous mission, Confucius first addresses the unhealthiness of the Confucian concern for names (*ming*). He clearly discerns that Yan Hui's primary motivation for going to Wei is the *latter's own desire to attain a good name.* Confucius here exposes a central aspect of the hypocrisy involved in the Confucian sincerity project: one's desire for the dual correspondence between one's actions and character and one's performance and (good) name implies a mutual confirmation of one's own persona and one's social recognition. One thereby not only defines oneself by socially constructed values but also presupposes that the goodness society will eventually ascribe to oneself reflects one's true personal goodness. By verifying social values, one thus intends to ultimately verify oneself. But this self-verification emerges paradoxically from an insincere desire to do and affirm that which is deemed good by society only in order to be acclaimed and considered—including by oneself—as sincerely good.

The problematic project of sincerity is attached to a personal affirmation of social values. Thus it also expresses itself in a form of moral "knowledge" (zhi 知)—one becomes ever more certain that one is right and knows better. The more intensely one internalizes socially constructed values, and the more social esteem one thereby harvests, the more one is prone to become self-righteous. From a Daoist perspective, this process eventually produces false sincerity, false names, and false knowledge. Rather than replacing false sincerity, false names, and false knowledge with true sincerity, true names, and true knowledge, as we already know, the Daoist alternative is to dissolve all these things into nothing. Exactly this "deconstructionist" process is what Confucius hopes to kick-start in Yan Hui. And, of course, from a Daoist perspective, one will be able to be effective in society (and thus capable of surviving a mission to Wei) only if one succeeds in this exercise.

Confucius asks Yan Hui if he "knows" (zhi) what undermines *de* (power, efficacy, health, virtuosity) and how knowledge (zhi) comes forth. This question is not without irony, because it paradoxically assumes that it is good or beneficial to know why knowing (or assuming to know better) is not good. In any case, the answer to the question is, "*De* is undermined by names; knowledge comes forth with contention" (*de dang hu ming; zhi chu hu zheng* 德蕩乎名；知出乎爭) (Zhuangzi 4.1). Confucius adds that both names and knowledge are "inauspicious tools" (*xiong qi* 兇器) that one should stay away from. In other words, Yan Hui's very desire for a good name undermines his effectiveness, and his insistence on moral knowledge not only endangers him but also is prone to produce social tension and conflict about what is right and wrong. In typical ancient Chinese fashion, Confucius illustrates his point with a few (pseudo-)historical examples—namely, those of two ancient moralists whose desire for a good name only led to their execution by tyrants, and, notably, those of the two Confucian sage-kings Yao and Yu, who, in their own moral pursuit of a good name, exterminated some rogue tribes and thus caused havoc and suffering. This reference corresponds to a "parody" (Ziporyn 2009, 17n24) in the second chapter of the *Zhuangzi* where Yao is presented as expressing the irresistible urge to eliminate the same rival tribes. Similarly, Confucius echoes accusations of genocide in the name of morality brought forth against the sage-kings by Robber Zhi in section 29.1. Obviously, Confucius is not impressed by Yan Hui's moral intentions and not only regards his motivations as closer to hypocrisy than to sincerity but also thinks that his proposed course of action will more likely cause disaster than ameliorate suffering.

After having been rebuked by Confucius in this way, Yan Hui attempts to defend his enterprise by concretely explaining in more or less standard Confucian terminology the attitudes he intends to display in order to impress the King of Wei and succeed with his mission. However, all these suggested approaches are dismissed by Confucius as inappropriate and ineffectual. Finally at the end of his wits, Yan Hui asks Confucius what he should do instead; Confucius tells him to practice the "fasting of the heart-mind" (*xin zhai* 心齋). This term, too, has had an expansive career in *dao jiao* practices (see Miura 2008a), and Confucius indeed first explains this fasting physiologically as a *qi* 氣 cultivation that eventually produces a presumably psychosomatic state of emptiness (*xu* 虛) in the heart-mind. Yan Hui then asks if this emptiness corresponds to a state where " 'myself' has never begun to exist" (Ziporyn 2009, 27). Confucius affirms this and thereby finally reveals the irony of his initial remark about having to first "establish it [the *dao*] in oneself" before being fit to do so for others. What has to be established in oneself is, for the Daoist Confucius, the emptiness of the self.

In conjunction with the physiological, psychosomatic, and spiritual descriptions of *xin zhai*, Confucius also offers a more social description of this state of the heart-mind. He says that on the basis of an empty self one can "ramble [*you* 遊] within one's social confinements without a concern for one's name" (*you qi fan er wu gan qi ming* 遊其樊而無感其名)—which is a pretty accurate ancient Chinese definition of genuine pretending. He then continues to describe how one might act in such a state: "When you gain access, do your crowing. When you do not get access, let it rest. Do not offer openings, do not distribute poison. Regard it as the one place and make yourself at home where you cannot but be" (Ziporyn 2009, 27; translation modified). As inner-social hermits, selfless genuine pretenders can accommodate themselves wherever they go. They are not concerned with verifying their names and can act effectively without causing tension but also—differently from Hundun—without being "penetrated": they do not let the situation get to them. They become smooth operators.

Confucius then presents Yan Hui with a series of rather poetically formulated comparisons between what is easy and what is difficult to achieve. In our view, they can be read as a guideline for testing how far one has come in mastering the art of genuine pretending. The first one is, "It is easy to wipe away your footprints, but difficult to walk without touching the ground" (Ziporyn 2009, 27). We understand this to say that it is easy to feign or fake or hide an identity, or to *simply pretend*—to act as if one had not been or is not there while one in fact was. The difficult thing is to *genuinely pretend*, to leave no footprints because one does not touch the ground. The genuine pretender is there without being there as him- or herself. There is no footprint by which he or she authenticates being there and makes a place or action his or her own. It is not so easy to move about socially without imprinting one's social roles with a sense of identity.

The second comparison is this: "When acting/in service as a person, it is easy to pretend/playact; when acting/in service by natural coincidence, it is difficult to pretend/playact" (*wei ren shi, yi yi wei; wei tian shi, nan yi wei* 為人使易以偽為天使難以偽). As far as we are concerned, this statement, too, distinguishes simple pretending from genuine pretending. It is easy to fake or feign. Just because we may have written an essay the night before it was due rather than properly working on it for weeks does not cause us to question our role as a proper student. Just because we surpassed the speed limit, we do not doubt that we are law-abiding citizens. And simply because we do not in every single instance tell our husbands or wives the complete truth, we do not lose confidence in ourselves as good spouses. Simple pretending is a daily habit. However, and perhaps surprisingly, genuine pretending, the playing of a role that we do not identify with, is much more difficult—that is, being a proper student, citizen, or spouse while regarding these roles as entirely contingent or as a natural coincidence (*wei tian shi* 為天使 or *ming* 命) that has nothing to do with a "real" self. On the one hand, we then have to accept that all we do is playacting, but on the other, we also have to accept that it is the playacting of an empty heart-mind and not our *own* playacting.

Semantically, this second comparison corresponds with the anti-Zhongyong 22 pronouncement in section 24.13 of the *Zhuangzi*, which says that *zhenren* "do not with their personality enter into is 'from heaven' " (*bu yi ren ru tian* 不以人入天). A *zhen*uine pretender is capable of playacting/pretending (*wei* 偽)

what he or she is destined to do by natural coincidence without regarding it as a personal activity rooted in his or her authentic self. We would also like to stress that, for reasons of parallelism, it seems philologically prudent to assume that the presumably difficult art of playacting or pretending when acting by natural coincidence is regarded as a positive rather than negative skill, as are "walking without touching the ground" in the preceding sentence and "flying without wings" as well as "knowing by nonknowledge" in the two following ones.

This brings us to the third comparison: "You have learned how to fly with wings, but not yet how to fly without wings" (Ziporyn 2009, 27). In our reading, this sentence, too, corresponds with the just-discussed pronouncement from section 24.13. *Zhenren* do what they do without conceiving of their persons as the creators of that action. To fly with wings metaphorically expresses the idea of personal agency; one does what one does on the basis of one's own initiative and by one's own efforts. Flying without wings, on the contrary, is a metaphor conveying the idea of a movement that no one owns.

Confucius's fourth comparison is as follows: "You have learned to know by having knowledge, but you have not yet learned 'to know by not having knowledge'" (*yi wu zhi zhi zhe* 以無知知者). This statement mirrors his previous remark to Yan Hui about the benefits of knowing why knowing (or thinking one knows better) is not beneficial. It was made in the context of a criticism of moral knowledge claims and their tendency to create conflict and provoke social disasters. In a wider sense, the statement also refers to the paradoxical "zhenuine knowledge" (*zhenzhi* 真知) of the *zhenren* as discussed in the preceding. Once more echoing chapter 71 of the *Daodejing* ("to know [or to master] nonknowledge is the best kind of knowledge" *zhi bu zhi shang* 知不知上), the text brings up the Daoist topos of cultivated stupidity. This kind of knowledge refrains not only from knowledge claims about what is morally right or wrong but also from knowledge claims about what one really is and what one is not. To know not to engage in knowledge games of this sort is a basic virtue of genuine pretenders—and one that Confucius thinks Yan Hui had better acquire before venturing out to see the King of Wei.

Read in this way, the dialogue about the visit to Wei illustrates the benefits of cultivating genuine pretending rather than moral sincerity when facing violent, destructive, and dangerous social powers—or, in moral terms not so often applied in the *Zhuangzi*, when facing evil. Genuine pretending helps to build immunity against these powers, which are, in various degrees, found everywhere. This immunity is twofold. On the one hand, one becomes less vulnerable by avoiding direct confrontations with these powers—one has a better chance of eschewing execution. On the other—and perhaps more importantly—one does not reinforce the evildoer's *mode of commitment* and one's own selfish desire for and commitment to the pursuit of a good name. For Robber Zhi in chapter 29 and Confucius in the dialogue about the visit to Wei, the brutal tyrants and the moralist heroes like Yao and Yu are two sides of the same coin. As chapter 11 in the *Zhuangzi* asks, "How do I know that [the moral exemplars] Zeng and Shi are not the whistling arrows which signal the attack of tyrant Jie and robber Zhi?" (Graham 2001, 213). The genuine pretender *deflates* the self-centered attitude that produces tyranny and thereby helps, as an empty role model, establish social immunity against taking names, possessions, rank, and success too seriously. As Confucius said, one has to first establish emptiness in oneself before one can establish it in others.

Genuine pretenders cultivate an indifference to social status and names; they paradoxically "match" the usefulness of their roles with no commitment to and no recognition of the values attached to them; they are not sure of themselves and they do not claim to know better. This incongruent attitude makes genuine pretenders outwardly useful while inwardly useless and outwardly skillful while inwardly stupid. Hence, they become empty exemplars who, like children, do not *know how to internalize* what is deemed valuable in society and how to make it their *own*. But from a Daoist perspective, precisely such internalization along with the desire to *own* a good name is among the major causes of evil.

THE ENVOY TO QI: DEALING WITH STRESS

The second story about a daunting mission in chapter 4 of the *Zhuangzi* has Zigao 子高, the Duke of She 葉, consult Confucius before going as an envoy to the state of Qi 齊. Unlike Yan Hui in the preceding story, Zigao is not naively optimistic but rather deeply worried about his task and looking for some sort of therapeutic advice from Confucius to calm his nerves. The dialogue does not address any extraordinarily perilous situation but rather the common feeling of what is nowadays called stress. Zigao feels overwhelmed by his job; with a clear hint of caricature he is depicted as saying, "I got my orders this morning and already I am sucking on ice chunks this evening, as if my insides were on fire! I have not yet begun the actual task and already my yin and yang are out of whack!" (Ziporyn 2009, 28).

Confucius treats Zigao's anxiety with a lesson on genuine pretending. This lesson is introduced with a remark on the general structure of society that humans normally find themselves in and cannot avoid—and as in the previous narrative, the recluse option is not even considered. Confucius explains that there are two great "constraints" (jie 戒) in life related, respectively, to the private and public spheres—namely, "fate" (ming 命) and "duty" (yi 義). Privately, we are necessarily members of a family and thus tied to kinship bonds. This is our fate, and it inevitably makes us affectionate beings. Publicly—that is, politically and economically—we are subject to hierarchical relations and subordination, wherever we are. This imposes a "duty" (Graham 2001, 70) or "responsibility" (Ziporyn 2009, 28) on us. The trick for achieving mental stability, and thus to avoid stress and anxiety as far as possible, is, according to Confucius, to manage to be at ease (an 安)[4] or "reconciled to" (Ziporyn 2009, 28) the private and public conditions of one's life without being "picky" (bu ze 不擇) about them. The assumption is of course that one does not choose one's family background and the sociopolitical environment one lives in, and that there is little one can do to freely shape or reshape those parameters—the modern Enlightenment conception of liberty was not yet common. Given these constraints, it seemed reasonable not to become "manic" in such affairs and minimize both the "sorrow and joy" (ai le 哀樂) they could elicit in oneself. Confucius suggests that such a "stoic" equanimity can best be accomplished by "absorbing oneself in the realities of the task at hand to the point of forgetting oneself" (28; translation modified).

Confucius's simple therapeutic message seems to be that anxieties in everyday life often develop if one takes things too personally. A fully pragmatic focus on the tasks at hand emerges when one is capable of decreasing one's own stakes in it. The depersonalization of an approach to everyday matters can not only reduce the potential for conflict with others but also emotionally stabilize the agent and thereby increase the efficaciousness of the action. Zigao is advised to approach his mission as a genuine pretender: he can be a less stressed out and thus more efficient envoy if he does not identify too much with the job and does not conceive of its success or failure as his own success or failure. He is encouraged to playact an envoy rather than sincerely become one—and to thereby become a less worried and better envoy.

Confucius concludes his session with the anxious Zigao by providing a further definition of genuine pretending in everyday affairs: "Let yourself be carried along by things so that you can let your heart-mind roam" (cheng wu yi you xin 乘物以遊心) (Ziporyn 2009, 29; translation modified). The freely wandering or roaming heart-mind (you xin 遊心), as we discuss in more detail further on, is not only at ease but also highly attentive to its surroundings and alert to changes. Its attentiveness is not driven by a preconceived agenda or worries about one's good name but, to the contrary, is open to changing circumstances. It is the modus operandi of a smooth operator.

THE TIGER TRAINER: TAMING BEASTS

The third and final dialogue between someone preparing for an assignment and an adviser in chapter 4 of the Zhuangzi involves a certain Yan He 顏闔, who "was appointed tutor to the crown prince of Wei" (Ziporyn 2009, 29) and Qu Boyu 蘧伯玉, who takes on the role of the consultant in a parallel manner to Confucius in the preceding two sections. Yan He appears a few times more in the Outer and Miscellaneous Chapters, where he is portrayed variously as an accomplished Daoist (19.12, 32.9) and a recluse (28.5). Here, however, he faces a proper but also very delicate job—namely, to educate a volatile and dangerous crown prince, who we learn "is just naturally no good" (Ziporyn 2009, 29). Yan He is depicted neither as a moral enthusiast wanting to make a name for himself by saving the world from evil (like Yan Hui) nor as a man (such as Zigao) in need of therapeutic assistance. He simply wonders how to deal with a difficult person. Qu Boyu is mentioned in another section of the Zhuangzi (25.8), where he is depicted as someone who, although already sixty years of age, never held on to a fixed opinion and thus did not fall into the trap of thinking he knew better. Paradoxically, this absence of knowledge is precisely what qualifies him as a Daoist teacher.

Qu Boyu is aware of the bad reputation of the crown prince and thus realizes the potentially hazardous nature of the enterprise. Simply opting out of the job is apparently no longer possible and thus not taken into consideration. So the question is mainly how Yan He can make it out alive. The major issue is thus, once again, the art of survival in a precarious social environment. Qu Boyu rises to the challenge and presents Yan He with a complex set of instructions, consisting partly of general maxims, partly of direct prescriptions, and partly of allegorical similes. The most famous of the last is the allegory of the praying mantis that "flailed its pincers around to stop an oncoming chariot wheel, not realizing the task was beyond its powers" (Ziporyn 2009, 29).

Obviously, it is never advisable to act in such a heedless and futile way. Instead, Qu Boyu recommends engaging in some basic genuine pretending: "If he's playing the baby, play baby with him. If he's being lawless and unrestrained, be lawless and unrestrained with him. If his behavior is unbounded and shapeless, be unbounded and shapeless with him" (29).

Given the circumstances and the distribution of power, there is little that Yan He will be able to do to restrain the crown prince, and acting like a praying mantis in front of an approaching chariot is certainly not a solution. Therefore, he adjusts himself to the shifting moods of the crown prince—but without sharing them, adopting them, or fueling them. Apprehensive accommodation of the "client" without personal attachment and actual sympathy is required. One can playact with a dangerous counterpart of far superior strength, but one has to maintain an inner distance.

Qu Boyu illustrates the art of engaging with precarious powers in society using two linked allegories. A trainer of tigers, he says, does not feed them live animals or uncut meat so as not to arouse their lust for killing. The trainer thereby accommodates or "goes along with" (shun 順) the tigers and manipulates them into not attacking him. Qu Boyu describes a good tiger trainer who plays with the tigers and makes them act friendly toward himself, but he never disregards their difference and does not take their affection to him *personally*. He does not make the mistake of believing that he truly is a friend of the tigers simply because he can play with them. Were he to make such a mistake, his life would be in danger, as Qu Boyu shows with a second allegory: "A man who loves horses even to the point of gathering their shit and piss in jeweled boxes may still get his skull or chest kicked in if he smacks away a mosquito on the unbridled animal at the wrong time" (Ziporyn 2009, 30). In a satirical fashion, Qu Boyu's allegory illustrates the idiocy of being personally carried away when accommodating others: "There is something pathological in caring [too much]" is a somewhat modernized (but still justifiable) translation of Qu Boyu's conclusion, *ai you suo wang* 愛有所亡.

When in the service of powerful superiors, one not only has to cautiously avoid rubbing them the wrong way but also, and even more important, remain in a state of genuine pretending and make sure not to let one's interactions be accompanied by a personal commitment. Otherwise, one is in danger of developing a false sense of attachment to them and, eventually, to one's own identity. One risks getting affected by the game that one had to play and taking oneself too seriously. And instead of a true friend, one will become, in effect, a self-deceiving idiot, like the caricature of the lover of horses who treasures their shit only to be smashed in the head by them later.

The dialogues of the more or less distressed messengers and the allegories of the trees in chapter 4 in the Zhuangzi show the enactment of genuine pretending in various social situations. They constitute a sort of Daoist "survival guide" for living in an often hostile or perilous society. While a dao jiao practitioner may aspire to transcend the constraints of a regular social life altogether and to spiritually escape into higher dimensions of being, and while a Daoist primitivist may permanently—and a bourgeois Daoist aesthete temporarily—withdraw to the fringes of social life, there are also Daoist inner-social hermits who practice the art of genuine pretending in everyday social interactions in order to maintain a certain sanity or achieve an unlikely level of contentment.[5] The stories depict various mundane predicaments: assignment to roles or functions one did not choose or could not avoid, having to deal with stressful everyday tasks in one's professional or family life, exposure to capricious superiors or powerful institutions, or facing the juvenile urge to change the world. In all cases, strategies of genuine pretending are recommended: a playful and skillful engagement with the tasks at hand without personal identification. The particular benefits of genuine pretending depend on the situation one faces. Genuine pretending can at times be a strategy for simply staying alive, sometimes a method for success, and in other contexts a therapeutically helpful attitude.

Cynical lying for selfish gain, however, is never advised. The purpose and practice of genuine pretending are geared toward selflessness. Social contexts may tempt one to engage in projects of making a name for oneself and stir feelings of entitlement and ownership. As inner-social hermits, genuine pretenders try not to get carried away by such desires and crazes; they aim at doing things reasonably well and smoothly. In most social contexts, excellence or perfection is hardly achievable. But there are exceptions, and they are addressed in the so-called knack stories found throughout the Zhuangzi.

DRUNK SKILLS: ON CONTINGENT EXCELLENCE

In the introduction to his translation of the Zhuangzi, A. C. Graham (2001) asserts that Daoism resists definitions. However, he nevertheless feels justified in identifying "one basic insight" shared by all those who have been labeled philosophical Daoists: one must "learn to reflect his situation like a mirror, and respond to it with the immediacy of an echo to a sound or shadow to a shape" (6). Graham calls this mirrorlike capacity spontaneity or spontaneous aptitude, and once Daoists have discovered this knack or skill, their hope is that they will be able to "forget themselves in their total absorption in the object, and then the trained hand reacts spontaneously with a confidence and precision impossible to anyone who is applying rules and thinking out moves" (6). Philosophers concerned with maximum conceptual precision or sinologists aiming for maximum historical accuracy will certainly be able to find fault with Graham's daring (or perhaps desperate) attempt at discerning at least one common ideal among Daoists, but we are quite happy with his general observation.[6] Obviously, Graham's account relates to two of the most central notions of spontaneity in the *Daodejing* and in the *Zhuangzi* and other Daoist texts: *wu wei* 無為 (nonaction or nonassertive action) and *ziran* 自然 (self-so).

Much more so than the *Daodejing*, the *Zhuangzi* illustrates the ideal of *wu wei* with concrete examples in the form of narratives. In the more recent English-language literature on the *Zhuangzi*, these are often referred to as knack stories (or "skill stories"), the most famous of which is that of Cook Ting or Butcher Ding (*Zhuangzi* 3.2), who is capable of dismembering oxen so beautifully that the slaughter sounds like a musical performance and so smoothly that his knife has lost none of its sharpness after nineteen years of use. A. C. Graham (2001, 143–57) collects many of the knack stories in a section he calls "The Advantages of Spontaneity" and ascribes to the "School of Zhuangzi," referring to the faithful followers of the presumed author of the Inner Chapters. Most of these episodes are actually taken from chapter 19 of the *Zhuangzi* on the art of *da sheng* 達生 (fathoming life).

Just as *wu wei* and *ziran* are—with full justification, of course—among the most discussed concepts in the scholarly literature on Daoism, the knack stories and the type of skill they depict are, with equal justification, among the most academically discussed passages of the *Zhuangzi*. It would be difficult to find anyone who has published work on the *Zhuangzi* and had not addressed any of the knack stories (or at least the issue of spontaneity) in one way or another. Accordingly, it is difficult to present an exhaustive account of all the research on this topic. Rather than engage in such an attempt, it may suffice for our present purposes to indicate three of the various trajectories in the more recent Western academic literature on skill and spontaneity in the *Zhuangzi*.[7]

These trajectories are not mutually exclusive, and while they may differ in important respects, they also overlap in others.

At present, probably the most influential take on the subject has been worked out by Edward Slingerland (2003), who can also be credited with the highly effective English rendering of *wu wei* as "effortless action." Although Slingerland's publications do not usually deal exclusively with the *Zhuangzi*, he makes ample use of this text and its knack stories. As depicted most pointedly in his book *Trying Not to Try* (2014), Slingerland aims at joining the *Zhuangzi's* philosophy with contemporary cognitive science. For him, the knack stories express some universally valid insights into human behavior and efficacy. Slingerland thereby connects with, but also critically distinguishes himself (Slingerland 2014, 108) from, previous attempts to align the philosophy of skill in the *Zhuangzi* with the psychology of skill associated with Mihaly Csikszent-mihalyi's notion of "flow experience" (Csikszentmihalyi 1990; see also Jochim 1998). On a much smaller scale, an attempt to link Daoist and contemporary understandings of skill has also been made by Moeller (2006) with respect to the psychological concept of "automaticity" (as discussed in the special issue on the subject in *American Psychologist* [54, no. 7]).

Another approach to spontaneous skill in the *Zhuangzi* has focused on highlighting its relevance for the formation of a genuinely Daoist philosophy (Wohlfart 2005) or on localizing it within a larger framework of thought taken to be distinctively ancient Chinese (Jullien 2004). These efforts should be understood in the wider context of a "Continental" philosophical method working toward building coherent networks of meaning rather than making sinological claims about "cultures." From such a perspective, spontaneity and skill in the *Zhuangzi* are integral aspects of an elaborate Daoist weltanschauung and a corresponding philosophical practice that, in their respective ways, authors such as Wohlfart and Jullien aspire to connect with in their writings.

A third way of looking at the knack stories and the issue of skill in the *Zhuangzi* is as setting up examples for a Daoist cultivation ideal. The skillful individuals depicted in the stories are understood as Daoist sages whom a practitioner should seek to emulate. This approach connects loosely with a traditional *dao jiao* reading of texts such as the *Zhuangzi* and takes the stories quite literally as illustrations of what one can achieve—if not physically then at least spiritually—if one becomes a devoted Daoist. The knack stories thereby take on a religious or soteriological meaning. They are read as encouraging readers to consign themselves to the same pursuit that the protagonists are assumed to have undertaken. They can show how to reach perfection and acquire truth. P. J. Ivanhoe (1993) thinks that Zhuangzi had an "unwavering faith in his Way," and accordingly "in his examples of skillful individuals, Zhuangzi completely abandons the perspectivist argument and reveals the foundation of his normative vision. It turns out that there is a proper perspective: the Heavenly view of the world" (652; emphasis in the original). Therefore, figures such as Cook Ding invite us to "follow Heaven": "There is a pattern in Nature and the Daoist sage follows it" (652). Echoing Ivanhoe's assessment, Nathaniel F. Barrett (2011, 699) believes that the *Zhuangzi*'s knack stories are about a superhuman skill providing "access to the spontaneous power of an ultimate reality such as the Dao or Heaven." They represent the "religious nature of Zhuangzi's ideal" (700) and express an "ultimate spiritual state" that has to be understood in "reference to a larger cosmic (or a-cosmic) framework." Barrett stresses that, moreover, the knack stories invite readers "to commit to some particular worldview" because "spirituality may not be possible without some such commitment" (700). In this view, the skillful craftsmen of the *Zhuangzi* function as religious models eager to achieve "personal transcendence" through a firm commitment to the "ultimate" (699). In other words, they strive toward a higher truth, and their skillfulness reflects the degree to which they have managed to unite themselves with it.

In an interesting blog entry, Erik Schwitzgebel (2007) has expressed some reservations about standard interpretations of the skill stories in the *Zhuangzi* associated with, for instance, Slingerland, Graham, and Ivanhoe (though not with European authors such as Wohlfart and Jullien, whom he seems not to have considered). He stipulates that these interpretations should be reevaluated and outlines a direction in which this could be done: "Maybe it's the commitment to caring about success and failure—and "right" and "wrong"—that is the root of the problem. The *Zhuangzi* of Chapter 2 might not praise the butcher who takes pride in his accomplishment. And who presumably would be disappointed if he broke his knife and ruined the ox, or even became only an average butcher—which most butchers must of course be."

We think that Schwitzgebel makes a valid point. Indeed, he provides a foundation for an alternative reading of the knack stories, one that conceives of their protagonists neither primarily as literary illustrations of certain physiological facts that we can now describe more accurately through science nor as role models for a religious union with the ultimate to be achieved on the basis of an unwavering faith in Dao or heaven. In his blog, Schwitzgebel does not elaborate on his position, but we believe the quoted statement contains an important clue that allows one to distinguish his approach to skill in the

Zhuangzi very clearly from the religious one represented by Ivanhoe and Barrett. Ivanhoe and Barrett use a vocabulary of "faith" and speak of a "normative vision" and "commitment" to "personal transcendence." This vocabulary not only rings quite a few (church) bells but also connotes the more secularized ideal of sincerely or authentically committing to what one identifies as right and true. Barrett in particular emphasizes the centrality of such a commitment to his religious reading of the *Zhuangzi*. Schwitzgebel, on the contrary, points out that exactly such a commitment is ironically questioned in the knack stories of the *Zhuangzi*. The skilled craftsmen *do not really care*, nor do they personalize their skills or accomplishments.[8] Upon closer inspection, it is rather obvious, we believe, that the strange artisans in the *Zhuangzi* paradoxically demonstrate a drastic noncommitment to the arts they practice—or, to use Schwitzgebel's terms, to the right and wrong or success and failure of their arts. In short, the artisans in the *Zhuangzi*'s knack stories, too, can be seen as smooth operators engaged in genuine pretending.

In order to substantiate our reading of the knack stories as portraying excellence through genuine pretending, it is important to once more emphasize the "queer" nature of the role models in the *Zhuangzi*. They are rarely, we contend, straight exemplars that one can simply take at face value and emulate. They are dissonant, grotesque, exaggerated, or empty role models, depicted with a *Verfremdungseffekt*; and they sometimes bear satirical and ironical features to the point that they resemble a parody of a role model. None of the standard interpretations addressed by Schwitzgebel acknowledge this. These standard interpretations treat the *Zhuangzi*'s model characters, including the master artisans, as supposedly more perfect or even holier alternatives to the exemplary persons constructed in the Confucian and other traditions of the time. We do not follow this basic assumption and instead see these figures as significantly less holy than (and as wholly distinct from) most of their counterparts in other writings of the time. Accordingly, we do not treat them with much reverence, and we feel justified in this because they, too, treat themselves and their arts irreverently.

At least one scholarly article comments on the humorous, bizarre, and thereby dissonant nature of one of the *Zhuangzi*'s famous knack stories, that of the swimmer at the Lüliang waterfall (section 19.10). In the context of quoting the parallel version of this story as it appears in the *Liezi* (section 8.6), Shirley Chan (2011, 85) notes that the narrative describes an "absurdly impossible challenge": the swimmer diving into a cascade where even "fish and turtles and crocodiles could not swim." Confucius, who coincidently sees the swimmer plunging into the water, is shocked by this sight and, overcome by feelings of pity, sends his disciple to rescue him. The swimmer, however, happily emerges from the water and stultifies the rescue effort. Questioned by Confucius, the swimmer then explains his superior skill. Chan rightly remarks that "we smile as we picture the discomfiture of the great sage who thought he was performing a meritorious act of saving a life" (86). The story bears many of the hallmarks of comedy, such as the absurdly exaggerated nature of the swimmer's task, the comical relief of anxiety, and the carnivalesque exposure of the wise and moral Confucius as a fool. These comical elements serve on their own to distance the reader from looking at the text as a straightforward emulation story. The swimmer is not merely a master of his art; he is a jester and a mocker.

Once readers get over some of their perhaps misplaced awe of the skillful craftsmen in the Zhuangzi, other, potentially comical, features of the knack stories emerge. Perhaps the Cook Ding narrative, the mother of all knack stories in the Zhuangzi, is a bit ridiculous from the start: What sort of ruler would stoop to learn about nourishing life from a butcher? And isn't the Zhuangzi introducing a satirical tone into the story when it describes the bloody and ghastly dismemberment of a carcass as a symphonic event, where the rhythm of "the thwacking tones of flesh falling from bone" accompanies the whizzing sound of the knife "with its resonant thwing" so that each stroke rings out "the perfect note, attuned to the 'Dance of the Mulberry Grove' or the 'Jingshou Chorus' of the ancient sage-kings" (Ziporyn 2009, 22)? Couldn't the text here be read as a bitingly sarcastic parody of the *ancient sage-king's butchering of people* that the Zhuangzi sometimes alludes to when, for instance, depicting sage-emperor Yao as lusting for potentially genocidal attacks against the "Zong, Kuai, and Xu'ao" (17) in the "Qiwulun" chapter (section 2.10), or when the "Robber Zhi" chapter (section 29.1) describes the Yellow Emperor's battles as having "made the blood stream for a hundred miles" (Graham 2001, 237)? And isn't there at least a hint of parody when the first example of skill in chapter 19 of the Zhuangzi is, in a most profane fashion, a story about a completely tanked drunkard falling off a cart? Do we have to take him as a face-value exemplar for our spiritual cultivation and for committing ourselves to finding heaven's patterns when it is said that "his bones and joints are no different from those of other men, but the degree of harm done by the fall differs radically, for the spiritual in him forms one intact whole" (Ziporyn 2009, 78)?

We are not arguing here that the knack stories in the Zhuangzi are all parodies or humorous throughout. They are not. But we find that some of them contain comical elements that, in conjunction with other recurrent features (such as absurd exaggerations or clearly profane elements), serve to dissociate the reader from their "heroes" and put any unwavering commitment to their tasks into question. It seems that if there is a pattern among the strange artisans and artists then it is precisely the insincerity in their undertakings. A drunkard, we assume, does not embrace the Way of Drinking as a Heavenly call, nor does he attain "personal transcendence" or impart a clearly discernible "normative vision." Yet we gladly admit that he nevertheless fits Graham's general definition of Daoist skill as quoted in the preceding since he is surely capable of *forgetting himself in total absorption of himself in the object* (i.e., in his liquor). And there can be no doubt that, when falling from a cart, he can do so "spontaneously with a confidence and precision impossible to anyone who is applying rules and thinking out moves" (Graham 2001, 6). Thus we ask on the basis of strong textual evidence that the drunkard be rehabilitated and that his art of surviving falling off carts be included in the hall of fame of Daoist knacks, right next to symphonic oxen slaughtering and extreme waterfall diving.

Irony and the surreal split us, the readers, from the Daoist artists and artisans in the *Zhuangzi* and set up a healthy distance between us and them so that we do not fall under their spell and are thus spared a mode of devotion and desires of imitation. At the very least, this is a hermeneutic function of irony and the surreal that readers can respond to if so inclined. They are set free not to emulate and still enjoy things and reflect. Perhaps more important from a philosophical perspective, these literary devices also serve to establish a difference between the artists depicted and their arts. Just as a drunkard does not normally identify himself with his art and does not see it as a profession that he has perfected and thereby enhanced his innermost potential to the utmost, many of the other model artists in the *Zhuangzi* dissociate themselves from their activities as well.

The most commonly noted aspect of this dissociation is the physiological and psychological disengagement process by which the artisans "disown" their activities. Cook Ding, for example, becomes good at carving up oxen once he no longer looks at them with his eyes. A similar process is described in more detail in the case of Woodworker Qing (*Zhuangzi* 19.11), who, before making a marvelous bell stand, engages for several days in an exercise of "fasting of the heart-mind" (*xin qi* 心齊), analogous to the exercise of *xin zhai* 心齋 recommended by Confucius to Yan Hui before his going on a mission to the ruler of Wei. The various forms of the fasting of the heart-mind correspond to the famous notion of losing one's self (*sang wo* 喪我), which is poetically described at the beginning of the second chapter of the *Zhuangzi* by the Daoist master practitioner Ziqi. They also correspond to the process of "sitting and forgetting" (*zuo wang* 坐忘) that Yan Hui famously depicts in a dialogue with Confucius at the end of chapter 6 (Ziporyn 2009, 49). All these cases represent archetypical forms of early Daoist meditation exercises, crucially informing a long and complex history of Daoist and Chinese Buddhist practices over the millennia. They constitute a core element of the "inward training" (*nei ye* 內業) of Daoist mysticism as explored, for instance, in Harold D. Roth's (1991) classical study on this subject. The physiopsychological nature of *nei ye* practices is obvious, and the knack stories in the *Zhuangzi* are clearly related to them. We therefore do not wish to doubt or minimize the spiritual or mystic dimensions of the knack stories stressed by many interpreters. However, we do not think that the spiritual or mystic dimensions exhaust all the hermeneutic possibilities opened up by the knack stories, or even by the more exclusively meditation-focused narratives such as those about Ziqi's losing his self and Yan Hui's sitting and forgetting. We think that both the meditation narratives and the knack stories in the *Zhuangzi* also contain a good dose of nonmystical or "socioexistential" ingredients. Thus, while they may be read in a *dao jiao* context as illustrations of specific achievements through spiritual self-forgetting exercises, they can also be read as stories about achieving a more mundane form of excellence through disowning one's actions via genuine pretending.

When Yan Hui has described to Confucius his *zuo wang* exercise, Confucius exclaims in admiration, "If you go along with it, you have no preferences; if you let your self transform, you have no permanence!" (Graham 2001, 92; translation modified). This could well be read as yet another definition of genuine pretending. Read from a social or existential perspective, Confucius's pronouncement praises the capacity to affirm the contingency of one's roles and tasks by "having no preference" for them, and to excel at them by not identifying with them as "permanent."

Clearly, the image of the excellent drunkard who has perfected the art of surviving falls off carts implies neither that one should embrace drunkenness as one's authentic state of being nor that one should permanently identify with this skill. The dissociation between the artist and his art and the corresponding emphasis on contingency becomes explicit in the conclusion of the story of the master swimmer. The swimmer says to Confucius, "I have no course [dao]" (Ziporyn 2009, 81). He does not *own* his art or his way of life—nor is he owned or defined by his art. On the contrary, he follows the course of the water while "not making it my personal thing" (bu wei si 不為私).[9] In fact, it does not matter to him where he moves about; he does not see himself as a swimmer with the water as "his element." Like the reclining and forgetting Yan Hui, the diver has no preference for any specific environment and can thus equally adjust to any: "I was born on land and am at ease on land"; but he also states, "I grew up with the water and am at ease in the water." He concludes by saying, in a literal English translation, "that which is the case is so while one does not know if it is so by me" (bu zhi wu suoyi ran er ran 不知吾所以然而然). In a free rendering this would be, "One cannot claim any ownership of whatever one is doing."[10] This is once more an ancient Chinese definition of genuine pretending, and in the cases of both the swimmer and the drunkard, it serves as an explanation of why one can be very good at what one is doing in an everyday life context (such as drinking, walking, or swimming) rather than in an extraordinary or mystical endeavor.

The process of disowning one's activities or dissociating oneself from an identification with one's profession is outlined in significantly more detail in the narrative of Woodworker Qing. When an interlocutor—namely, the woodworker's political and economic superior, his ruler and employer, the Marquis of Lu—attempts to ascribe to him a specific talent or art (shu 術), Qing refuses such an identification. Echoing the swimmer who refuses to "own up to" any dao of his own, the woodworker admits to being in a profession and having a social role but does not see his social role as a personal quality: "I am an artisan, but what art would I have?" When further explaining the details of the "fasting of the heart-mind" (xin qi) that eventually enables him to make a perfect bell stand, he describes not only a physiopsychological "cleansing" process but also a social and existential dissociation from his profession, role, and activity. Just as he no longer regards his body and mind as his own, he also distances himself from all potentially ensuing social praise or failure—even from his employer, the very person to whom he is talking. After seven days of fasting, he says that "there is no kingly court" to him anymore. Paradoxically, the woodworker claims to be best at the tasks tied to his profession when his practice is completely void of any personal investment; in other words, he serves his lord best by not caring about him anymore.

It is crucial to note here that in ancient China, as in many other societies, one typically did not decide on but rather inherited one's profession as a craftsman and was thus "born into it." The tasks that artisans in the *Zhuangzi* perform are not freely chosen by them but encountered according to "fate" (*ming* 命), to use the terminology employed by the swimmer in section 19.10. Rather than pretending that a profession they did not and could not pick is truly theirs, these artisans disown it and thereby accept it impersonally.

In Wang Bo's terms, Woodworker Qing undergoes "inner emigration"; he neither flees society nor retreats to its fringes but instead remains active in its midst and fulfills his duties with excellence. At the same time, he shows no devotion to his position and treats his superior with disrespect—he forgets about the marquis and even tells him as much. While complying perfectly with his role, Qing engages in *xin qi* and thereby sets himself apart from the social commitment that is labeled as doing one's job with one's heart in it. Qing is playing his role perfectly but refrains radically from becoming it. In resonance with Schwitzgebel's reflections quoted previously, the story illustrates how one can do something that is regarded as highly valuable and "right" precisely by abandoning and ignoring these very values. Woodworker Qing's mode of action can be understood, with Edward Slingerland, not only as an instance of acting by not trying to try (or, spiritually speaking, as reaching a mystical state of being one with nature) but also as an instance of the efficacy of a smooth operator who is able to maneuver well through life precisely because he or she resists the temptation to identify with the praise or condemnation that one or one's work receives.

Seen in this way, the great accomplishments that these Daoist artisans achieve in the eyes of others do not mean that much to themselves. By disowning their crafts, they protect themselves against a social reification on the basis of their roles or presumed talents; they avoid becoming "celebrities"— at least in their own estimation. At the same time, they become immune to idolizing their arts. They do what they happen to find themselves entrusted or assigned with, or what their present circumstances demand. They face the two great "constraints" (*jie* 戒)—namely, natural contingencies (or "fate" [*ming* 命]) and social contingencies (or "duty" [*yi* 義]). Their activities are radically conditional: the swimmer swims not because he regards the art of swimming as greatly meaningful or spiritually rewarding but because he grew up with the water (this is his *ming*). The only apparent reason for the woodworker to make bell stands out of trees is that the Marquis of Lu commissions him to do so because he happened to be born into the profession concerned with making bell stands (this is his *yi*). Neither he, nor the *Zhuangzi* for that matter, says anything to the effect that bell stands are the most beautiful things humans can produce; in fact, the text says nothing about the general purpose of art at all. And while, as Cook Ding shows, butchering oxen can be aesthetically rewarding, the art of slaughtering is never assigned a higher value in the *Zhuangzi*. Conspicuously, all the arts of the excellent craftsmen depicted in the *Zhuangzi* are characterized as being contingent on either the natural (*ming*) or social (*yi*) circumstances that the artisans have been born into. There is no ultimate need for any of those arts—while we may arguably need butchers, there is no need for cutting up oxen musically—and none of the artisans set out to embellish their craft as essential, nor do they specifically justify what they do. On the contrary, the swimmer, for example, points out that he refrains from "knowing" any particular reason for why he is doing what he happens to excel at. As Guo Xiang's commentary highlights, he simply "attained" (*de* 得) (Wang Xiaoyu 2012, 657) this skill.

The radical contingency of the Daoist masters' arts as portrayed in the *Zhuangzi* is thus not a Kantian purposelessness of the beautiful or artistic that derives its necessity and reason precisely from this negative quality. Just as one finds no genius in cultivating subjectivity through artistic performance in the knack stories of the *Zhuangzi*, one finds no veneration of the sublime either. The skills that the Daoist masters excel at are coincidental and mundane, or, as in the case of the drunkard, even vulgar. They are common crafts practiced by common people by virtue of birth or circumstances. The difference between the master artisans and "normal" practitioners lay only in the degrees of excellence. In the knack stories, practical excellence is associated with affirmation of contingency and a capacity to disown one's position and role in society, with neither developing a sense of sincerity nor showing a personal preference for what one does, and with being able to maintain a distance to one's profession.

The affirmation of contingency entailed in the knack stories is perhaps most evident in the drunkard allegory, which is also the most carnivalesque of them all. Since we read the allegory of the drunkard who falls off a cart humorously, we do not see it as advocating the adoption of sober or cultivated variations of a drunken cognitive or spiritual state. For us, the allegory of the drunkard is not so much a model for emulation as a comical critique of those who are keen on internalizing their social persona by committing to their roles and developing sincerity. The drunkard is a profane *zhenren* who is good at taking a fall because he does not consider himself to be an artist or celebrity when he's falling. He simply falls when he falls. But he does not "with his person-ality enter into what is 'from heaven'" (*bu yi ren ru tian* 不以人入天); he is not, we presume, a committed alcoholic. This is to say, he does not give rise to the creation of an ideal of falling off carts and is thus immune to all sorts of vani-ties that may arise from identifying oneself with what one happens to be good at. The drunkard thus mocks the social construction of excellence and by extension the inability to survive a fall from grace that may come with the per-sonal investment in being regarded as truly good at something.

"Naturally" contingent skills may easily be reified into constraining social constructions of excellence. Likewise, one who is capable of enacting an activ-ity skillfully may easily come to regard oneself as a master whose own *dao* or art (*shu* 術) others ought to emulate. The knack stories in the *Zhuangzi* respond to this danger via humoristic means that are most obvious in the allegory of the drunkard falling off the cart and the story of the swimmer without a *dao*. With humor, the knack stories discourage readers from all too easily adopt-ing a mode of mere adoration and its accompanying desire for emulation. They create resistance against becoming an all-too-Daoist Daoist. As paradoxical models of skillfulness through disowning skills, the models, too, need to be disowned and emptied out. Only if one perceives one's skills as a drunk person sees the skill of falling off carts—by not knowingly possessing them and thus not regarding oneself as skillful—is it possible to remain unharmed by one's skills. Otherwise, if one has one's skills in an all-too-conscious way and identifies with them strongly, one may eventually succumb to "the disease of conceit."

The danger of idealizing excellence and attempting to make sincere com-mitments that result only in perverting and destroying it makes the Daoist masters ambiguous figures who often exercise contingent crafts, profane arts, or grotesquely exaggerated skills. The paradoxical nature of being an empty Daoist exemplar is particular evident with respect to Carpenter Chui 工倕, who could draw the shapes of the things he built with his magically skillful hand alone, without any tools such as compasses or T squares. He is briefly praised for these talents in section 19.13 as just one more example of skillful craftsmanship, in addition to the many other knack stories and illus-trations of effortless action in this chapter. However, in contradistinction to the other narratives, Carpenter Chui's short appearance in the chapter is devoid of ambiguity. As if the composer(s) of the *Zhuangzi* had become uneasy with such a straightforward and nondissonant knack episode, Carpenter Chui also appears in section 10.2, where he is treated in a rather different way—here, the idol meets his twilight and the hammer has been taken out: "Only when we destroy the hooks and rope levels, abandon the compasses and T-squares, and break Carpenter Chui's fingers will the people of the world be able to retain their skills" (Ziporyn 2009, 64–65; translation modified).

For us, this section does not contradict the knack stories of the *Zhuangzi* but rather confirms one central aspect of them—their emphasis on genuine pretending by means of empty role models. Once a figure like Carpenter Chui becomes an idol in search of emulation (e.g., through unambiguous praise such as in chapter 19 in the *Zhuangzi*), it only serves to "hero-worship completeness" (*xiong cheng* 雄成) and needs to be disowned by the text.[11] Typically, the knack stories in the *Zhuangzi* present masters who distance themselves from their skillfulness and enact it contingently. Whenever there is a tendency to establish a figure who internalizes their skill, idolatry may arise. The *Zhuangzi* reacts drastically to such a danger and "shockingly" undermines potentially dogmatic readings.

The skillful excellence of genuine pretenders is not based on a personal dedication to a craft that one has inherited through social convention or acquired by coincidence but on an indifference toward it. Genuine pretenders are capable of developing an impersonal attitude toward the tasks they happen to face. This allows them to become genuinely or spontaneously skillful at them. There is nothing extraordinary about the activities they excel at, such as swimming or butchering. They learn to fulfill their daily chores with mastery through habituation, or, in contemporary psychological terms, automaticity, just as one learns to drive a car, speak one's native language, or write text messages. One becomes good at these skills more often than not while being neither personally invested in them nor regarding them as venerable arts (which may be only arguably so in the case of texting). Such mundane and profane skills are examples of smooth operating by genuine pretending; we can engage with them effortlessly and achieve excellence without idolizing ourselves as masters. We obtain significant existential relief, and potentially even enjoyment, if only we can enact day jobs and move about the places we live in with the same ease and spontaneity that a master drunkard displays when he falls off a cart. This is what the knack stories in the *Zhuangzi*, when read using the genuine pretending hermeneutic, are all about.

WHERE WE COME FROM: ON RAMBLING AND THE ART OF PHILOSOPHIZING

The mundane way of moving about playfully in everyday life with ease, spontaneity, and unspectacular excellence has a name in the *Zhuangzi*: it is called *you* 遊. The term can well be understood as an emblematic abbreviation of the title of the first chapter of the *Zhuangzi*, "Xiaoyao you" (逍遙遊), which A. C. Graham (2001, 8) translates as "going rambling without a destination" and Burton Watson (1968, 23) (perhaps more famously) as "free and easy wandering." A more recent translation suggested by Chris Fraser (2014, 550) is "meanderingly wandering." *You* is a common word in the *Zhuangzi*. It occurs ninety-five times in the text, and if adding the ten occurrences of the practically synonymous character *you* 游, written with the "water" radical, more than one hundred times. There are few philosophically significant terms that are used with such frequency in the book. A definition of *you* in the *Zhuangzi* as a "eudaimonistic ideal" is presented by Fraser (563): he depicts it as essentially "marked by cognitively aware, affectively calm, adaptive, and generally enjoyable or zestful activity" (556).

Looking at the numerous occurrences of *you* in the *Zhuangzi* it becomes clear, however, that the mundane use of *you* as characterized by Fraser—which indicates an itinerant, aimless, and attentive way of moving around in life—is complemented, and arguably even overshadowed, by a more spiritual use of the term illustrating an elevated form of existence. A Daoist sage may "roam in the wilderness where no humans are" (*you yu wu ren zhi ye* 遊於無人之野, section 20.2), "roam the realm of Nothingwhatever" (*you wu he you zhi xiang* 遊無何有之鄉, section 1.7; see Graham 2001, 95), "roam the land without borders" (*you wu ji zhi ye* 遊無極之野, section 11.3), "roam the boundless" (*you wu duan* 遊無端, section 11.5), or be "someone who roams in nonpresence" (*you yu wu you zhe* 遊於無有者, section 7.4). In many instances, *you* appears along with the term *xin* 心 (heart-mind). Here it is used verbally in a "causative" fashion such that, following A. C. Graham (2001), *you xin* 遊心 means "to let the heart-mind roam." There are cases where this phrase is used exactly parallel to *you* on its own: just as there is a "roaming the limitless" (*you wu qiong* 遊無窮, section 1.3), one can also "let the heart-mind roam in the limitless" (*you xin yu wu qiong* 遊心於無窮, section 25.4; see Graham 2001, 154). In other cases, one is encouraged to "let the heart-mind roam in the flavourless" (*you xin yu dan* 遊心於淡, section 7.3; Graham 2001, 95; translation modified), and Laozi is praised for being able to let "the heart-mind roam at the beginning of things" (*you xin yu wu zhi chu* 遊心於物之初, section 21.4; Graham 2001, 130; translation modified).

In these instances, the sages who engage in *youing* are not simply strolling around but seem to have entered into some extraordinary state. The prevalence of such mystical usages of *you* and *you xin* in the *Zhuangzi* has given rise to what may be called a standard *dao jiao* understanding of *xiaoyao you* and its terminological derivatives or variations as religious notions. This approach is nicely represented by Liu Xiaogan's (2011, 54) entry on "Daoism: Laozi and Zhuangzi" in *The Oxford Handbook of World Philosophy*. Liu says there that the *Zhuangzi* attributes to *you* the implication that

> the place in which one roams freely is mysterious as well as remote. The wilderness or the "Never-never land" (*wu-he-you-zhi-xiang* 無何有之鄉) refers to such a place, far beyond the world. Moreover the compound *you-xin* (mind's wandering) appears repeatedly, indicating quite directly that it is the mind, rather than the body, that roams. Thus, by combining *xiao-yao* and *you*, the *Zhuangzi* depicts a free soul roaming in the boundless world of imagination where the mysterious union with Dao can be attained. *Xiao-yao* and *you* mean gaining access to the infinite panorama of a spiritual world.

A religious reading of *you* as representing "the mysterious union with Dao" somewhere "far beyond the world" is certainly justified if one is inclined to approach the *Zhuangzi* with intentions of a spiritual ascent to some higher realm, as countless readers have done. However, given the multidimensionality of the text, this "mainstream" interpretation by no means disqualifies more secular readings. Such readings have been attempted, for instance, by Fraser (2011 and 2014), Moeller (2015b), and Levinovitz (2012). Adopting Brook Ziporyn's image, Levinovitz (2012, 495) conceives of *you* as representing an existential and epistemological "wild card" given out by the *Zhuangzi* rather than a ticket to transcendence. He writes, "There is *you*, the wild card, completely open, versatile and ready to become whatever the hand you are dealt with requires. Like a spillover-goblet the wild card is neither scepticism or relativism nor any single position at all, really. It is not constantly empty, but rather changes according to its context. And its form (more than its 'meaning') frees us so that we are not normatively bound to imitate the *you* of sages, Zhuangzi, or other exemplars."

We very much embrace this mundane understanding of *you* in the *Zhuangzi* as a rambling mode of being that allows one to take on whatever task or attitude that the "hand you are dealt with requires." Indeed, we regard this notion of *you*, as well as the accompanying image of the wild card, as proper depictions of genuine pretending. Understood in relation to genuine pretending, the existential and epistemological "freedom" of *you* that Levinovitz speaks of is the mundane counterpart to the religious conceptions of entering a "realm of Nothingwhatever," or the "limitless" and "boundless" associated with *you*. From a wild card and genuine pretending perspective, those poetic expressions do not necessarily indicate an otherworldly excursion of the mind or soul but a very *inner*-worldly nonessential way of being and remaining nothing while having the capability of playing anything. In particular, we agree with Levinovitz's observation that the versatility or playfulness implied in the notion of *you* is so radical that it resists not only essential identification but also veneration. It is a mode of living or thinking that is indifferent to its content, so that there is nothing exemplary about it that can be specified—like genuine pretending, it does not imply a commitment to anything specific.

When the notion of *xiaoyao you* is introduced right at the beginning of the *Zhuangzi* in the title of the first chapter, it is immediately associated with transformation and movement. Famously, the first chapter begins with the allegorical depiction of the giant fish Kun who transforms into the equally giant bird Peng and traverses the world moving great distances at a time. It is significant that *you* is thereby associated with the (at least seemingly) roaming movement of animals rather than of humans. As opposed to terms referring to human movement such as "traveling," "journeying," or "going," "roaming" designates an *aimless* wandering that is not focused on getting from point A to a final destination B. It is neither spatially nor temporally framed by an intentional beginning and end. In this sense, it may well be comparable to being asleep, a mode of consciousness that one also cannot consciously get into or out of and that does not lead from a purposeful start to a finish. Its endlessness and limitlessness do not necessarily point to any beyond but can be perfectly immanent. Peng's *you*ing allows the bird to fly and rest anywhere in the world while never leaving it altogether. The association of *you* with the movement of animals, however, suggests not only a "free and easy wandering" but also a capacity for intense perception. Roaming animals are aware of their surroundings and have, for instance, a strong sense of the nearness of food or water or an approaching enemy. Thus *you* connotes not only the absence of stress but also excellence in adaptation and sensibility.

An image occurring once in the second chapter of the *Zhuangzi* corresponds well to the notion and can serve to illustrate it a little further. Section 2.12 introduces an "exile since childhood" (Graham 2001, 59), or *ruo sang* 弱喪, as someone who "has no sense of returning home" (*bu zhi gui* 不知歸). Guo Xiang (1954, 49) explains the term as follows: "Exile since childhood [*ruo sang*] is a name for someone who has lost their former home at an early age. Such exiles will consequently be at ease wherever they are and will not know of returning to their hometown" (少而失其故居，名為弱喪。夫弱喪者，遂安於所在而不知歸於故鄉也。).

An exile since childhood has never developed a sense of belonging to one particular place as opposed to any other. Accordingly, the exile does not identify him- or herself with a specific location, so the notion of "home" loses its meaning. Such persons can never be exiled for good; they can feel at home anywhere. Their lack of identification with a particular place also prevents them from building a potentially precarious relationship with a place they regard as their own. By disowning their own place, they "dis-disown" the world at large. They transform themselves into a giant Kun or Peng whose "home" is limitless and without boundaries. Understood in connection with the allegories of Kun and Peng and the image of the *ruo sang*, both of which erase the boundary between home and not home, the boundlessness of *you* does not have to be taken to indicate an entry into another dimension. *You* is boundless and limitless because one is not bound or limited by any commitment to a place, be it geographical or social, that one identifies as belonging to oneself. This radical homelessness is the ontic condition, so to speak, for engaging in *you*. In the state of *you*, one becomes the wild card, or, even more appropriately, the *joker* who, without limits, can smoothly move into any hand of cards and make it look good.

The aimless motion of *you* has no provenance and no destination but implies an acute sense of fit. It meanders through places and positions that it provisionally occupies. For those rambling without destination through society, the roles or names (*ming*) they take on are, as section 14.5 says, "tools for public use," and "one should not have too-strong preferences for them." For us, unlike for Liu Xiaogan and the *dao jiao* approach that his interpretation represents, the wandering metaphor of *you* does not necessarily lead one to a potentially disembodied and remote realm but right into the midst of social life. *You* speaks directly to who and where you are. We like to understand *you* as a form of roaming or rambling on this very ground.

Once one conceives of *you* as an intrasocial and easygoing explorative stroll taking one here and there, it becomes possible to see how this notion informs the famous narrative of the Happy Fish (*yu zhi le* 魚之樂, section 17.13) and supplies it with an often unacknowledged philosophical register. On its surface, the story depicts an epistemological debate between Zhuangzi the Daoist and Hui Shi the School of Names (*ming jia* 名家) representative about what we can and cannot know, as outlined, for instance, in Chen Guying's (2012) reading thereof (see also Moeller 1990). However, this story, too, can be seen as a multidimensional text that simultaneously addresses another topic—the notion of *you*:

> Zhuangzi and Hui Shi were roaming around [*you*] and got to a bridge above the Hao River. "The minnows swim around [*you*] so free and easy," said Zhuangzi, "that's how the fish are happy." Hui Shi said: "You are not a fish, whence [*an* 安] do you know that the fish are happy?" Zhuangzi replied: "You aren't me, whence do you know that I don't know the fish are happy?" Hui Shi said: "We'll grant that not being you I don't know about you. You'll grant that you are not a fish, and that completes the case that you don't know the fish are happy." Zhuangzi said: "Let's go back to where we started. When you said '*whence* [*an* 安] do you know that the fish are happy?' you asked me the question already knowing that I knew. I knew it from up above the Hao."
>
> (Graham 2001, 123; translation modified)

In the narrative, the epistemological debate between Zhuangzi and Hui Shi is clearly introduced by the theme of *you*, here variously translated as "roaming around" with respect to Zhuangzi's and Hui Shi's stroll and as "swim around" with respect to the fish in the water. In the end the story implicitly returns to this theme when Zhuangzi takes Hui Shi's question literally and understands the interrogative pronoun *an* in the sense of "whence" rather than simply as "how." In this way, he not only supplies the story with a humorous twist but also changes the philosophical key of the conversation. The story is now no longer an "analytic" inquiry into the conditions of knowledge claims or the validity of certain propositions but a meditation on the existential conditions of philosophizing about unlikely topics such as the happiness of fish.

Once one understands social life and the thoughts and ideas that come with it sub specie *you*, or under the aspect of a playful but attentive rambling without destination—and thus as analogous to the (probably biologically incorrectly) perceived way of minnow life—one can see that we arrive at certain philosophical insights (such as the insight into the emotions of fish) not so much because we have a capacity to attain objective knowledge but because a sociointellectual journey has led one to certain beliefs, feelings, language games, and worldviews. In other words, what we hold to be true or debate about passionately is not so much due to what we really know or are, or to the a priori conditions of understanding, or to the nature of things, but due to the *contingencies of where we come from*.

Crucially, where we come from, as "exiles since childhood" engaged in a *you* movement without provenance and aim, is never a true home but always a preliminary point on a journey without a center. Accordingly, what one holds true and values is not so because it is "in itself" so or because of a privileged knowledge or mode of cognition one possesses but rather because it is something that one's shifting path has led one to see—and that is subject to change again when one moves on. Just as the joker in a card game "may put up for a night but does not settle for long" in a role he plays, as philosophers, too, we do not reach stable insights and final conclusions, or, in Cartesian terms, certainty, or, in Rorty's terms, a "final vocabulary." We will never be certain about such things as the happiness of fish, but our philosophical ramblings can lead us temporarily, when a conversation with a good philosopher friend gets us there, to a moment of grasping such things. The reason that Zhuangzi can know about the happiness of fish is precisely that his intellectual rambling with Hui Shi has brought him there. This is the limitlessness and boundlessness of intellectual rambling. While it does not give us certainty, it allows one's "heart-mind to roam at the beginning of things," to use the flowery language of the *Zhuangzi* in a secular sense.

Therefore, we fully agree with Levinovitz (2012, 492), who suggests—and thus sets himself apart from Moeller's (2004a, 55–61) earlier reading of the Happy Fish allegory—a triple meaning of *you* in the narrative: the fish swim around, Zhuangzi (and Huizi) roam around, and Zhuangzi and Huizi philosophically or intellectually ramble around. All these movements are playfully attentive, aimlessly provisional, and intensely enjoyable. Indirectly, the significance of *you* as a philosophical method consisting of nonteleological, "nongeometrical," and contingent conversational excursions was recognized by one of the major philosophers of the twentieth century. Ludwig Wittgenstein experienced a shift in attitude toward philosophy that led him from his early attempts to philosophize in a strictly systematic and linear fashion to the insight that, at least for him, doing philosophy meant rambling through a landscape and putting together an album of sketches made on the way. He says as much in the preface to his *Philosophical Investigations* (Wittgenstein 1953, vii):

> It was my intention at first to bring all this together in a book whose form I pictured differently at different times. But the essential thing was that the things should proceed from one subject to another in a natural order and without breaks. After several unsuccessful attempts to weld my results together into such a whole, I realized that I should never succeed. The best that I could write would never be more than philosophical remarks; my thoughts were soon crippled if I tried to force them on in any single direction against their natural inclination.—And this was, of course, connected with the very nature of the investigation. For this compels us to travel over a wide field of thoughts, criss-cross in every direction.—The philosophical remarks in this book are, as it were, a number of sketches of landscapes which were made in the course of these long and involved journeys. The same or almost the same points were always being approached afresh from different directions, and new sketches made. Very many of these were badly drawn or uncharacteristic, marked by all the defects of a weak draughtsman. And when they were rejected a number of tolerable ones were left, which now had to be arranged and sometimes cut down, so that if you looked at them you could get a picture of the landscape. Thus this book is really an album.

Perhaps often unbeknownst to their authors, most philosophical books, if not all of them, are such albums—including the *Zhuangzi*. It is a widespread illusion that philosophical writings are, or at least potentially are, capable of proceeding "from one subject to another in a natural order and without breaks," or that they express the authentic standpoint of one author. From the perspective of genuine pretending, all positions one assumes, be they social roles, professional assignments and titles, or the opinions or views one expresses, are preliminary and momentary and come not so much from either oneself or the facts of the matter but from where a complex path—consisting of geographical components, of career paths, and of intellectual trajectories— has taken one. Specific motions in life may consist of passages from point A to point B, and individual texts (like the present one) may set out from somewhere and lead to certain points. But seen in a larger context, and also when going into the smaller details, it turns out that one rambles through life as well as through communication and thoughts in a highly contingent way and under the influence of innumerable factors—among which of course are also the people around oneself. *Identifications* with a point of view, with an insight, or with a specific position on the way depend on contingent abstractions and decomplexifications. In order to authenticate a position or belief or insight, one has to disregard the "criss-crossing" journey of *you* that veers out in "every direction" and construct a home and a feeling of belonging and purpose; one has to reduce the "where from" to a singular point of departure and the "where to" to an ultimate goal. Genuine pretenders playfully and happily engage with such abstractions, but they do not authenticate them; rather, they remain in the mode of *you*. As a philosophical method—or better yet, mode—*you* affirms and reflects contingency.

Of interest is Wittgenstein's observation that his "thoughts were soon crippled if [he] tried to force them on in any single direction against their natural inclination." For him, it seems, to give in to the wavering course of *you* and its "natural inclination" rather than forcing himself to subscribe to a supposed "natural order" was also a matter of staying *healthy*, if one takes seriously the metaphor he used. Thus, he relates the art or method of philosophizing to a project of maintaining sanity. So here, too, Wittgenstein shows a family resemblance to Daoism, which, as Girardot (2008, 33) has said, is fundamentally " 'medicinal' in intention and structure."

Sanity and Health: Immune to Afflictions and Conceit

The connection between *you*—which is for us not only an existential mode of genuine pretenders but also a mode of philosophizing—and sanity has been highlighted by Chris Fraser (2014, 560), who states clearly and simply that *you* "promotes psycho-physiological well-being." We agree not only with this assessment but also with his suggestion that a very close connection between *you* and *de* 德 (power, efficacy, health, virtuosity) informs the idea of a good life in the *Zhuangzi*: "Insofar as good health and the ability to carry out projects are requirements for a flourishing life, . . . *de* and wandering [*you*] are crucial to such a life" (550). In other words, *you* "is a characteristic expression or exercise of *de*" (545). *De*, in turn, is understood by Fraser as "a form of non-moral power, potency, or virtuosity" (543), and we agree with this understanding as well. Therefore, for Fraser as well as for us, *you* as "roaming," "rambling," or "wandering" and *de* as "power" or "virtuosity" are crucial ingredients of a

Daoist notion of well-being. However, while Fraser explores the normative and ethical potentials of the notion of well-being in the *Zhuangzi*, we prefer to approach the *Zhuangzi*'s views on sanity and health in the context of a philosophy of genuine pretending.

Before looking into *de* as a concept of sanity, which is, in the *Zhuangzi*, connected with the mode of "rambling through life" associated with *you* and genuine pretending, it is in order to once again acknowledge more common interpretations of power or health in the *Zhuangzi* tied to a *dao jiao* reading of the text. A general *dao jiao* understanding of the *Zhuangzi* tends to read the many designations of extraordinary beings, such as the "utmost persons" (*zhiren* 至人)—or, using a term that rarely occurs in the *Zhuangzi* but is much more widely associated with a Daoist cultivation ideal in popular contexts, the "immortals" (*xian* 仙)—quite literally as models of health whom one should try to match. The most improbable protagonists in the narratives of the *Zhuangzi* thus become idols of psychosomatic cultivation. Michael Strickmann (2015) provides a representative account of this hermeneutic approach:

> Among the strange figures that people the pages of the *Zhuangzi* are a very special class of spiritualized beings. Dwelling far apart from the turbulent world of men, dining on air and sipping the dew, they share none of the anxieties of ordinary folk and have the smooth, untroubled faces of children. These "supreme persons," or "perfected persons," are immune to the effects of the elements, untouched by heat and cold. They possess the power of flight, and are described as mounting upward with a fluttering motion. Their effortless existence was the ultimate in autonomy, the natural spontaneity that Zhuangzi ceaselessly applauds. These striking portraits may have been intended to be allegorical, but whatever their original meaning, these immortals (*xian*), as they came to be called, were to become the center of great interest. Purely literary descriptions of their freedom, their breathtaking mobility, and their agelessness were construed as practical objectives by later generations. By a variety of practices, people attempted to attain these qualities in their own persons, and in time Zhuangzi's unfettered paragons of liberty were to see themselves classified according to kind and degree in a hierarchy of heavenly hosts.

We will not pursue here the historically dominant *dao jiao* reading of the "utmost persons" in the *Zhuangzi* as a "very special class of spiritualized beings" who became exemplars for emulation. Instead, we look at them as allegorical figures, which, as Strickmann says, they "may have been intended to be" in the first place. Therefore, we do not follow them into realms "far apart from the turbulent world of men" but bring them right back into the mundane. Thus, "the power of flight" that they possess and the "fluttering motion" that they adopt are for us poetic depictions of an inner-worldly *you*; and their "effortless existence" and "breathtaking mobility" point to the smooth operations of genuine pretenders. That they are "ageless" and have the "faces of children" hints at their nonidentification with any of the "mature" social roles and functions they are capable of adopting while remaining *zhenuinely* selfless. Perhaps most important with respect to the issue of sanity, they "share none of the anxieties of ordinary folk"—and we take this to apply to life in this world rather than to one among "a hierarchy of heavenly hosts." This lack of anxiety makes them "immune to the effects of the elements," and again, such immunity is, for us, very much at the center of the sanity of an accomplished Daoist in the midst of society and the hostile climate it often engulfs one in.

Our approach to health and sanity in the *Zhuangzi* is not concerned primarily with its fanciful depictions of the *zhiren* 至人 but with the more specific conception of a *zhi de zhe* 至德者, "one who has attained perfect *de*" or perfect sanity, power, or virtuosity. The *Zhuangzi* itself defines such people very much in terms of a Daoist kind of immunity noted by Strickmann: section 17.7 says that those having attained perfect *de* "do not harm themselves with things" (*bu yi wu hai ji* 不以物害己), and the *Zhuangzi* then continues with a typical description of the degree of immunity they have reached. Such a person "can enter fire without feeling hot, enter water without drowning. Neither heat nor cold can harm him; the birds and animals do not impinge upon him" (Ziporyn 2009, 72). This description not only uses the exact same imagery depicting the *zhenren* in chapter 6 but also connects nicely with chapter 50 of the *Daodejing* as discussed in connection with the Hundun parody. Just as those who are "good at holding on to life" in that chapter are immune to the spears of soldiers and the claws of animals, those with perfect *de* remain unharmed in the midst of danger because they do not allow the hostile elements around them to enter into them. Echoing this metaphor, chapter 55 of the *Daodejing* says that those having a "thickness of *de*" (*de zhi hou* 德之厚) are neither bitten by "wasps, scorpions, vipers, and snakes" nor seized by "birds of prey and wild beasts." These images clearly show how the "thickness of *de*" and therefore the Daoist notion of sanity and health is conceived as an "immunization."[12] We read the penetration and seizing imagery of the *Daodejing*—in line with our interpretation of the Hundun parody—as referring to various kinds of socially inflicted injuries that come along with internalizing an imposed identity: anxiety, stress, emotional afflictions, or conceited and hypocritical forms of behavior.

We think that the notion of *de* as a concept connoting psychological and physiological (or psychosomatic) sanity and health in Daoism is essentially immunological, and that personal dissociation and distancing are among the methods by which one can achieve immunity. One can achieve thickness of *de* by rambling through life—that is to say, by playfully going out and about in society (*you*) while avoiding the internalization of one's roles; *de* and *you* mutually constitute each other. Section 26.8 of the *Zhuangzi* confirms this when it stipulates that those who are capable of rambling (*neng you* 能遊) also have a "thick *de*" (*hou de* 厚德).

Hence, there is a paradoxical core to the Daoist notion of *de* that sets it apart from the Confucian or "mainstream" understanding of it in the period when the *Zhuangzi* was composed. It is not only stripped of its moralist connotations but imbued with dissonance; it is detached from the idea of a sincere enactment of one's social roles and of an exemplary person or sage-ruler whom others should look up to as a model. Because of the detachment of the Daoist *de* from sincerity and commitment via its identification with *you*, it becomes an inversion, or even a parody, of the "regular" moral *de* of the times. The paradoxical and ironical aspects of the Daoist *de* are not only illustrated, as we previously indicated, by the array of cripples in chapter 5 of the *Zhuangzi*, along with their incongruent "complete *de*," but also emblematically expressed in the first lines of chapter 38 of the *Daodejing*, which point out that "higher *de* is not *de*; therefore it has efficacy [*de*]. Lower *de* does not let go of *de*; therefore it has no efficacy [*de*]."

The absence of a personal investment in one's social roles produces emotional immunity from socially induced afflictions of the heart-mind and from the stress and anxieties that these afflictions produce. This state of psychosomatic immunity can be called the empty heart-mind (*xu xin* 虛心), to borrow an expression from chapter 3 of the *Daodejing*. Chris Fraser (2011, 100) has convincingly shown that, despite having an empty heart-mind, the Daoist "virtuoso" is "not utterly emotionless" but rather "free from strong, disruptive emotions, whether pleasant, positive ones such as joy or unpleasant, negative ones such as sorrow," and that this state of having emotions while not being afflicted by them is not "defeatism" but actually "empowering." Thus, contrary to the classic traits of a psychopath who combines total insensitivity and absence of empathy with a narcissistically amplified sense of ego and self-centeredness (Hare 1999), the Daoist person of *de*—the "virtuoso" in Fraser's terminology or the genuine pretender in ours—combines a diminished sense of ego with the ability to possess emotions in a harmless manner. *Immunity to emotional afflictions does not mean being immune to feelings altogether but being immune to getting hurt by what one feels.* It means to remain personally and socially healthy while joyful or sad. And the capacity to remain emotionally sane in this way is, once more, tied to the incongruent capacity to not identify with one's emotions too deeply.

The emotional immunity of the genuine pretender can be illustrated with an everyday experience pointing to its mundane nature rather than to any spiritually elevated or extraordinary qualities. When watching a movie one can feel intense joy or sorrow and react somatically by laughing out loud or shedding tears. The actuality of these feelings is undeniable; they are not mere illusions or faked, nor are they displayed for the sake of social conformity or to put on a show. One experiences them on one's own just as intensely as in company, and in the latter case, one may even feel a bit embarrassed about them. While one's emotional experiences when watching a movie are thoroughly *genuine*, one is normally not personally afflicted by them and does not relate them to oneself; precisely because of this, when watching a tragedy one can, just as Mengsun Cai did at his mother's funeral, "remain unsaddened in the depths of one's heart." Genuine pretending does not mean insane coldness or unhealthy insensitivity; on the contrary, it enables one—again, like Mengsun Cai—to participate effectively in society (including an emotional participation) without being overpowered by one's emotional experience. Movie audiences and genuine pretenders can have feelings and dissociate themselves from them at the same time. They are immune to emotional affliction—but not to emotions as such—because they refrain from authenticating their feelings.

The genuine empathy that movie audiences and genuine pretenders feel on the basis of "emptying their heart-minds" may well be compared to the dispassionate empathy one might find in a therapist or a judge. Both therapists and judges are expected to be capable of emotionally understanding and empathically relating to the people who appear before them in their professional role and to be guided by this understanding and empathy in their interactions with them. At the same time, it is also expected that they do not allow their emotions to become personal—they should refrain from developing any interpersonal emotional dependencies or treating their clients as if they have a personal stake in the matter. This dissociation from their feelings not only enables them to stay healthy but also forms the basis for doing their job effectively. Or, paraphrasing Fraser, their emotional attitude is not defeatist but empowering.

As shown in our analysis of the Mengsun Cai story, the emotional immunity—or, to use a term employed more commonly in the secondary literature, equanimity (see, e.g., Raphals 1996)—ascribed to the Daoist virtuoso or genuine pretender in the Zhuangzi extends, most importantly, to what is arguably the primary source of the existential angst of humans: death. The philosophical "strategy" to develop an anxiety-fee and thus psychosomatically healthy attitude toward death in the Zhuangzi is based once more on dissociation. Allegories and narratives such as the famous butterfly dream point out the futility of our worries about death in view of the fact that the transformation of things is so radical that there is no substantial continuity of beings (Moeller 2004a, 44–54). We will not be dead but simply replaced by something else when no longer alive. Nothing happens to us when we die. We end, and another life begins—and this new life may well be as enjoyable as or even more so than the previous one. In this way, just as the notion of you disowns us spatially and makes us "homeless" only to "dis-disown" space in general and to allow us to transitorily settle anywhere, a Daoist philosophy of life and death disowns our lifetime only to dis-disown time in general and allow us to transitorily exist in whichever presence we may encounter.[13] By not identifying with our present form of existence, by genuinely pretending not only our roles in society but also our life in general, we become empowered to overcome our greatest fear and attain equanimity.

The difficulty of attaining such ease, equanimity, or emotional immunity is not underestimated in the Zhuangzi. In addition to the fear of death, many people regularly find themselves in distressing circumstances that they cannot easily dissociate themselves from. The hands people are dealt are often calamitous, not to speak of the minor causes of anxiety, discomfort, or anger that even an otherwise comfortable life has in stock on a daily basis. A rarely discussed episode at the end of chapter 6 depicts how hard it is to find equanimity in the midst of all too common misery. Differing from the better-known stories of some Daoist friends who are able to more or less happily welcome death, here we are presented with two men who are not very cheerful. As the text says, "after ten days of freezing rain" (Ziporyn 2009, 49), Ziyou worries about the well-being of his friend Zisang. He sets out to visit him and bring him some rice. When he arrives, he hears Zisang singing and crying out in desperation the words "Father? Mother? Heaven? Man?" (49). When asked by Ziyou why he is uttering these words, Zisang replies, "My mother and father would surely never wish to impoverish me like this. Heaven covers all equally, earth supports all equally, so how could heaven and earth be so partial as to single me out for impoverishment? I search for some doer of it all but cannot find anything—and yet here I am in this extreme state all the same. This must be what is called fate [ming 命], eh?" (49).

When having to put up with misfortune, one's suffering is often only enhanced by taking it personally and asking oneself the question, why me? One is easily led to take one's destitution personally—as if one had been "singled out" by some curse or unjust punishment. The identification with one's misery amplifies it, or, as the English saying goes, adds insult to injury. A genuine pretender will be able to subtract the insult from the injury, and it seems that Zisang is working on this difficult subtraction process. As a result, it may become possible for him to accept his bad luck by dissociating himself from it—there is no need to internalize unfortunate circumstances by committing oneself to them. A healthy attitude will accept them impersonally as fate (ming 命). After all, as Confucius told Zigao, the distressed envoy to Qi in section 4.3 in the Zhuangzi, the perfection of de, or of sanity, power, or virtuosity (de zhi zhi 德之至) consists in being at ease with (an 安) or "reconciled to" (Ziporyn 2009, 28) what one cannot do anything about by "taking it as fate" (ruo ming 若命)—or as entirely contingent.

The equally unhealthy and thus non-de counterpart of taking misfortune personally is to identify with moral luck or social success. The resulting "disease of conceit" is, as we have tried to show, the object of ridicule in some of the satirical stories of the Zhuangzi, such as in the narrative of Robber Zhi's meeting with Confucius. The Confucian de ethos of the ethics of sincerity is focused on the correspondence between social rank and performance and inner commitment to outer behavior. Accordingly, the socially successful and powerful are encouraged to feel good about and identify with their positions and successes. If they sincerely commit to their powerful positions, they have all the reason to see themselves as truly virtuous and to not "let go of de." Connecting with the Daodejing's claim to the contrary that higher de consists, paradoxically, in letting go of it, section 13.13 of the Zhuangzi claims that "in the era of perfect *de*" (*zhi de zhi shi* 至德之世) "the worthies were not esteemed." Likewise, "being upright and correct was not known of as righteous; caring for one another was not known of as humane; to be for real was not known of as loyal; doing the right thing was not known of as trustworthy." The establishment of moral praise and the idea that social rank should correspond with it then only foster self-righteousness and corrupt *de*.

Just as it is healthy not to personalize social misfortune or exclusion and to instead regard it as contingent fate, it is also healthy to refrain from personalizing social success and esteem and to not become enthralled by such success. There are many stories about Zhuang Zhou's rejecting official appointments in the *Zhuangzi* (see Graham 2001, 118–23). The most famous of them occurs in section 32.15 and, in an extended version, in the biography of Zhuangzi in chapter 63 of the *Shiji*. Here, the perils of social acclaim are illustrated with the image of the sacrificial ox who, after being pampered for a long time, is eventually dressed up richly only to be killed. This allegory is usually read in a Yangist way (117) as pointing to the physical dangers involved in a life in politics. Alternatively, it may also be understood as satirically indicating the unhealthiness—and conceited stupidity—of believing that identifying with rather than playing an exalted social role makes one something better than an ox.

The nonconceitedness of those who incongruently play their social roles without commitment, dedication, or belief not only makes them healthy and sane because their *de* remains powerful and intact but also can actually make them attractive. Horsehead Hunchback, the ugly seducer, was strangely attractive to the young women around him, and Robber Zhi, the cannibal, was most handsome and strong. These two humoristic characters are carnivalesque counterimages of the Confucian ideal of sincere beauty. Just as the sincere affirmation of one's social esteem is unhealthy, the internalization of one's beauty makes one not more sincerely beautiful but paradoxically unattractive. Not without irony, a story about two concubines in section 20.9 of the *Zhuangzi* shows this:

> Yangzi, travelling to Song, spent a night at an inn. The innkeeper had two concubines, one of them beautiful, the other ugly. The ugly one he valued, the beautiful one he neglected. When Yangzi asked the reason, the innkeeper's boy answered: "The beautiful one thinks herself beautiful; we do not notice she is beautiful. The ugly one thinks herself ugly; we do not

notice she is ugly." "Make a note of that, my disciples," said Yangzi. "If you act excellently, and do so without regarding this excellence as yours, where will you go and not be liked?"

(Graham 2001, 141–42; translation modified)

Truly claiming to be something, rather than merely playing it (even if it is something obviously nice), can be off-putting to others.

CONCLUSION

I hazard the guess that man will be ultimately known for a mere polity of multifarious, incongruous, and independent denizens.
—Robert Louis Stevenson, *Strange Case of Dr. Jekyll and Mr. Hyde*

A PARADOXICAL UNPRETENTIOUSNESS OF GENUINE PRE-tending lies at the heart of a Daoist art of maintaining sanity and achieving efficacy. Genuine pretending allows one to operate smoothly in the midst of a social environment full of hypocrisies and, at times, perils. This art is referred to in the statement in *Zhuangzi* 20.9, cited at the end of the preceding chapter, which recommends not regarding one's excellence as one's own. By practicing genuine pretending, it is suggested, one can manage to remain *unharmed* (*bu shang* 不傷) like Huzi, the miraculous face changer in sections 7.5–6 in the *Zhuangzi*, who avoids turning into "a corpse presiding over [his] good name [*ming* 名]" (Ziporyn 2009, 53). Huzi's shifting appearances make him unidentifiable and thereby preclude any narcissist infatuation with the images that society reflects back onto him. As a *zhenuine* pretender, the *zhenren* in the *Zhuangzi* can, as illustrated by such characters as Huzi, "assume any appearance on the way" (*deng jia yu dao* 登假於道; section 6.1).

The *Zhuangzi* identifies the sociopolitical and psychological powers of role-indicating names as a perfidious danger to a sane and flourishing life. Ironically, it depicts Confucius, the spokesperson for the "rectification of names" in other texts such as the *Analects*, warning his favorite disciple, Yan Hui, that one's *de* 德—one's "virtuosity," "power," or, by extension, one's general psychosomatic health—is "undermined by names" (*de dang hu ming* 德蕩乎名; *Zhuangzi* 6.1). Names, as the *Zhuangzi* has Confucius insist, are "inauspicious tools" (*xiong qi* 兇器). In a satirically exaggerated manner, the same passage identifies the desire of the great sage-rulers Yao and Yu to match their names with actuality (*shi* 實) as the main reason for their committing genocide against rogue tribes—all in the name of virtue. It is intimated that they became so obsessed with their own greatness that they felt entitled to engage in a brutal slaying of those they deemed immoral. Their ultimate commitment to their own excellence reverted into a violent moral frenzy and brought about a terrible insanity that conquered them and the society over which they ruled. With reference to this "unconventional" (to say the least) historical anecdote, Confucius admonishes Yan Hui, "If names and actualities are something that even sages cannot resist, then how about you!?" (*ming shi zhe shengren zhi suo bu neng sheng ye, er kuang ruo hu* 名實者聖人之所不能勝也而況若乎) (*Zhuangzi* 6.1).

If supposed sages like Yao and Yu got carried away by their lofty roles and names and thus felt personally empowered to actualize them in a most terrible commitment to them, then how difficult is it for us "normal" people not to fall prey to the same pattern of name-fueled self-aggrandizement in our everyday lives? Unlike in the curious legend of Yao and Yu's genocide, we are normally not in the position to become mass murderers. However, we may, induced by an insane identification with social positions and ranks, nonetheless give in to all kinds of vanities and conceitedness, albeit on a much smaller scale.

Mirroring the problems arising from the identification with positive roles and names, a sincere identification with negative roles and names can have equally devastating effects. Chapter 5 of the *Zhuangzi* shows a number of cripples and criminals who do not live up to these roles at all. In a carnivalesque fashion, they defy the stigmatization indicated by their social rank and are consequently able to thrive despite their handicaps. By not committing to the names that would designate them "correctly," they are able not only to escape humiliation but also, ironically, to greatly succeed even in the unlikeliest circumstances. As bizarre and comically portrayed counterheroes, they are satirical counterimages of the genocidal sages Yao and Yu. While a sincere commitment to their socially ascribed sagacity turns the latter into grotesque monsters, a noncommitment to their socially ascribed monstrosity turns the former into weird sages.

Genuine pretending is recommended as an antidote to the potentially unhealthy effects of a total commitment to social roles and the feelings of entitlement or nonentitlement—or the hubris and depression—that may come with it. Hubris, it has to be stressed, may also lie in assuming that one is a "true" Daoist master or model. Therefore, the figure of the genuine pretender is not and cannot be simply another role model that differs from the Confucian ones only in content or with respect to the "virtues" it is supposed to manifest. Just as much as the *Zhuangzi* tends to ridicule and thereby deconstruct conventional (Confucian) role models on the one hand—just as much as it engages in this kind of iconoclasm—it also subverts, on the other hand, the tendency to idolize the genuine pretender as a more "authentic" role model that one ought to sincerely imitate. The prescription to be authentic or sincere would obviously be not only paradoxical but also self-refuting and counterproductive. To follow this prescription would mean not to follow it. Therefore, genuine pretenders in the *Zhuangzi* are not straightforward role models but "queer" and otherwise "distorted" antimodels whose names are only the "guest" of their forms and who cannot be emulated as such.

The figure of the genuine pretender is inherently dissonant and incongruous. And this dissonance and incongruity first and foremost reflects a disjunction between name and form or name and actuality. Important protagonists in the *Zhuangzi* such as the cripples and criminals of chapter 5, the genuinely pretending tree, and Robber Zhi are introduced as exemplifying such a disjunction, which also implies having no fixed identity or particular merit. Most paradigmatically, section 6.7 in the *Zhuangzi* says that Mengsun Cai "does not have the actuality, but has got the name" (*wu qi shi er de qi ming* 無其實而得其名).

We have tried to show that a similar dissonance and incongruity extends to many of the famous knack stories of the *Zhuangzi* and their strange protagonists. The "extreme waterfall diver" at Lüliang, the nameless drunkard mastering the art of falling off carts unharmed, and Cook Ding, the symphonic slaughterer, are oddly exaggerated "players," partly surreal and partly comical, partly mundane and partly miraculous. They are larger than life and at the same time most average, wonderful, and ordinary. Their stupefying skills are accompanied by the utmost unpretentiousness. These paradoxical artists *disown* their arts. Just as Song Rongzi detaches from his knowledge, deeds, and virtuosity, or Ziqi and Yan Hui forget their selves, the drunkard is not committed to his falls, and the anonymous diver at Lüliang points out the coincidental nature of his capacities that he happened to acquire merely by chance of birth and for which he claims no personal credit or intentional devotion. The resistance of such a casual kind of expertise to idealization is most radically expressed in the *Zhuangzi*'s self-iconoclastic and self-deconstructing—and thus, of course, also ironical—demand in section 10.2 that, for the sake of attaining skillfulness, master carpenter Chui's fingers need to be broken. The association between skill and name or art and fame that turns artists into "celebrities" is thereby effectively undermined. Thus, both the artisans and their arts are de-idolized and "normalized," and a routine of a paradoxically common and contingent excellence that one may or may not engage in emerges.

The core term in the *Zhuangzi* reflecting and affirming a common and contingent exercise of excellence—and the sanity of being or acting that can come along with it—is *you* 遊. Genuine pretending is a mode of being that allows one to enjoy with unquestioned ease "foreign" existences and capacities and to get along with what happens in a situation (*yin shi* 因是 or *yi hu tianli* 依乎天理), like a butterfly in a dream, a tree functioning as a shrine, or a keeper of monkeys. One can act without self-conscious worries because one does not own or essentially become such existences and capacities. *Youing* accepts radical transformation and alteration (*hua* 化) by going along with what is obvious (*yi ming* 以明), and this radical transformation allows for the genuineness in genuine pretending. Since no essential self underlies them, the "pretended" or "played" (*jia* 假) temporary existences or capacities are not attributes of a more fundamental substance or subject. Not despite but precisely because of this lack of grounding or *inessentiality*, they are fully real and *zhenuine* and not merely qualities of something more essential. If, echoing the title of a novel by Robert Musil, a genuine pretender is a "man without qualities," then genuine pretending is a "quality without a man." The itinerant and nonteleological way of moving through life of a man without qualities is *youing*. Such a motion provides immunity from reification and, to allude to the title of another twentieth-century novel, so, too, the possibility of an actually bearable lightness of being in a social environment that is perhaps otherwise unbearable.

In the *Zhuangzi*, *you* as a roaming movement through life is associated with the notion of *de* 德, which represents an encompassing understanding of

health, vigor, and vitality. Section 26.8, for instance, states that the ability to
"roam aimlessly" (neng you 能遊) corresponds to having a "thick de" (hou de
厚德). In this way, a philosophy of genuine pretending in the Zhuangzi confirms Norman J. Girardot's (2008, 33) diagnosis that Daoism is "fundamentally
'medicinal' in intention and structure." It is noteworthy that the medicinal or
therapeutic effect of "releasement" from an obsession with achieving a sincere dual correspondence between one's social roles on the one side and one's
actions and inner commitment on the other is brought about by humor in the
Zhuangzi. Once read in a humorous key, the allegories and philosophical rumi-
nations in the Zhuangzi set their readers free from a commitment to social
roles, names, or to right and wrong (shi fei 是非) statements. They thereby
break out of a propositional mold that some contemporary academic interpretations of Daoist philosophy set out to reconstruct. At the same time, a
humorous viewpoint allows readers to distance themselves from the absurd
protagonists of those narratives and so avoid any imperative of emulation or
role modeling. The text thus undermines the same dao jiao devotion to spiritual cultivation that it encourages when read in a more mystical fashion. The
humor of the Zhuangzi—acknowledged by many readers yet philosophically
examined by few—does not eliminate the possibility of nonhumorous
understandings but sheds a decisively different light on the text. When read
humorously, the text distances itself from the doctrines, morals, or isms that
one finds in it when looking for straightforward arguments or positions;
likewise, it deprives the sages and masters depicted of their dignified and
transcendent aura and equalizes these characters and their arguments (qi wu lun
齊物論). From a comical perspective, the Zhuangzi infuses itself with irony
and performatively engages in a mode of genuine pretending: it de-essentializes itself and becomes skillful play. The text, then, operates and enacts genuine pretending. It nonetheless leaves it to its readers to be willing and able to
engage with it on this level. Genuine pretending and humor are generous
offers one remains perfectly free to refuse—they function as an emergency
exit available to those who prefer not to restrict themselves to binding interpretations of the world and of oneself.

It seems that a genuine pretending reading of the Zhuangzi intertwines an
existential mode of "rambling without destination" (you) with a thoroughly
humorous approach to meaning and language. As such, this observation
presents nothing new. In fact, in a last ironic turn in section 33.6, the text
describes itself along these lines: "Since all the ten thousand things are inex-
tricably netted together around us, none is worthy of exclusive allegiance.

This is where the ancient art of the *dao* 道 lies. Zhuang Zhou got wind of it and was delighted. He used ridiculous and exaggerated descriptions, absurd and preposterous sayings, senseless and shapeless phrases, indulging himself unrestrainedly as the moment demanded, uncommitted to any one position, never looking at things from any one corner" (Ziporyn 2009, 123; translation modified).

With our reading of the *Zhuangzi*, we have tried, on the one hand, to situate the text within the wider debates on names and actualities of its time and thus to provide a historically embedded interpretation. On the other hand, we have also tried to delineate an—in our view—intriguing ancient view of life and sanity, and of society, language, and art. While we certainly sympathize with this view and admire the eloquence and simultaneous complexity with which it is expressed, we do not wish to claim that it can be seamlessly incorporated into contemporary philosophical, theoretical, or sociopolitical contexts. It remains a challenge to test how a philosophy of genuine pretending can be transformed and adapted to current discourses. However, by articulating how the modern semantics of sincerity and authenticity has not only influenced philosophy, literature, and the broader culture of our age as described by Trilling, Taylor, and others but also significantly impacted the reception of ancient Chinese philosophy, we have identified a potential framework for taking on that challenge. If the philosophy of genuine pretending in the *Zhuangzi* evolved as a critical response to an ancient Chinese philosophy of sincerity, then maybe a contemporary philosophy of genuine pretending can be developed as a critical response to a modern "jargon of authenticity," to use Adorno's expression. Such an endeavor would without a doubt have to distance itself from the problems and issues discussed by early Chinese Confucians and Daoists and from the vocabularies they employed. But it may nevertheless draw inspiration from the philosophy of genuine pretending that we find in the *Zhuangzi* in order to see what a Daoism of today could look like.

If one follows authors such as Trilling and Taylor and assumes that there is a specifically modern concept of authenticity, then this modern concept of authenticity will also be connected to specifically modern forms of inauthenticity. In a modern context, the authentic-inauthentic distinction becomes specifically relevant with the emergence of technological and social developments that produce copies on an unprecedented scale—and thus also inevitably produce a lack of originals. The more copies there are the rarer the original is. New levels of the mass production of copies were reached in modernity with the proliferation of mass media communication in the form of, for instance, printed matter, film, television, or the new so-called social media. It seems that the modern quest and demand for authenticity occurs in a world filled with copies, where the question of genuineness is posed in a new way. Now, the value of genuineness is not so much attached to the degree of sincere commitment to a social role as it is transposed to the claim that an object or person has to be an original rather than a mere copy. Uniqueness has become more prestigious than mere honesty. According to Niklas Luhmann (2000, 142n12), "the desire to experience things authentically for oneself is itself a desire first suggested by the creation" of the very distinction between authenticity and inauthenticity brought to the fore by mass media representations and their dissemination. And so, a notion of "culture" as something having its peculiar and original characteristics that set it apart as interesting, recognizable, and special emerges: "Without reproduction there would be no originals; without [its] mass media [representation] culture would not be recognizable as culture. And the fact that this reflective culture, this culture which knows itself as culture, produces its counter-conceptuality of 'authenticity,' 'the real thing,' 'spontaneity' etc. just serves to confirm that what is involved here is a universal phenomenon which includes self-reference" (86; translation modified).

Through mass media representation—for example, in novels, newspapers, movies, or on websites—peculiar individuals or events or (not so) artistic products are introduced as peculiar because only the peculiar is worthy of mass media representation in the first place. "Culture" thus emerges as that which is somehow unique or special and accordingly deserves recognition and to be displayed, observed, and respected. However, its very representation in mass media paradoxically constructs and undermines the uniqueness of the represented character, event, or work of art. Through being displayed in a mass format, the unique is simultaneously designated as unique and prone to lose its uniqueness as a consequence of its mass display. The paradoxical social construction of originality and uniqueness built into mass media representation in turn fuels a demand for authenticity as true originality or uniqueness or peculiarity. An originality that puts itself into question through its public display—in a way similar to how the public display of sincerity puts sincerity into question—only falls prey to suspicion and gives rise to calls for an ever-purer form of itself—that is, a call for ever more authentic authenticity. This self-referential mechanism is paradoxical and, on an existential level, absurd by simultaneously requiring of and making it impossible for an individual or an object to be truly authentic.

Unlike its historic predecessor in an age of sincerity, a contemporary philosophy of genuine pretending would have to react to the paradoxes and absurdities of an age of authenticity, and to the—in our opinion, impossible—social demands, hubris, obsessions, and stress it produces. It would have to deconstruct the incongruity of authenticity ideals and the perfidy of calls to emulate them. It would have to undermine the semantics of authenticity with humor and thereby "carnivalize" its appeal—or at least show how this can be done. It could also outline how it may be possible to skillfully ramble without destination, or at least how to remain unharmed as a social hermit in the midst of a society busy with, among other things, reinforcing a regime of authenticity onto itself and demanding that everyone be special, interesting, and innovative—including the authors of academic and philosophical texts.

NOTES

PREFACE

1.   Chapters 1 and 2 in this book are developments of Paul D'Ambrosio's PhD dissertation, "Hypocrisy, Lying, and Deception in Early Chinese Philosophy" (University College Cork), which was supervised by Hans-Georg Moeller.

INTRODUCTION: A JOKER IN THE FOLD

1.   For a critical analysis, see Heubel (2015, 67–71).
2.   We would like to stress here, as we point out in more detail in the subsequent chapters of this book, that what interests us in a reading of Confucian ethics as relational or role oriented is not the now hotly debated question of whether or not this conception allows for autonomous agency (and we do not think that this question had much influence on the *Zhuangzi*, in any case), but rather that it prescribes sincerity.
3.   According to Feng Youlan 馮友蘭 (Fung 1970, 80), the difference between Confucians and Daoists boils down to this: "The Confucianist sages were

enthusiastic souls, the [D]aoist sages were men of imperturbable calm." In our reading, we develop this difference by highlighting the importance of sincerity in those "enthusiastic souls" and the lack of it in the "unperturbed."

4. Zhang Liwen 張立文 (1999, 57) notes that pre-Qin Confucian and Daoist texts are both concerned with people "falsely appearing good, and pretending." Daoist texts tend to respond to problems of falsity, hypocrisy, and selfishness that arise as a result of Confucian practice.

5. See, e.g., chapters 18 and 80.

6. We also recognize that Guo Xiang may have "borrowed" much of Xiang Xiu's 向秀 (d. 272) work.

7. Interestingly, Ren Jiyu overturns traditional interpretations, arguing that the Inner Chapters actually represent the thoughts of later followers of Zhuang Zhou.

8. While Feng Youlan (Fung 1931) does not think that the Inner Chapters are necessarily the work of a single author, and that Zhuang Zhou may have "brushed" some of the outer or miscellaneous chapters, he does claim that the first two chapters contain the core ideas in the text.

1. SINCERITY, AUTHENTICITY, AND ANCIENT CHINESE PHILOSOPHY

1. As is the case for Roger Ames and Henry Rosemont Jr.

2. Tu Weiming (forthcoming) insists, as many critics of Ames and Roesemont do, that the notion of the Confucian self includes autonomous agency independent of social roles. However, Tu (as well as many other contemporary Confucians) remains stringently opposed to any moral insincerity—and thus reaffirms the traditional "regime of sincerity." Tu (1999, 98) writes, for example, "Since man's nature is imparted by Heaven, the creative power of sincerity is inherent in the very structure of man. To learn how to be sincere is ultimately an attempt to become truly human."

3. To this effect, Chen Lai (2015, 52) writes, "In Chinese culture the person is not atomic, but rather a relational being that is one of the parties in the continuum of social relations."

4. For more on the comparison between contemporary Chinese accounts of Confucianism and Ames and Rosemont's Confucian role ethics, see D'Ambrosio (2016).

2. THE CONFUCIAN REGIME OF SINCERITY

1. Throughout the history of textual commentary on the *Zhuangzi*, interpreters have noted that the self described therein is defined in opposition, or as a reaction

to, the Confucian perspective on the person. Yang Guorong's (2009b, 200–201) description provides a good example: "Once humaneness, duty, and other Confucian values come to define the self, the individual loses his or her original state and becomes a ritualized and dutified 'self.' . . . Zhuangzi wants to dissolve the [Confucian] ritualized and dutified 'self.' "

2. Cai Qinghua describes how the pre-Qin debates were further developed during the Wei-Jin period in the form of commentaries on the *Analects*, the *Book of Changes*, the *Zhuangzi*, and the *Daodejing*.

3. A variation of this is given in the *Hou Han shu* 後漢書, "Zuo Zhou Huang Liezhuan 左周黃列傳" 55.27.

4. Wang Deyou (2010, 145) argues that for the *Zhuangzi* once persons are molded by Confucian values, they become "a man-made and empty and false thing" (*yi zhong renwei de, xujia de dongxi* 一種人為的，虛假的東西)."

5. Chenyang Li (2014, 89) expresses this point well, saying, "A person's self-cultivation cannot be separated from his effort to harmonize the rest of the world, as he becomes more mature his focus expands from self-refinement, to fostering a good family, to contributing to a good society, and so forth."

6. Chen Lai 陳來 (forthcoming) argues that, from a Confucian perspective, politics and a sincere commitment to morality are inseparable, and when they are not, hypocrisy arises.

7. This terminology is first introduced in David Hall and Roger Ames's *Thinking Through Confucius* (1987) and later expanded on in Ames and Rosemont's work.

8. More recently, Puett seems to have altered his view, rejecting the "mistaken idea that we should answer to some 'core' self" (Puett and Gross-Loh 2016, 45).

3. PHILOSOPHICAL HUMOR AND INCONGRUITY IN THE ZHUANGZI

A more detailed version of the section "Hundun's Death: A Parody of a Myth" has been published in *Philosophy East and West* 67 (3) (Moeller 2017). We are grateful to Roger Ames for allowing us to use some of its material here.

An earlier version of the section "Huzi, the Face Changer: A Parody of a Didactic Tale" has been previously published (Moeller 2016). We are grateful to Springer, the publisher of *Dao: A Journal of Comparative Philosophy*, for permission to use some of its materials here.

An earlier version of the section "Horsehead Humpback and the Freaks: Parodies of the 'Ideal Man'" has been published as Moeller (2015a). We are grateful to Livia Kohn and Three Pines Press for permission to use some of its materials here.

1. On humor and Chan Buddhism, see also Morreall (2009, 133–37) and Hyers (1989).

2. We are grateful to Richard Garner for translating this joke into English.

3. We are aware that Wang Bo (2014) is a translation of Wang Bo (2004). English translations from the latter are our own unless otherwise noted.

4. For a refutation of the hypothesis that China lacks creation myths, see Goldin (2008).

5. Chen Guying (2008, 265) notes that the "good" intentions of the Emperors of the North and South are met with unexpected and disappointing results and asks rhetorically (and humorously), "Who would affirm or accept this type of good intention?"

6. In the following sections of this chapter we explore figures in the Zhuangzi who possess the art of avoiding identification.

7. Cf. Daodejing 28.

8. Cf. Daodejing 20 and 25.

9. Bernard Faure (1994, 90) has related Chan Buddhist tricksters to Daoist trickster predecessors as found in the Zhuangzi. Susan Debra Blum (2007, 142) states that "Zhuangzi in China could almost be considered a trickster."

10. We are thankful to Suzanne Murphy for pointing out this parallel.

11. Commenting on this line, Chen Guying (2008, 245) notes, "having 'de' and not placing importance on external forms or appearances, this is the most perfect 'de.'"

12. Chen Guying (2008, 241) has also picked up on this point.

13. Traditional commentators have made similar observations, albeit often without explicitly mentioning specific Confucian texts but rather Confucian ideas or values in general. For example, Wang Fuzhi (1964, 47), in his commentary to the title of this chapter, contrasts de in the Zhuangzi and Daodejing with ritual (li 禮) and music (yue 樂) in Confucianism.

14. Guo Xiang (see Wang Xiaoyu 2012, 209) notes that Horsehead Humpback does not harm creatures and can even get along with animals or birds without causing disturbances.

15. This may or may not indicate a homophony or near homophony in ancient Chinese pronunciations, depending on time and region. According to Baxter (1992), the words were not homophonic in ancient China.

16. Franklin Perkins (2014, 180) has offered a succinct summary of the Zhuangzi's amoral perspective on evil or badness. Arguing that, for the Zhuangzi, nothing is good or bad from the perspective of heaven, he concludes, "This may be the ultimate consequence of a thorough reflection on the problem of evil: the fact

that the world is bad according to our categories ultimately negates the very category of bad."

17. Chen Guying (2008, 366–67) similarly notes that Robber Zhi is targeting Confucian hypocrisy, specifically as it is related to Confucian conceptions of a stratified society.

18. Wang Bo (2004, 178) also argues that the *Zhuangzi* maintains and moreover celebrates the distinction between heart-mind (*xin* 心) and form (*xing* 形).

19. Ziporyn (2009, 31) translates the single character *yi* 義—which stands for the Confucian moral value of "righteousness," or proper dual correspondence fit— here as "does what is or is not called for by its position, by what role it happens to play."

4. SMOOTH OPERATORS: THE ARTS OF GENUINE PRETENDING

The section "Where We Come From: On Rambling and the Art of Philosophizing" follows, in part, Moeller 2015b. We are grateful to the University of Hawai'i Press for permission to use some of the materials from that essay here.

1. For historical-philological overviews of the terms *zhen* and *zhenren*, see Coyle (1998) and Miura (2008b).

2. While such negative depictions abound, there are also a few slightly more positive depictions of the *zhenren* in other sections of the *Zhuangzi*, as indicated in Shen (2003).

3. In Chinese Buddhism, the term *jia* 假 takes on a very similar meaning; see Kantor (2014, 2015).

4. Recently, Fei Xiaotong (2012) and Li Zehou (2008a, 2014) have argued that being "at ease" is an important concept also in the Confucian tradition.

5. Wang Bo (2004, 178–79) notes that "one can choose a lifestyle where one hides in human society . . . it is a type of 'psychological hiding,' which means that one's physical body is not hidden. One can live in the world and every day do things such as eating, drinking, playing, and partying just like everyone else, however one's heart-mind is special, it is different from others."

6. Many Chinese scholars have been content to make a similar general observation; see Hu Shi (1919); Na Wei (2003); Ren Jiyu (1963); Tang Yijie (2004); Tang Yongtong (1962); Wang Bo (2004); Wang Deyou (2012); Youru Wang (2003); Yang Guorong (2009b); and Yang Lihua (2010).

7. In modern Chinese secondary literature, the knack stories tend to be read in mystical (Chen Guying 2008), aesthetic (Li Zehou 1981, 1985), or spiritual (Fung 1997) contexts.

8. Cook Ding, for example, spends more time explaining his knife than his own actions and seems to attribute his skill to an ability to harmonize the knife, the carcass, and himself (see Li Zehou 1985; Wang Bo 2004; Wang Deyou 2010; Yang Guorong 2009b; D'Ambrosio 2012a).

9. Or, as Cheng Xuanying 成玄英 (d. 669) interprets this expression, he "does not impose his personal feelings" (bu shi si qing 不使私情) (see Wang Xiaoyu 2012, 656).

10. Our interpretation reflects Guo Xiang's notion of "not going by the personal" (bu ren ji 不任己) (Wang Xiaoyu 2012, 656).

11. Guo Xiang seems to affirm the Zhuangzi's critique of role-modelling and "hero-worshipping" when he points out that it is "not required that people become carvers, in that every thing can have its own function (bu qiu zhi yu gongjiang, ze wan wu ge you neng ye 不求之與工匠，則萬物各有能也 [Wang 2012, 364]).

12. We do not intend to make any claim here about a potential compatibility or incompatibility of the Daoist concept of "immunization" with Roberto Esposito's notion of "immunitas" (Esposito 2011).

13. Zhuangzi 6.2 highlights this notion of a paradoxical homelessness that allows one to be at home anywhere with its discussion of "hiding the world in the world" (cang tianxia yu tianxia 藏天下於天下). See also Chen Guying's (2008, 249–50) explanation of this passage.

BIBLIOGRAPHY

Adorno, Theodor. 1964. *Jargon der Eigentlichkeit: Zur deutschen Ideologie* [The jargon of authenticity: On German ideology]. Frankfurt am Main: Suhrkamp.

Allen, Barry. 2015. *Striking Beauty: A Philosophical Look at the Asian Martial Arts*. New York: Columbia University Press.

Allinson, Robert E. 1989. *Chuang-Tzu for Spiritual Transformation: An Analysis of the Inner Chapters*. Albany: State University of New York Press.

Ames, Roger. 1996. "The Classical Chinese Self and Hypocrisy." In *Self and Deception: A Cross-Cultural Philosophical Enquiry*, edited by Roger T. Ames and Wimal Dissanayake, 219–40. Albany: State University of New York Press.

——. 1998. Introduction to *Wandering at Ease in the "Zhuangzi,"* edited by Roger T. Ames, 1–14. Albany: State University of New York Press.

——. 2011. *Confucian Role Ethics: A Vocabulary*. Hong Kong: Chinese University Press.

Ames, Roger T., and Henry Rosemont Jr. 1998. *The Analects of Confucius: A Philosophical Translation*. New York: Ballantine Books.

Angle, Steven. 2012. *Contemporary Confucian Political Philosophy*. Cambridge: Polity Press.

Bai, Tongdong. 2012. *China: The Political Philosophy of the Middle Kingdom*. London: Zed Books.

Bakhtin, Mikhail [Michail M. Bachtin]. 1990. *Literatur und Karneval: Zur Romantheorie und Lachkultur* [Literature and carnival: On the theory of the novel and the culture of laughter]. Frankfurt am Main: Fischer.

Bao Qinggang 暴慶剛. 2004. "Lun Zhuangzi ziyou sixiang zhi chaoyue pinge" 論莊子自由思想之超越品格 [Transcendence of freedom: Zhuangzi's thoughts on freedom]. *Dong fang lun tan* 2004 (1): 89–92.

Barrett, Nathaniel F. 2011. "*Wuwei* and Flow: Comparative Reflections on Spirituality, Transcendence, and Skill in the Zhuangzi." *Philosophy East and West* 61 (4): 679–706.

Baxter, William H. 1992. *A Handbook of Old Chinese Phonology*. Berlin: Mouton de Gruyter.

Bergson, Henri. 1924. *Le rire: Essai sur la signification du comique* [Laughter: An essay on the meaning of the comic]. Paris: Alcan.

Berkowitz, Alan. 2000. *Patterns of Disengagement: The Practice and Portrayal of Reclusion in Early Medieval China*. Stanford, Calif.: Stanford University Press.

Blum, Susan Debra. 2007. *Lies That Bind: Chinese Truth, Other Truths*. Plymouth, U.K.: Rowman and Littlefield.

Braak, André van der. 2011. *Nietzsche and Zen: Self-Overcoming Without a Self*. Plymouth, U.K.: Lexington Books.

Brecht, Bertolt, and Eric Bentley. 1961. "On Chinese Acting." *Tulane Drama Review* 6 (1): 130–36.

Cai Qinghua 才清華. 2013. *Yan yi zhi bian yu yuyan zhexue de jiben wenti: Dui Wei-Jin yan yi zhi bian de zai quanshi* 言意之辨與語言哲學的基本問題：對魏晉言意之辨的再詮釋 [On the differentiation between language and meaning and basic problems in the philosophy of language: A study on the differentiation between language and meaning during the Wei-Jin period]. Shanghai: Shanghai renmin chubanshe.

Carr, Karen L., and P. J. Ivanhoe. 2000. *The Sense of Antirationalism: The Religious Thought of Zhuangzi and Kierkegaard*. New York: Seven Bridges Press.

Chai, David. 2009. "Music and Naturalism in the Thought of Ji Kang." *Dao* 8 (2): 151–71.

Chan, Alan K. L. 2014. "Embodying Nothingness and the Ideal of the Affectless Sage in Daoist Philosophy." In *Nothingness in Asian Philosophy*, edited by JeeLoo Liu and Douglas L. Berger, 213–29. New York: Routledge.

Chan, Shirley. 2011. "Identifying Daoist Humor: Reading the Liezi." In *Humour in Chinese Life and Letters: Classical and Traditional Approaches*, edited by Jocelyn Chey and Jessica Milner Davis, 73–88. Hong Kong: Hong Kong University Press.

Chen Guying 陳鼓應. 1983a. *Laozi jinzhu jinyi* 老子今注今譯 [Contemporary annotation and interpretation of the *Laozi*]. Beijing: Zhonghua shuju.

——. 1983b. *Zhuangzi jinzhu jinyi* 莊子今注今譯 [Contemporary annotation and interpretation of the *Zhuangzi*]. Beijing: Zhonghua shuju.

——. 2008. *Lao-Zhuang xin lun* 老莊新論 [New theories on Laozi and Zhuangzi]. Rev. ed. Beijing: Commercial Press.

——. 2012. *Daojia de renwen jingshen* 道家的人文精神 [The humanist spirit of Daoism]. Beijing: Zhonghua shuju.

Chen Lai 陳來. 2014. *Renxue bentilun* 人學本體論 [On the ontology of humaneness]. Beijing: SDX Joint Publishing.

——. 2015. *Zhonghua wenming de hexin jiazhi* 中華文明的核心價值 [The core values of Chinese civilization]. Beijing: SDX Joint Publishing.

——. Forthcoming. "Discussing Michael Sandel's Democracy's Discontent from a Confucian Perspective." Translated by Robert Carleo III and Paul J. D'Ambrosio. In *Michael Sandel and Chinese Philosophy*, edited by Michael Sandel and Paul J. D'Ambrosio.

Chen, Xunwu. 2004. *Being and Authenticity*. Amsterdam: Rodopi.

Chen Yun 陳贇. 2009. "Xiaoyao jingjie de zhengzhi xiangdu—Zhuangzi xiaoyaoyou 'Zhixiaoyiguan' zhang de wenben xue shidu" 逍遙境界的政治向度—《莊子一逍遙遊》知效一官章的文本學釋讀 [Political dimension of the free and unfettered realm—interpretation of the "He Whose Understanding Is Sufficient to Fill Some One Post" passage]. *Academica Bimestrio* 2:123–30.

Chey, Jocelyn, and Jessica Milner Davis, eds. 2011. *Humour in Chinese Life and Letters: Classical and Traditional Approaches*. Hong Kong: Hong Kong University Press.

Chong, Kim-chong. 2011. "The Concept of Zhen 真 in the *Zhuangzi*." *Philosophy East and West* 61 (2): 324–46.

Colebrook, Claire. 2004. *Irony*. London: Routledge.

Connolly, Tim. 2011. "Perspectivism as a Way of Knowing in the *Zhuangzi*." *Dao* 10 (4): 487–505.

Coutinho, Steve. 2013. *An Introduction to Daoist Philosophies*. New York: Columbia University Press.

——. 2015. "Zhuangzi (Chuang-Tzu, 369–298 B.C.E.)." In *Internet Encyclopedia of Philosophy*, http://www.iep.utm.edu/zhuangzi/.

Coyle, Daniel. 1998. "On the Zhenren." In *Wandering at Ease in the "Zhuangzi,"* edited by Roger T. Ames, 197–210. Albany: State University of New York Press.

Csikszentmihalyi, Mihaly. 1990. *Flow: The Psychology of Optimal Experience*. New York: Harper and Row.

Dai Mingyang 戴明揚. 1962. *Ji Kang ji jiao zhu* 稽康集校注 [Collected annotations and commentaries on Ji Kang]. Beijing: Renmin wenxue chubanshe.

D'Ambrosio, Paul. 2012a. "Hypocrisy, Lying, and Deception in Early Chinese Philosophy." PhD diss., University College Cork.

——. 2012b. "The Role of a Pretending Tree: Hermits, Social Constructs and 'Self' in the *Zhuangzi*." In *Selfhood East and West: De-Constuctions of Identity*, edited by Jason Dockstader, Hans-Georg Möller, and Günter Wohlfart, 57–70. Nordhausen, Ger.: Bautz.

——. 2014. "Going Along—A Daoist Alternative to Role Ethics." In *Landscape and Travelling East and West: A Philosophical Journey*, edited by Hans-Georg Moeller and Andrew K. Whitehead, 197–210. London: Bloomsbury Academic.

——. 2015. "Authenticity in the *Zhuangzi*? Contemporary Misreadings of *Zhen* 真 and an Alternative to Existentialism." *Frontiers of Philosophy in China* 10 (3): 353–79.

——. 2016. "*Against Individualism* and Comparing the Philosophies of Rosemont and Sandel." *Comparative and Continental Philosophy* 8 (2): 224–35.

Davis, Jessica Milner, and Jocelyn Chey, eds. 2013. *Humour in Chinese Life and Culture: Resistance and Control in Modern Times*. Hong Kong: Hong Kong University Press.

Defoort, Carine. 2012. "Instruction Dialogues in the *Zhuangzi*: An 'Anthropological' Reading." *Dao* 11 (4): 459–78.

Denecke, Wiebke. 2010. *The Dynamics of Masters Literature: Early Chinese Thought from Confucius to Han Feizi*. Cambridge, Mass.: Harvard University Asia Center.

de Sousa, Ronald. 1987. "When Is It Wrong to Laugh?" In *The Philosophy of Laughter and Humor*, edited by John Morreall, 226–49. Albany: State University of New York Press.

Eoyang, Eugene. 1989. "Chaos Misread: Or, There's Wonton in My Soup!" *Comparative Literature Studies* 26 (3): 271–84.

Esposito, Roberto. 2011. *Immunitas: The Protection and Negation of Life*. London: Polity Press.

Faure, Bernard. 1994. *The Rhetoric of Immediacy: A Cultural Critique of Chan/Zen Buddhism*. Princeton, N.J.: Princeton University Press.

Fei Xiaotong 費孝通. 2012. *Xiangtu Zhongguo* 鄉土中國 [From the soil: Foundations of Chinese society]. Translated by Gary G. Hamilton and Wang Zheng. Beijing: Foreign Language Teaching and Research Press.

Franke, William. 2014. *A Philosophy of the Unsayable*. Notre Dame, Ind.: University of Notre Dame Press.

Fraser, Chris. 1997. Review of *Classifying the "Zhuangzi" Chapters*, by Liu Xiaogan. *Asian Philosophy* 7 (2): 155–59.

——. 2011. "Emotion and Agency in the *Zhuangzi*." *Asian Philosophy* 21 (1): 97–121.

——. 2013. "Xunzi versus Zhuangzi: Two Approaches to Death in Classical Chinese Thought." *Frontiers of Philosophy in China* 8 (3): 410–27.

——. 2014. "Wandering the Way: A Eudaimonistic Approach to the Zhuāngzǐ." *Dao* 13 (4): 541–65.

Freud, Sigmund. 1922. *Wit and Its Relation to the Unconscious*. London: Kegan Paul.

——. 1930. *Das Unbehagen in der Kultur*. Vienna: Internationaler Psychoanalytischer Verlag.

Fried, Daniel. 2007. "A Never-Stable Word: Zhuangzi's 'Zhiyan' 厄言 and 'Tipping Vessel' Irrigation." *Early China* 31:145–70.

Froese, Katrin. 2007. *Nietzsche, Heidegger, and Daoist Thought: Crossing Paths In-Between*. Albany: State University of New York Press.

——. 2014. "The Comic Character of Confucius." *Asian Philosophy* 24 (4): 295–312.

Fung, Yu-lan. 1931. *Chuang Tzu: A New Selected Translation with an Exposition of the Philosophy of Kuo Hsiang*. Shanghai: Commercial Press.

——. 1970. *The Spirit of Chinese Philosophy*. Translated by E. R. Hughes. Westport, Conn.: Greenwood Press.

——. 1997. *A Short History of Chinese Philosophy*. Edited by Dirk Bodde. New York: Free Press.

Galvany, Albert. 2009. "Debates on Mutilation: Bodily Preservation and Ideology in Early China." *Asiatische Studien/Études asiatique* 63 (1): 67–91.

Gier, Nicholas F. 2000. *Spiritual Titanism: Indian, Chinese, and Western Perspectives*. Albany: State University of New York Press.

Girardot, Norman J. 2008. *Myth and Meaning in Early Daoism: The Theme of Chaos (Hundun)*. St. Petersburg, Fla.: Three Pines Press.

Goldin, Paul. 2008. "The Myth That China Has No Creation Myth." *Monumenta Serica* 56:1–22.

Goossaert, Vincent. 2008. "Quanzhen." In *The Routledge Encyclopedia of Taoism*, edited by Fabrizio Pregadio, 2:814–20. London: Routledge.

Graham, A. C., trans. 1981. *Chuang-tzu: The Seven Inner Chapters and Other Writings from the Book of "Chuang-tzu."* London: Allen and Unwin.

——. 1989. *Disputers of the Tao: Philosophical Argument in Ancient China*. Chicago: Open Court.

——, trans. 2001. *Chuang-Tzu: The Inner Chapters*. Indianapolis: Hackett.

Granet, Marcel. 1919. *Fêtes et chansons anciennes de la Chine* [Ancient Chinese festivals and songs]. Paris: Albin Michel.

——. 1959. *Danses et légendes de Chine ancienne* [Ancient Chinese dances and legends]. Paris: Université de France.

——. 1969. *La pensée chinoise* [Chinese thought]. Paris: Albin Michel.

Guo Xiang 郭象. 1954. "Zhuangzi jishi" 莊子集釋 [Collected annotations on the *Zhuangzi*]. In *Zhuzi jicheng* 諸子集成 [A collection of masters' works]. Beijing: Zhonghua shuju.

Guo, Xuezhi. 2002. *The Ideal Chinese Political Leader: A Historical and Cultural Perspective.* Westport, Conn.: Praeger.

Hall, David L., and Roger T. Ames. 1987. *Thinking Through Confucius.* Albany: State University of New York Press.

Han Shuifa 韓水法. 2011. "Das Subjekt der Aufklärung" 啟蒙的主體. In *Im Namen der Aufklärung* 以啟蒙的名義, edited by Otfried Höffe, 28–51. Tübingen: Francke.

Harbsmeier, Christoph. 1989. "Humor in Ancient Chinese Philosophy." *Philosophy East and West* 39 (3): 289–310.

——. 1990. "*Confucius Ridens:* Humor in the Analects." *Harvard Journal of Asiatic Studies* 50 (1): 131–61.

Hare, Robert D. 1999. *Without Conscience: The Disturbing World of the Psychopaths Among Us.* New York: Guilford Press.

Hawkes, David. 1985. *The Songs of the South: An Anthology of Ancient Chinese Poems by Qu Yuan and Other Poets.* London: Penguin.

Hegel, Georg Wilhelm Friedrich. 1986. *Phänomenologie des Geistes* [Phenomenology of spirit]. Frankfurt am Main: Suhrkamp.

Heidegger, Martin. 1962. *Being and Time.* Translated by John Macquarrie. New York: Harper and Row.

Heubel, Fabian. 2015. "Entdramatisierung der Subjektivität: Über das Buch Zhuāngzǐ als Quelle für eine Demokratie der Zukunft" [De-dramatization of subjectivity: On the book *Zhuangzi* as a source for a democracy of the future]. *Bochumer Jahrbuch für Ostasienforschung* 38:63–88.

Hu Shi 胡適. 1919. *Zhongguo zhexue shi dagang* 中國哲學史大綱 [An outline of the history of Chinese philosophy]. Shanghai: Shanghai Commercial Press.

Hyers, Conrad. 1989. "Humor in Zen: Comic Midwifery." *Philosophy East and West* 39 (3): 267–77.

Iser, Wolfgang. 1989. *Prospecting: From Reader Response to Literary Anthropology.* Baltimore: Johns Hopkins University Press.

Ivanhoe, Philip J. 1993. "Zhuangzi on Skepticism, Skill, and the Ineffable Dao." *Journal of the American Academy of Religion* 61 (4): 639–54.

——. 2002. *Ethics in the Confucian Tradition: The Thought of Mengzi and Wang Yangming.* Indianapolis: Hackett.

Jauss, Hans Robert. 1982. *Toward an Aesthetic of Reception.* Translated by Timothy Bahti. Minneapolis: University of Minnesota Press.

Jia, Jinhua. 2015. "Redefining the Ideal Character: A Comparative Study between the Concept of Detachment in the Aṣṭasāhasrikā and Guo Xiang's Theory of Eremitism at Court." *Dao* 14 (4): 545–65.

Jiang Zhongyue 蔣重躍. 2010. *Hanfeizi de zhengzhi sixiang* 韓非子的政治思想 [Hanfeizi's political thought]. Beijing: Beijing Normal University Publishing Group.

Jochim, Chris. 1998. "Just Say No to 'No Self' in Zhuangzi." In *Wandering at Ease in the "Zhuangzi,"* edited by Roger T. Ames, 35–74. Albany: State University of New York Press.

Jullien, François. 2004. *A Treatise on Efficacy: Between Western and Chinese Thinking.* Honolulu: University of Hawai'i Press.

Kaltenmark, Max. 1969. *Lao Tzu and Taoism.* Stanford, Calif.: Stanford University Press.

Kant, Immanuel. 1911. *Kant's Critique of Aesthetic Judgment.* Translated by J. C. Meredith. Oxford: Clarendon Press.

Kantor, Hans-Rudolf. 2014. "Philosophical Aspects of Sixth-Century Chinese Debates on 'Mind and Consciousness.' " In *A Distant Mirror: Articulating Indic Ideas in Sixth and Seventh Century Chinese Buddhism,* edited by Chen-kuo Lin and Michael Radich, 337–95. Hamburg: Hamburg University Press.

——. 2015. "Concepts of Reality in Chinese Mahāyāna Buddhism." In *Chinese Metaphysics and Its Problems,* edited by Chenyang Li and Franklin Perkins, 130–51. Cambridge: Cambridge University Press.

Kelly, Adam. 2010. "David Foster Wallace and the New Sincerity in American Fiction." *Consider David Foster Wallace: Critical Essays,* edited by David Hering, 131–46. Los Angeles: Sideshow Media Group Press.

——. 2014. "Dialectic of Sincerity: Lionel Trilling and David Foster Wallace." *Post 45* (October 17). http://post45.research.yale.edu/2014/10/dialectic-of-sincerity-lionel -trilling-and-david-foster-wallace/.

Kjellberg, Paul, and Philip J. Ivanhoe, eds. 1996. *Essays on Skepticism, Relativism, and Ethics in the "Zhuangzi."* Albany: State University of New York Press.

Klein, Esther. 2010. "Were There 'Inner Chapters' in the Warring States? A New Examination of Evidence about the Zhuangzi." *T'oung Pao* 96:299–369.

Knechtges, David R. 1970–1971. "Wit, Humor, and Satire in Early Chinese Literature (to A.D. 220)." *Monumenta Serica* 29:79–98.

Kohn, Livia. 2014. *"Zhuangzi": Text and Context.* St. Petersburg, Fla.: Three Pines Press.

——. 2015. "Daoism and the Origins of Qigong." *Abode of the Eternal Tao.* http://abode tao.com/daoism-and-the-origins-of-qigong/.

Komjathy, Louis. 2013. *The Way of Complete Perfection: A Quanzhen Daoist Anthology.* Albany: State University of New York Press.

Kupperman, Joel J. 1989. "Not in So Many Words: Chuang Tzu's Strategies of Communication." *Philosophy East and West* 39 (3): 311–17.

Lai, Karyn L. 2015. "Cosmology, Divinity, and Self-Cultivation in Chinese Thought." In *The Routledge Handbook of Contemporary Philosophy of Religion*, edited by Graham Oppy, 93–113. Abbingdon, U.K.: Routledge.

Latta, Robert L. 1999. *The Basic Humor Process: A Cognitive-Shift Theory and the Case against Incongruity*. Berlin: Mouton de Gruyter.

Lee, Jung H. 2014. *The Ethical Foundations of Early Daoism: Zhuangzi's Unique Moral Vision*. New York: Palgrave MacMillan.

Levinovitz, Alan. 2012. "The *Zhuangzi* and *You* 遊: Defining an Ideal Without Contradiction." *Dao* 11 (4): 479–96.

Li, Chenyang. 2014. *The Confucian Philosophy of Harmony*. New York: Routledge.

Li Zehou 李澤厚. 1981. *Mei de licheng* 美的歷程 [The path of beauty]. Beijing: Cultural Relics Press.

——. 1985. *Zhongguo gudai sixiang shilun* 中國古代思想史論 [On traditional Chinese intellectual history]. Beijing: People's University Press.

——. 2008a. *Lunyu jindu* 論語今讀 [Reading the *Analects* today]. Beijing: SDX Joint Publishing.

——. 2008b. *Zhongguo gudai sixiang shilun* 中國古代思想史論 [On traditional Chinese intellectual history]. Beijing: SDX Joint Publishing.

——. 2011. *Zhexue gangyao* 哲學綱要 [Outline of philosophy]. Beijing: Peking University Press.

——. 2014. *Huiying Sangdeer ji qita* 回應桑德爾及其他 [A response to Michael Sandel and other matters]. Beijing: SDX Joint Publishing.

Liu Jianmei. 2016. *Zhuangzi and Modern Chinese Literature*. Oxford: Oxford University Press.

Liu Liangjian 劉梁劍. 2015. *Hanyuyan zhexue fafan* 漢語言哲學發凡 [Introduction to linguistic philosophy based on the experience of Chinese language]. Beijing: Higher Education Press.

Liu Qingping. 2003. "Filiality versus Sociality and Individuality: On Confucianism as 'Consaguinitism.'" *Philosophy East and West* 52 (2): 234–50.

——. 2009. "To Become a Filial Son, a Loyal Subject, or a Humane Person? On the Confucian Ideas about Humanity." *Asian Philosophy* 19 (2): 173–88.

Liu Xiaogan 劉笑敢. 1995. *Classifying the Zhuangzi Chapters*. Ann Arbor: University of Michigan Center for Chinese Studies.

——. 2010. *Zhuangzi zhexue jiqi yanbian* 莊子哲學及其演變 [The evolution of Zhuangzi's philosophy]. Rev. ed. Beijing: People's University Press.

———. 2011. "Daoism: Laozi and Zhuangzi." In *The Oxford Handbook of World Philosophy*, edited by Jay L. Garfield and William Edelglass, 47–57. Oxford: Oxford University Press.

Lloyd, G. E. R. 2014. *The Ideal of Inquiry: An Ancient History*. Oxford: Oxford University Press.

Lou Yulie 樓宇烈. 1999. *Wang Bi ji jiao shi* 王弼集校釋 [Collected explanations and annotations of Wang Bi]. Beijing: Zhonghua shuju.

Luhmann, Niklas. 2000. *The Reality of the Mass Media*. Translated by Kathleen Cross. Stanford, Calif.: Stanford University Press.

Luo Linhui 羅琳會. 2003. *Haidegeer yu Daojia renshengguan zhi bijiao* 海德格爾與道家人生觀之比較 [A comparison of Heidegger's and Zhuangzi's perspectives on human life]. *Journal of Chengdu University* 1:14–16.

Magill, R. Jay, Jr. 2012. *Sincerity: How a Moral Ideal Born Five Hundred Years Ago Inspired Religious Wars, Modern Art, Hipster Chic, and the Curious Notion That We All Have Something to Say (No Matter How Dull)*. New York: Norton.

———. 2014. "Irony, Sincerity, Normcore: Jon Stewart, Stephen Colbert, David Foster Wallace and the End of Rebellion." *Salon.com* (May 18). http://www.salon.com/2014/05/18/irony_sincerity_normcore_jon_stewart_stephen_colbert_david_foster_wallace_and_the_end_of_rebellion/.

Major, John S., Sarah A. Queen, Andrew Seth Meyer, and Harold D. Roth. 2010. *The Huainanzi: A Guide to the Theory and Practice of Government in Early China*. New York: Columbia University Press.

Makeham, John. 1994. *Name and Actuality in Early Chinese Thought*. Albany: State University of New York Press.

Maraldo, John C. 2012. "Four Things and Two Practices: Rethinking Heidegger Ex Oriente Lux." *Comparative and Continental Philosophy* 4 (1): 53–74.

McCraw, David. 2010. *Stratifying Zhuangzi: Rhyme and Other Quantitative Evidence*. Taipei: Institute of Linguistics, Academia Sinica.

Miles, M. 2002. "Disability on a Different Model: Glimpses of an Asian Heritage." *Journal of Religion, Disability and Health* 6 (3): 89–108.

Miura Kunio. 2008a. "Xinzhai." In *The Routledge Encyclopedia of Taoism*, edited by Fabrizio Pregadio, 2:1110–11. London: Routledge.

———. 2008b. "Zhenren." In *The Routledge Encyclopedia of Taoism*, edited by Fabrizio Pregadio, 2:1265–66. London: Routledge.

Moeller, Hans-Georg. 1990. "Cong haoliang zhi bian kan Zhuangzi de 'zhen' guan" 從濠梁之辯看莊子的 '真' 觀 [The concept of truth in the Zhuangzi]. In *Zhuangzi yu Zhongguo wenhua* 莊子與中國文化 [Zhuangzi and Chinese culture], edited by

Huangshan wenhua shuyuan 黃山文化書院, 380–87. Hefei: Anhui renmin chubanshe.

——. 2004a. *Daoism Explained: From the Dream of the Butterfly to the Fishnet Allegory*. Chicago: Open Court.

——. 2004b. "The 'Exotic' Nietzsche—East and West." *Journal of Nietzsche Studies* 28:57–69.

——. 2006. "Frei von menschlichen Regungen: Antihumanismus in Ost und West" [Devoid of human emotions: Antihumanism in East and West]. In *Symposiums-Beitrage: Drittes Internationales Symposium der Katholischen Fu Jen Universität; Personen- und Individuumsbegriff in China und im Westen—der Beitrag der Bonner Sinologischen Schule um Professor Rolf Trauzettel* [Symposium contributions: Third international symposium of the Catholic Fu-Jen University; The notion of the person and the individual in China and the West—the contribution of Professor Rolf Trauzettel and the Bonn school of philosophy], edited by Z. Wesolowski, 501–38. Taipei: Institute Monumenta Serica.

——. 2007. *Daodejing*. Chicago: Open Court.

——. 2008. "Idiotic Irony in the *Zhuangzi*." CLEAR 30 (December): 117–23.

——. 2009. *The Moral Fool: A Case for Amorality*. New York: Columbia University Press.

——. 2011. "Emotional Immediacy: Emotions and Morality in Confucianism." In *Disan ji shijie Ruxue dahui xueshu lunwen ji* 第三屆世界儒學大會學術論文集 [Proceedings of the third session of the world Confucian conference], edited by Jia Leilei and Yang Chaoming, 507–16. Beijing: Wenhua yishu.

——. 2015a. "Paradoxes of Health and Power in the *Zhuangzi*." In *New Visions of the "Zhuangzi,"* edited by Livia Kohn, 76–88. St. Petersburg, Fla.: Three Pines Press.

——. 2015b. "Rambling Without Destination: On Daoist 'You-ing' in the World." In *Zhuangzi and the Happy Fish*, edited by Roger T. Ames and Takahiro Nakajima, 248–60. Honolulu: University of Hawai'i Press.

——. 2016. "Liezi's Retirement: A Parody of a Didactic Tale in the *Zhuangzi*." Dao 15 (3): 379–92.

——. 2017. "Hundun's Mistake: Satire and Sanity in the *Zhuangzi*." *Philosophy East and West* 67 (3): 783–800.

Møllgaard, Eske. 2007. *An Introduction to Daoist Thought: Action, Language, and Ethics in Zhuangzi*. New York: Routledge.

Monro, D. H. 1963. *Argument of Laughter*. Notre Dame, Ind.: University of Notre Dame Press.

Morreall, John. 2009. *Comic Relief: A Comprehensive Philosophy of Humor*. Malden, Mass.: Wiley.

——. 2013. "Philosophy of Humor." In *The Stanford Encyclopedia of Philosophy*, edited by Edward N. Zalta. http://plato.stanford.edu./archives/spr2013/entries/humor/.

Morris, Pam, ed. 1994. *The Bakhtin Reader: Selected Writings of Bakhtin, Medvedev, and Voloshinov*. London: Edward Arnold.

Morrow, Carmine. 2016. "Metaphorical Language in the Zhuangzi." *Philosophy Compass* 11 (4): 179–88.

Na Wei 那薇. 2003. "Daojia de fanpu guizhen he Haidegeer de benzhen cunzai" 道家 的返璞歸真和海德格爾的本真存在 [Returning to the genuine in Daoism and Heidegger's authentic existence]. *History of Chinese Philosophy* 2:114–21.

——. 2005. "Daojia de dao yu Haidegeer de kaipi daolu" 道家的道與海德格爾的開 闢道路 [Daoism's "Dao" and Heidegger's blazing the way]. *Journal of Northwest Normal University* 42 (4): 25–30.

Needham, Joseph. 1956. *Science and Civilisation in China, Volume 2: History of Scientific Thought*. Cambridge: Cambridge University Press.

Nelson, Eric S. 2004. "Responding to Heaven and Earth: Daoism, Heidegger and Ecology." *Environmental Philosophy* 2 (1): 65–74.

Nienhauser, William H., Jr., ed. 1994. *The Grand Scribe's Records, Vol. 7: The Memoirs of Pre-Han China*. Bloomington: Indiana University Press.

Parkes, Graham. 1987. Introduction to *Heidegger and Asian Thought*, edited by Graham Parkes, 1–14. Honolulu: University of Hawai'i Press.

——. 2013. "Zhuangzi and Nietzsche on the Human and Nature." *Environmental Philosophy* 10 (1): 1–24.

Parlett, David. 1992. *A Dictionary of Card Games*. Oxford: Oxford University Press.

Patterson, Orlando. 2006. "Our Overrated Inner Self." *New York Times*, December 26. http://www.nytimes.com/2006/12/26/opinion/26patterson.html.

Perkins, Franklin. 2014. *Heaven and Earth Are Not Humane: The Problem of Evil in Classical Chinese Philosophy*. Bloomington: Indiana University Press.

Pregadio, Fabrizio. 2008. "Liuyi Ni." In *The Routledge Encyclopedia of Taoism*, edited by Fabrizio Pregadio, 1:697–98. London: Routledge.

Puett, Michael J. 2002. *To Become a God: Cosmology, Sacrifice, and Self-Divinization in Early China*. Cambridge, Mass.: Harvard University Asia Center.

Puett, Michael J., and Christine Gross-Loh. 2016. *The Path: What Chinese Philosophers Can Teach Us About the Good Life*. New York: Simon and Schuster.

Raphals, Lisa. 1996. "Skeptical Strategies in the Zhuangzi and Theaetetus." In *Essays on Skepticism, Relativism, and Ethics in the "Zhuangzi,"* edited by Paul Kjellberg and Philip J. Ivanhoe, 26–49. Albany: State University of New York Press.

——. 2013. *Divination and Prediction in Early China and Ancient Greece*. Cambridge: Cambridge University Press.

Rapp, John A. 2012. *Daoism and Anarchism: Critiques of State Autonomy in Ancient and Modern China*. London: Bloomsbury Academic.

Ren Fuxin 任付新. 2013. "Haidegeer zhexue yu Zhuangzi zhexue bijiao" 海德格爾哲學與莊子哲學比較 [Comparison of Heidegger's philosophy and Zhuangzi's philosophy]. *Journal of Sichuan University for Nationalities* 22 (2): 47–54.

Ren Jiyu 任繼愈, ed. 1963. *Zhongguo zhexue shi* 中國哲學史 [A history of Chinese philosophy]. Beijing: Renmin chubanshe.

Robinet, Isabelle. 2008. "Hundun." In *The Routledge Encyclopedia of Taoism*, edited by Fabrizio Pregadio, 1:523–25. London: Routledge.

Rorty, Richard. 1989. *Contingency, Irony, and Solidarity*. Cambridge: Cambridge University Press.

Rosemont, Henry, Jr. 1991. "Rights-Bearing Individuals and Role-Bearing Persons." In *Rules, Rituals, and Responsibility: Essays Dedicated to Herbert Fingarette*, edited by Mary I. Bockover, 71–102. Chicago: Open Court.

———. 2015. *Against Individualism: A Confucian Rethinking of the Foundations of Morality, Politics, Family, and Religion*. Lanham, Md.: Lexington Books.

Roth, Harold D. 1991. *Original Tao: Inward Training (Nei-yeh) and the Foundations of Taoist Mysticism*. New York: Columbia University Press.

Sample, Joseph C. 2011. "Contextualizing Lin Yutang's Essay 'On Humour': Introduction and Translation." In *Humour in Chinese Life and Letters: Classical and Traditional Approaches*, edited by Jocelyn Chey and Jessica Milner Davis, 169–90. Hong Kong: Hong Kong University Press.

Scharfstein, Ben-Ami. 1995. *Amoral Politics: The Persistent Truth of Machiavellism*. Albany: State University of New York Press.

Schneider, Laurence A. 1980. *A Madman of Ch'u: The Chinese Myth of Loyalty and Dissent*. Berkeley: University of California Press.

Schumm, Darla, and Michael Stoltzfuss. 2011. "Beyond Models: Some Tentative Daoist Contributions to Disability Studies." *Disability Studies Quarterly* 30 (3): 103–22.

Schwermann, Christian. 2011. *"Dummheit" in altchinesischen Texten: Eine Begriffsgeschichte* ["Stupidity" in ancient Chinese texts: A conceptual history]. Wiesbaden: Harrassowitz.

Schwitzgebel, Erik. 1996. "Zhuangzi's Attitude Toward Language and His Skepticism." In *Essays on Skepticism, Relativism, and Ethics in the "Zhuangzi,"* edited by Paul Kjellberg and Philip J. Ivanhoe, 68–96. Albany: State University of New York Press.

———. 2007. "Flow and the Not-So-Skillful Zhuangzi?" *The Splintered Mind* (blog). http://schwitzsplinters.blogspot.com/2007/03/flow-and-not-so-skillful-zhuangzi.html.

Seligman, Adam B., Robert P. Weller, Michael J. Puett, and Bennett Simon. 2008. *Ritual and Its Consequences: An Essay on the Limits of Sincerity*. New York: Oxford University Press.

Sellmann, James D. 1998. "Transformational Humor in the Zhuangzi." In *Wandering at Ease in the "Zhuangzi,"* edited by Roger T. Ames, 163–74. Albany: State University of New York Press.

Shang, Ge Ling. 2007. *Liberation as Affirmation: The Religiosity of Zhuangzi and Nietzsche*. Albany: State University of New York Press.

Shen, Vincent. 2003. "Zhenren (Chen-jen): The True, Authentic Person." In *Encyclopedia of Chinese Philosophy*, edited by Antonio S. Cua, 872–74. New York: Routledge.

Sigurðsson, Geir. 2015. *Confucian Propriety and Ritual Learning: A Philosophical Interpretation*. Albany: State University of New York Press.

Sim, May. 2007. *Remastering Morals with Aristotle and Confucius*. Cambridge: Cambridge University Press.

Slingerland, Edward. 2003. *Effortless Action: Wu-wei as a Conceptual Metaphor and Spiritual Ideal in Early China*. Oxford: Oxford University Press.

——. 2014. *Trying Not to Try: Ancient China, Modern Science, and the Power of Spontaneity*. New York: Broadway Books.

Smuts, Aaron. 2015. "Humor." In *Internet Encyclopedia of Philosophy*. http://www.iep.utm.edu/humor/.

Sommer, Deborah. 2007. "Images for Iconoclasts: Images of Confucius in the Cultural Revolution." *East-West Connections* 7 (1): 1–23.

Strickmann, Michael. 2015. "Daoism." In *Encyclopaedia Britannica*. https://global.britannica.com/topic/Daoism.

Tang Yijie 湯一介. 2004. *Guo Xiang yu Wei-Jin Xuanxue* 郭象與魏晉玄學 [Guo Xiang and Wei-Jin neo-Daoism]. Beijing: Peking University Press.

Tang Yongtong 湯用彤. 1962. *Wei-Jin Xuanxue lungao* 魏晉玄學論稿 [Essays on Wei-Jin neo-Daoism]. Beijing: Zhonghua shuju.

Taylor, Charles. 1992. *The Ethics of Authenticity*. Cambridge, Mass.: Harvard University Press.

——. 2007. *A Secular Age*. Cambridge, Mass.: Harvard University Press.

Trauzettel, Rolf. 1999. "A Sophism by the Ancient Chinese Philosopher Gongsun Long: Jest, Satire, Irony—Or Is There a Deeper Significance?" *Journal of Chinese Philosophy* 26 (1): 21–36.

Trilling, Lionel. 1972. *Sincerity and Authenticity*. Cambridge, Mass.: Harvard.

Tu Weiming. 1999. *Humanity and Self-Cultivation: Essays in Confucian Thought*. Boston: Cheng and Tsui.

——. Forthcoming. "Discussion on Tu Weiming's Talk." In *Encountering China: Michael Sandel and Chinese Philosophy*, edited by Michael Sandel and Paul J. D'Ambrosio. Cambridge, Mass.: Harvard University Press.

Van Norden, Bryan W. 2008. *Mengzi: With Selections from Traditional Commentaries*. Indianapolis: Hackett.

——. 2011. *Introduction to Classical Chinese Philosophy*. Indianapolis: Hackett.

Wang Bo 王博. 2004. *Zhuangzi zhexue* 莊子哲學 [The philosophy of Zhuangzi]. Beijing: Peking University Press.

——. 2014. *Zhuangzi: Thinking Through the Inner Chapters*. St. Petersburg, Fla.: Three Pines Press.

Wang Deyou 王德有. 2010. *Wei-Jin Xuanxue: Gaodao piaoyi de xianshi rensheng* 魏晉玄學: 高蹈飄逸的閒適人生 [Wei-Jin neo-Daoism: Leisurely living hermits]. Shanghai: Oriental Publishing Center.

——. 2012. *Yi Dao guan zhi: Zhuangzi zhexue de shijiao* 以道觀之：莊子哲學的視角 [From the viewpoint of Dao: The perspective of Zhuangzi's philosophy]. Beijing: Renmin chubanshe.

Wang Fuzhi 王夫之. 1964. *Zhuangzi jie* 莊子解 [Annotations to the *Zhuangzi*]. Beijing: Zhonghua shuju.

Wang Limei 王麗梅. 2002. "Lun Zhuangzi de shengcun fangshi" 論《莊子》的生存方式 [On the *Zhuangzi*'s mode of existence]. *Northern Forum* 3:66–70.

Wang Xiaoyu 王孝鱼. 2012. *Zhuangzi jishi* 莊子集釋 [Collected annotations on the *Zhuangzi*]. Beijing: Zhonghua shuju.

Wang, Youru. 2003. *Linguistic Strategies in Daoist Zhuangzi and Chan Buddhism: The Other Way of Speaking*. London: RoutledgeCurzon.

Watson, Burton. 1968. *The Complete Works of Chuang Tzu*. New York: Columbia University Press.

Weinrich, Harald. 1976. "Ironie" [Irony]. In *Historisches Wörterbuch der Philosophie* [Historical encyclopedia of philosophy], edited by Karlfried Gründer, 4:577–82. Basel: Schwabe.

Wittgenstein, Ludwig. 1953. *Philosophical Investigations*. Translated by G. E. M. Anscombe. Oxford: Blackwell.

Wohlfart, Günter. 1999. "The Death of the Ego: An Analysis of the 'I' in Nietzsche's Unpublished Fragments." *Journal of Chinese Philosophy* 26 (3): 323–41.

——. 2000. "Gesichts-Drill: Zhuangzis traurige Geschichte von der Tod-Bohrung des guten Herrn Hundun" [Face drill: Zhuangzi's sad story of the lethal drilling of the good man Hundun]. In *Philosophieren im Dialog mit China* [Philosophizing in dialogue with China], edited by Helmut Schneider, 53–70. Cologne: Chora.

———. 2005. *Die Kunst des Lebens und andere Künste: Skurrile Skizzen zu einem euro-daoistischen Ethos ohne Moral* [The art of life and other arts: Whimsical sketches of a Daoist ethos without morality]. Berlin: Parerga.

———. 2010. "Transcendental Laughter Beyond Enlightenment." In *Laughter in Eastern and Western Philosophies*, edited by Hans-Georg Moeller and Günter Wohlfart, 224–32. Freiburg: Alber.

Wu, Kuang-ming. 1990. *The Butterfly as Companion: Meditations on the First Three Chapters of the Zhuangzi*. Albany: State University of New York Press.

Wu, Meiyao. 2014. "Hundun's Hospitality: Daoist, Derridean, and Levinasian Readings of Zhuangzi's Parable." *Educational Philosophy and Theory* 46 (13): 1435–49.

Xiao Dong Yue. 2010. "Exploration of Chinese Humor: Historical Review, Empirical Findings, and Critical Reflections." *Humor* 23 (3): 403–20.

Xu, Weihe. 2004. "The Confucian Politics of Appearance—and Its Impact on Chinese Humor." *Philosophy East and West* 54 (4): 514–32.

Xu Yinchun 徐陰春. 2006. "Xianqin mingshi zhi bian de yuyan zhexue yiyi" 先秦名實之辯的語言哲學意義 [The linguistic-philosophical significance of the names and actuality debate in pre-Qin thought]. *Jiangxi shehui kexue* 8:54–58.

Yan Beiming 嚴北溟. 1980. "Yingdui Zhuangzi chongxin pingjia" 應對莊子重新評價 [Zhuangzi needs to be reevaluated]. *Philosophical Researches* 1 (January): 40–48.

Yang Guorong 楊國榮. 2009a. *Shan de licheng: Rujia jiazhi tixi yanjiu* 善的歷程：儒家價值體系研究 [The course of the good: A study of the Confucian value system]. Shanghai: East China Normal University Press.

———. 2009b. *Zhuangzi de sixiang shijie* 莊子的思想世界 [Zhuangzi's world of thought]. Shanghai: East China Normal University Press.

———. 2011. *Lunli yu cunzai* 倫理與存在 [Ethics and existence]. Beijing: Peking University Press.

Yang Lihua 楊立華. 2010. *Guo Xiang Zhuangzi zhu yanjiu* 郭象《莊子注》研究 [On Guo Xiang's commentary to the *Zhuangzi*]. Beijing: Peking University Press.

Yang Rubin 楊儒賓. 2008. "Rumen nei de Zhuangzi" 儒門內的莊子 [Zhuangzi in a Confucian realm]. *Zhongguo zhexue yu wenhua* (Guilin: Guangxi shifan daxue chubanshe) 4:112–44.

Yang, Rur-bin. 2003. "From 'Merging the Body with the Mind' to 'Wandering in Unitary Qi' 氣: A Discussion of Zhuangzi's Realm of the True Man and Its Corporeal Basis." In *Hiding the World in the World*, edited by Scott Cook, 88–127. Albany: State University of New York Press.

Yearley, Lee H. 2005. "Daoist Presentation and Persuasion: Wandering among Zhuangzi's Kinds of Language." *Journal of Religious Ethics* 33 (3): 503–35.

Zhang Hengshou 張恒壽. 1983. *Zhuangzi xin tan* 莊子新探 [New inquiries into Zhuangzi]. Wuhan: Hubei renmin chubanshe.

Zhang Liwen 張立文. 1999. *Lun jianben Laozi yu Rujia sixiang de hubu huji* 論簡本《老子》與儒家思想的互補互濟 [On the complementarity of the Laozi slips and Confucian thinking]. Vol. 17 of *Daojia wenhua yanjiu* 道家文化研究 [On Daoist culture], edited by Chen Guying 陳鼓應. Beijing: SDX Joint Press.

Zhang, Shi Ying. 1992. "Heidegger and Taoism." In *Reading Heidegger: Commemorations*, edited by John Sallis, 307–22. Bloomington: Indiana University Press.

Zhu Xi 朱熹. 2011. *Sishu zhangju jizhu* 四書章句集注 [Annotations to the Four Books]. Beijing: Zhonghua shuju.

Zhuangzi yinde 莊子引得 [A Concordance to Chuang Tzu]. 1956. Harvard-Yenching Institute Sinological Index Series, supplement no. 20. Cambridge, Mass.: Harvard University Press.

Ziporyn, Brook. 2003. "How Many Are the Ten Thousand Things and I? Relativism, Mysticism, and Privileging the Oneness in the 'Inner Chapters.' " In *Hiding the World in the World*, edited by Scott Cook. Albany: State University of New York Press.

——, trans. 2009. *Zhuangzi: The Essential Writings with Selections from Traditional Commentaries*. Indianapolis: Hackett.

——. 2012. *Ironies of Oneness and Difference: Coherence in Early Chinese Thought; Prolegomena to the Study of Li*. Albany: State University of New York Press.

——. 2015. "Zhuangzi as Philosopher." Hackett Publishing Company. http://www.hackettpublishing.com/zhuangziphil.

INDEX

ability, 66, 93, 117, 121, 171, 175
abnormalities, 95
actuality, 5, 23, 42–44, 49, 84, 97, 108, 110, 113–14, 117–20, 129, 175
Adorno, Theodor W., 35. *See also* jargon of authenticity
aesthetics, 31, 57, 61, 93, 151, 161
Against Individualism (Rosemont), 29. *See also* Rosemont, Henry, Jr.
age of authenticity, 9–10, 19, 25, 27–30, 33–34, 36, 39, 41, 124. *See also* Taylor, Charles; Trilling, Lionel
allegory, 150, 178; butterfly dream, 4–5, 120, 129–30, 136, 176; drunkard, 161–62; fishnet, 4; Happy Fish, 169; Hundun (Emperor of the Center), 6, 12–13, 15, 78–86, 93–94, 113, 125, 145, 174; Kun and Peng, 77; praying mantis, 149; tree, 110, 117–18, 138, 140–41, 151, 160
Allen, Barry, 13
Allinson, Robert E., 74
Ames, Roger T., 7, 23, 28–29, 36, 51, 53, 55; translations of the *Analects* by, 8, 43, 45–47, 49–51, 126–27
amoralism, 107, 121. *See also* antimoralism
amputees, 98, 101
Analects, 6–8, 21, 42–43, 45–47, 49–52, 54–55, 80, 114, 118, 127, 130–32, 139. *See also* Confucianism; Confucius
Angle, Steve, 28
Angst, 3, 176
anthropocentrism, 80
antimoralism, 8, 70. *See also* amoralism

antirationalism, 73

apophaticism, 15, 31

arché, 79

arhat, 127. *See also* Buddhism

aristocracy, 31, 99, 108, 110

Aristophanes, 80

Aristotle, 4, 54, 61, 68. *See also* eudaimonia;
Rhetoric (Aristotle)

art, 10, 27, 31, 35, 59, 66, 83–84, 86, 91, 93,
98, 138, 149–50, 152, 156–62, 164, 171;
of genuine pretending, 4, 60, 123,
137–38, 140, 145–46, 151; of Laozi, 6;
martial arts, 13; of mask changing,
93–94

arts, 6, 13, 90, 135, 155, 157, 160–63

authenticity, 16, 19–42, 48, 56–57, 59, 75,
78, 92, 101, 104–5, 112, 124–28, 135,
145–46, 155, 158, 170–71, 175; age of,
9–10, 19, 25, 27–30, 33–34, 36, 39, 41, 124,
188; and Daoism (*see* Daoism)

automaticity, 153, 163

autonomy, 24–25, 27, 29, 32–33, 55, 172

Bakhtin, Mikhail, 63, 69–70

Barrett, Nathaniel F., 154–55

Being and Time (Heidegger). *See* Heidegger,
Martin;

being-with, 35–36. *See also* Heidegger,
Martin; hermeneutics

being-with-others, 36. *See also* Heidegger,
Martin; hermeneutics

Bergson, Henri, 60, 74

Berkowitz, Alan, 106

Bernard, Tristan, 19

bianlian 變臉 (mask changing), 93. *See also*
Huzi 壺子 (face changer)

Bible, 68

Bo Yi 伯夷, 103

boundlessness, 164–67, 169

Brecht, Bertolt, 81–82, 93

Buddhism, 15, 33, 68, 71, 73, 127, 158; Chan
禪, 15, 33, 68, 73–74, 156; Tiantai 天台,
33; Zen, 68

Butcher Ding. *See* Cook Ding

butterfly dream allegory, 4–5, 120, 129–30,
136, 176

Calabash, Master. *See* Huzi 壺子
(facechanger)

cards, 2–3, 167

caricatures, 81, 89–91, 97, 108–9, 111, 113,
125, 147, 151

carnivalesque, 13, 69–71, 99–103, 108–9,
111, 125, 156, 161

Carpenter Chui 工倕, 162–63

Casanova, Giacomo, 123–24

catharsis, 4. *See also* Aristotle

Chan, Shirley, 74, 155

chaos, 78, 87, 110

characteristics of humoristic
communication, 64

Chen Duxiu 陳獨秀, 39

Chen Guying 陳鼓應, 7, 13–14, 38–39,
41–42, 84, 93, 106, 168

Chen Lai 陳來, 29, 52

Chen Shan 陳善, 52

Chen, Xunwu, 19, 39

Chinese history, 128; contemporary, 38;
Cultural Revolution, 106; Han dynasty,
6, 50, 74, 105, 127–28; Qin dynasty, 42,
106, 115, 128; Warring States period, 74,
105; Wei-Jin 魏晉 period, 33, 135;
Zhou dynasty, 103

Chong, Kim-chong, 106, 111

Christianity, 38, 69

Chu, madman of, 72, 138–39

Chuci 楚辭, 135–36, 139

Civilization and Its Discontents (Freud), 69.
See also Freud, Sigmund

cognitive science, 13, 153

comedy, 65–66, 68–69, 74–76, 80, 113,
156

commodity, 140

conceit, 91, 107, 110, 142, 162, 171, 174

concubine, 95, 100

conformity, 8, 23, 27, 111, 118, 175

Confucianism, 5–10, 20, 25, 28–30, 38–49,
52–57, 59–60, 72, 74–75, 83, 90, 97–99,

101–7, 111–16, 119–20, 124–25, 127, 130–33, 135, 137, 141–44, 155, 174, 177–78, 183, 186; anti-Confucian, 6–7, 48, 74, 98, 106–7, 142; ethics, 7–10, 20, 28–30, 34, 45, 48, 54, 56, 119–20, 130; filial piety, 43–45, 51–52; filial responsibility, 51–52, 66, 103–4, 148; moral demands of, 8–9; role ethics, 23–24, 28–29, 41–42; self or person, 28, 39, 41–42, 54–55, 127; sexual connotations of ruler-minister relationship, 99; sincerity (dual correspondence), 7–9, 23, 28–30, 34, 38–44, 48, 54, 56, 59, 101, 111, 114, 120, 124, 127, 129–33, 143; tradition, 5–6, 12, 16, 19–20, 28, 30, 39–42, 44, 49–50, 54–55, 60, 72, 99, 103–4, 108–9, 114, 124–25; Yao and Shun (founders of civilization), 49–50, 125, 147

Confucius, 5–6, 43–44, 47, 49, 51–52, 54–55; and his students, 45–46; in the *Mencius*, 49; in the *Zhuangzi*, 6–7, 74–75, 95, 97, 102, 105–12, 118–19, 121, 131–32, 138, 141–49, 155–58

Conrad, Joseph, 41

consummate person, 94, 115–17

Continental philosophy, 153

contingency, 2–3, 5, 31–34, 126, 140, 145, 151, 158, 160–63, 169–71

Cook Ding, 152, 154, 156–57, 161, 183, 194

correspondence of names and actuality, 7–8, 22–23, 43–46, 56, 104, 110, 113, 115, 119, 131–32. See also *ming shi* 名實

cosmogony, 79–82

cosmology, 12, 79–80

Coutinho, Steve, 36, 96–97

Coyle, Daniel, 36, 126–27, 132, 134

craftsman, 93, 154–56, 160–63

Critique of Judgment (Kant), 15, 61

Csikszentmihalyi, Mihaly, 153

dai 待 (to treat as a guest), 85

D'Ambrosio, Paul, 35, 49, 117, 140

dao 道, 2, 38, 51, 103

Daodejing 道德經, 6, 8–9, 13, 24, 83–84, 90, 100, 115, 127–28, 130, 132, 138, 146, 152, 173–74

daojiao 道教 tradition, 12, 77, 79, 87–88, 97, 99, 102, 127–28, 134–35, 139, 144, 151, 153, 158, 165, 167, 172

Daoism, 12–13, 15, 20, 30, 32–34, 38, 40–42, 48, 63, 68, 72, 74, 77, 79, 86, 88, 97, 102, 104, 125, 128, 132, 138–39, 151–52, 165, 171, 174, 185–86; anarchist trajectories, 104–6, 108–10; and authenticity, 9, 30, 33, 36, 38, 40; neo-Daoism (*see* neo-Daoism); primitivist trajectories, 8, 15, 90, 105–6, 109–10, 139, 151; Yangist trajectories, 15, 105–6, 108–10, 138. See also medicinal aspects of Daoism

Daoist texts, 152. See also *Daodejing* 道德經; Inner Chapters (*Zhuangzi*); Miscellaneous Chapters (*Zhuangzi*); Outer Chapters (*Zhuangzi*); *Zhuangzi* 莊子

Dasein, 35, 37, 40. See also Heidegger, Martin

de 德 (efficacy), 6, 14–15, 19, 25, 37–38, 49–50, 69, 82, 93, 95–102, 108, 112–13, 128, 138, 142–43, 161, 171–75

death, 46, 64, 78–79, 81–87, 92, 94, 103, 118–21, 132, 134, 137, 176

deconstruction, 6, 10, 48, 57, 70, 73, 82, 113, 143. See also Wang, Youru

Defoort, Carine, 86, 88–89

Denecke, Wiebke, 88–89

depersonalization, 135–36, 148

Derrida, Jacques, 73. See also deconstruction

Descartes, Rene, 68, 169

dialectic, 6, 14, 19, 21–22, 24, 27, 30, 34, 40

dialectical materialism, 106, 140

Diderot, Denis, 25

disability, 141

disease, 83, 162

dissonance, 31, 45, 54, 72, 110, 124–25, 129, 136, 155, 174

diver. See Lüliang waterfall diver

drunkard, 156–59, 161–63

dual correspondence, 7–8, 41, 44–47, 49–51, 55–56, 79, 115, 143

Duke Jing of Qi, 46

Duke of Lu, 95

efficacy, 45, 99–100, 102, 127, 153, 160, 181; as *de* 德 (see *de* 德)

effortlessness, 64, 92

Eigentlichkeit. See authenticity; ownness

eisegesis, 10

Emperor Xuanzong of Tang 唐玄宗, 11

Enchiridion (Epictetus), 69

Enlightenment, 27, 61, 68, 148

Epictetus, 69

epistemology, 6, 165–66, 168

ethics of authenticity, 25, 27–28, 30, 59. See *also* ethics of sincerity

ethics of sincerity, 8, 20, 24–30, 40, 48, 56, 59, 113, 130, 132. See *also* ethics of authenticity

eudaimonia, 164

everydayness, 35–36. See *also* Heidegger, Martin; hermeneutics

existentialism, 27, 33, 36, 38–40; and authenticity, 38; and Daoism, 34, 38, 40

face changing, 86, 121

fame, 53, 99, 116, 137, 157

Fast (Shu 儵) and Furious (Hu 忽), 78, 80–81, 94

Fei Xiaotong 費孝通, 45

Feng Youlan 馮友蘭, 16

first principle. See *arché*

flourishing, 5, 171. See *also* eudaimonia

formlessness, 78, 102, 132

Foucault, Michel, 48

Franke, William, 31

Fraser, Chris, 16, 37, 96, 164–65, 171–72, 174–76; "Zhuangzist Virtuoso View," 37

freaks, 95–103

Freud, Sigmund, 60–69, 71; *Civilization and Its Discontents*, 69; *Galgenhumor* (see

gallows humor); psychoanalysis, 5; *Wit and Its Relation to the Unconscious*, 65

Froese, Katrin, 38, 74–75, 126

Galgenhumor. See gallows humor

gallows humor, 63–64, 67; see *also* Freud, Sigmund

Galvany, Albert, 98

games, 3, 146, 169. See *also* cards

genocide, 144, 156

genuine pretender, 3, 32–34, 40, 57, 76, 94, 101, 111, 114–15, 119, 121, 124, 130, 140, 142, 144–48, 151, 171, 173, 175–77, 183–84; as alternative to Confucian sincerity, 9; as antimodel, 183; and ironist, 32, 34; as joker card, 2–3, 9; as persons of *de* 德, 175–76; as a mode of philosophizing, 171; and personality, 40; and skill, 163; as spirit of the *Zhuangzi*, 14; and *zhenren* 真人, 126, 134, 136

genuineness, 36, 94, 112–13, 127–29. See *also* zhenuineness

Gier, Nicholas F., 80, 93

Girardot, Norman J., 12–13, 78–79, 81, 83–84, 171

Graham, A. C., 5, 11, 15, 86, 89, 104, 106, 113, 116, 132, 137, 148, 152, 154, 157, 164; translation of the *Zhuangzi* by, 78, 80, 105, 107, 108–11, 113, 131, 132, 147, 151, 156–58, 164–65, 167–68, 178–79

grotesque, 99–101, 107–8, 111, 125, 135, 155, 162

Guo Xiang 郭象, 15, 86, 93, 161, 164–65, 167

Guodian 郭店 (excavation site), 5

Han dynasty, 6, 50, 74, 105, 127–28

Hanfeizi 韓非子, 44, 50, 56

Hao River, 168

Happy Fish (*yu zhi le* 魚之樂), 168–69

Hawkes, David, 135

health, 95, 97–98, 142, 171–72, 174–75. See *also* sanity

heart-mind, 7, 43, 49, 89, 92, 103, 111, 115, 117–18, 144, 164–65, 174; completed or perfect, 102, 115, 132; empty, 144–45, 174–75; fasting of, 142, 157, 159, 169; roaming of, 149, 164–65

heaven, 79, 87–88, 129–30, 134, 136–37, 145, 154, 157, 162, 172–73, 177; as nature, 9, 129, 154; patterns of, 114, 156; way of, 53, 130

Hegel, G. W. F., 5, 8, 13–14, 21–22, 24–27. *See also* spirit

Heidegger, Martin, 4, 9, 16, 35–38, 40, 126

hermeneutics, 10–11, 13, 15–16, 20, 34, 73, 77, 157–58, 163, 172; Constance school, 10; Heideggerian interpretations, 9–10, 16, 36–38, 40, 126; humoristic key, 11; reception theory, 10; sacred key, 11–13

hermits, 111, 138–40, 144, 151

heroism of dumb service, 8

hierarchy, 25, 69, 109, 172–73

History of My Life (Casanova), 124–25

Hobbes, Thomas, 61, 68

holes, 78, 81–82

Horsehead Humpback, 95–102, 112–13, 125, 128

Huainanzi 淮南子, 79, 81, 86, 127, 132–34, 141

huaji 滑稽 (humorists), 74. *See also* humor

Huangdi neijing 皇帝內經, 128

hubris, 82

Hui Shi 惠施, 5, 168–69

Huizi, 169

humaneness, 45, 52–53, 136–37

humanity, 27, 53, 56, 103–4, 134

humor, 3–4, 6, 10, 13–15, 32, 34, 48, 57, 59–121, 124, 126, 162. See also *huaji* 滑稽 (humorists)

humor, six features of, 63–71. *See also* humor; philosophy of humor

humorist, 69, 72, 74, 82, 113. See also *huaji* 滑稽 (humorists)

Hunchback Limpleg, 95–96, 99, 102. See *also* freaks

Hundun 渾沌 (Emperor of the Center), 6, 12–13, 15, 78–86, 93–94, 113, 125, 145, 174

Huzi 壺子 (face changer), 86–94, 100–101, 113, 121, 133

hyperbole, 74, 109, 135

hypocrisy, 3, 8, 54, 59, 84, 101, 105, 107–9, 111, 126, 142–44, 174

idiotic irony, 34

idolatry, 160, 163, 172

Iliad, 20–21

imagination, 57, 72, 81, 135, 139, 165

immortals, 70, 103–4, 107, 139, 142, 172

impostor, 91, 104

inauthenticity, 26, 35–36, 75, 105, 112, 137. *See also* authenticity

incongruity, 3, 5, 15, 57, 60–121, 124–26, 129–31, 147, 174–75

individualism, 27–31, 33, 57

ineffable, 31, 73

inefficacy, 59, 102, 144. See also *de* 德 (efficacy)

ineptitude, 83, 90–91, 125

Inner Chapters (*Zhuangzi*), 12, 16, 75, 78–79, 86, 93, 95, 104–5, 118, 128, 134, 139, 152

inner emigration, 140, 160

insanity, 84–85, 110–11, 126. *See also* sanity

insincerity, 24–26, 48–51, 55–56, 59, 67, 94, 99, 112, 131, 143, 157; suspicion of, 8, 24–25, 48, 52, 54, 56, 75–76, 99, 107, 115

interdependency, 23, 37

intoxication, 89, 92, 103, 151, 156–59, 161–63, 166, 183

inward training, 158

irony, 11, 30–32, 34, 73–74, 76, 90, 143–44, 157

Iser, Wolfgang, 10

Ivanhoe, P. J., 11, 73, 75, 77, 98–99, 104, 106, 154–55

jargon of authenticity, 35, 186. *See also* Adorno, Theodor W.

Jarsized Goiter, 95–96, 99, 102. *See also* freaks; Horsehead Humpback

Jauss, Hans Robert, 10

jesters, 3, 74, 91–93, 99, 113, 156

jie 戒 (constraints), 148, 160

jingshen 精神 (spirit), 14, 39. *See also* Hegel, G. W. F.

Jixian 季鹹 (physiognomist), 86–87, 91–92, 94. *See also* Huzi 壺子 (face changer); Liezi 列子

joker card, 2–4, 9, 167, 169. *See also* wild card

junzi 君子 (gentleman), 51, 127, 131

Kaltenmark, Max, 80

Kant, Immanuel, 15, 45, 61–63, 67–68, 71, 161; *Critique of Judgment*, 15, 61

Kelly, Adam, 30

Kelly, Allen, 27

Kierkegaard, Søren, 4, 35, 75

Klein, Esther, 16, 104, 106

knack stories, 151–58, 161–63

Knechtges, David R., 71–72, 74, 77

Kohn, Livia, 12, 87–88

Kongzi 孔子. *See* Confucius

Kuang-ming Wu, 74

Kun 鯤 and Peng 鵬, 77, 166–67

Lai, Chen, 42, 52

Lai, Karyn L., 87–88

Laozi 老子, 6, 38, 72, 86, 165

Latta, Robert, 62–64, 66–67

laughter, 4, 15, 61–64, 67–70, 74, 76, 83

Legalism, 42, 44, 48, 56

Legend of Qin, The (television series), 106

Legge, James, 133

Levinovitz, Alan, 165–66, 169

Li Dazhao 李大釗, 39

Li Zehou 李澤厚, 29, 42, 45, 52

liberty, 39, 148, 172. *See also* Enlightenment

Liezi 列子, 5, 74, 79, 86–92, 94, 101, 117, 125, 127, 134, 155

Liji 禮記, 130, 132

Lin Yutang, 72, 76; "On Humor" (*Lun youmo* 論幽默), 72

Linguistic Strategies in Daoist Zhuangzi and Chan Buddhism (Wang), 73. *See also*

Buddhism: Chan 禪; deconstruction; Wang, Youru

linguistics, 60, 73, 131, 136

Liu Qingping 劉清平, 29

Liu Xiaogan 劉笑敢, 11, 104, 117, 165, 167

Liuxia Ji 柳下季, 105, 107

loser, 91, 108. *See also* player; player hater

Lu Xun 魯迅, 39

Lu 魯 (Chinese state), 102, 107, 118–19

Lu, Marquis of, 159–60

Luhmann, Niklas, 187. *See also* mass media

Lüliang waterfall diver, 39, 155–56, 158–62

Lun youmo 論幽默. *See* "On Humor" (*Lun youmo* 論幽默) (Lin Yutang)

lunli 倫理 (ethics), 28

Lunyu 論語. *See* Analects

Luo Linhui 羅琳會, 36

madman of Chu; *see* Chu, madman of

Magill, R. Jay, 19–20, 31

Maraldo, John, 40

mask changing, 93–94, 113

mass media, 186–87. *See also* Luhmann, Niklas

master swimmer. *See* Lüliang waterfall diver

Mawangdui 馬王堆 (excavation site), 5

maxim, 9, 11, 14, 68, 149

McCraw, David, 16

medicinal aspects of Daoism, 12–13, 83, 171

meditation, 158, 168

Mencius (*Mengzi* 孟子), 7, 9, 21, 42, 47, 49, 52–54, 80–81, 98–99, 127, 133–34

Mengsun Cai, 42, 97, 118–21, 132, 175–76

Mengzi 孟子, 7. *See* Mencius (*Mengzi* 孟子)

metaphor, 1–4, 14, 74, 114, 117, 132, 134, 136, 146, 167, 171, 173

metaphysics, 31, 73, 77, 79–80, 119–20

ming jia 名家. *See* School of Names

ming shi 名實 (names and actualities), 7, 42

Miscellaneous Chapters (Zhuangzi), 78, 103, 130, 149

mockery, 70, 73, 111, 130, 156

Moeller, Hans-Georg, 34, 40, 45, 103, 106, 119, 129, 153, 165, 168–69, 176; translations of the *Daodejing*, 115; translations of the *Zhuangzi*, 118, 121

Mohism, 6, 42, 116

Møllgaard, Eske, 39, 72

Monty Python's Life of Brian (film), 63–64, 68

moral ontology, 49. *See also* morality

morality, 21–22, 27–28, 51, 68, 70–71, 104, 107, 113, 144; antimorality, 70; Confucian, 8, 28, 45, 50, 107–8, 113

Morreall, John, 60–64, 66–70, 75

mourning, 46, 118–21

Musil, Robert, 184

mysticism, 12, 70, 73, 135, 158–60, 165

mythology, 12, 78–82, 86, 125

Na Wei 那微, 36–38

Nan de hutu 難得糊塗 (it is difficult to be muddled), 138. *See also* Zheng Banqiao 鄭板橋

Nanhua zhenjing 南華真經, 11

negation, 22, 24, 26, 70, 73, 101, 114–15

negative ethics, 69, 121. *See also* amoralism; antimoralism

Nelson, Eric, 40

neo-Daoism, 33, 135–36. *See also xuanxue* 玄學

New Sincerity, 29. *See also* ethics of sincerity

New Testament, 63

Nietzsche, Friedrich, 4, 35–36, 38–41, 68, 106, 126–27; and herd mentality, 38, 41; *On the Genealogy of Morality*, 68; slave morality, 68; *Übermensch*, 39–40, 127. *See also* nihilism

nihilism, 26, 68–69. *See also* Nietzsche, Friedrich

no-self, 115

nonaction, 152. See also *wu wei* 無為

Old Fisherman, 106

old man at the fort, 141. See also *Huainanzi* 淮南子

"On Humor" (Lun youmo 論幽默) (Lin Yutang), 72. See also Lin Yutang

ontic, 167. *See also* Heidegger, Martin; hermeneutics

ontology, 6, 37–38, 52–53, 56, 84, 94, 99, 115, 119–21

Outer Chapters (*Zhuangzi*), 75, 78, 103, 149

outlaw, 106, 113

ownness, 35–36, 38, 41, 57. *See also* authenticity

Ox Mountain, 53

paradox, 23, 73, 127, 139

Parkes, Graham, 40

parody, 63–64, 76, 83, 95, 98–100, 106, 109, 125, 139, 144, 155–56, 173–74; of Horsehead Humpback, 98, 100 (*see also* Horsehead Humpback); of Hundun, 6, 78, 80–82, 85, 89, 125, 174 (*see also* Hundun 渾沌 [Emperor of the Center]); of Huzi, 86 (*see also* Huizi); of Liezi, 91 (*see also* Liezi 列子); of Robber Zhi, 103, 109 (*see also* Robber Zhi 盜跖); use in the *Zhuangzi*, 73

Patterson, Orlando, 26

pedagogics, 88–89

pedantry, 20, 107

personae, 9, 22–23, 40, 54–56, 67, 84, 101, 126, 143, 161

personalization, 45, 131, 135, 155

perspectivism, 11, 56, 77, 110, 154

philology, 16, 74, 89, 104, 137, 146

Philosophical Investigations (Wittgenstein), 170. *See also* Wittgenstein, Ludwig

philosophy of humor, 4, 59–60; hybrid theories, 63; incongruity theories, 61–62; play theories, 61–64; relaxation theory, 10, 62–64, 66–67, 69; relief theories, 61–62, 69, 75, 83, 104, 156, 163; superiority theories, 61, 75–76

physiognomy, 86–87, 89–92, 94

pity, 64–65, 71, 83, 156

Plato, 41, 61, 68

playacting, 94, 145–46, 148, 150

player, 2, 30, 113, 124. *See also* player hater

player hater, 113. *See also* player

playfulness, 57, 61–62, 68, 70–71, 73, 76, 86, 103–4, 131, 151, 164, 166, 168–69, 171; and irony, 31; playfully assume (roles or values), 2, 7, 40, 85, 103, 137, 151, 174; playful pretense, 4, 66

pleasure, 34–35, 62–66, 69, 76, 92, 109–10, 124. *See also* Freud, Sigmund

pomposity, 106–7

postmodern, 30–34

praying mantis allegory, 149–50

pretending, 66–67, 112, 138–39, 141, 145–46, 160. *See also* genuine pretending

profane, 156–57, 161–63

psychogenesis, 66

psychosomatic, 13, 52, 61, 144, 172, 174, 176

Puett, Michael, 49, 55, 87–88

puns, 74, 76, 104

Pyle, Howard, 59

qi 氣 (vital force), 38, 87, 119, 143–44, 157, 159–60

Qi 齊 (state), 77, 147

Qinshi mingyue 秦時明月. See *Legend of Qin, The* (television series)

Qu Boyu 蘧伯玉, 149–50

Qin dynasty, 42, 106, 115, 128

rambling, 11, 14, 34, 136, 144, 164, 166–72, 174

Rameau's Nephew, 25–27, 31, 34

rebel, 26, 51, 103, 106, 109, 111–13

reclusion, 138–40, 148–49. *See also* Wang Bo

recognition, 13, 93, 116, 143, 147

rectification of names, 7, 41, 43, 46, 51, 55–56, 110, 143

relativism, 11, 21, 103, 165

religion, 12–13, 29, 70, 79

Remastering Morals with Aristotle and Confucius (Sim), 54. *See also* Sim, May

ren 仁 (humaneness): in Confucianism, 9, 45, 51–53, 134; critique of, 119

Ren Fuxin 任付新, 36

Ren Jiyu 仁繼愈, 16

Republic (Plato), 41. *See also* Plato

reverence, 12, 80, 92, 97, 100, 105, 139–40, 155

Rhetoric (Aristotle), 61. *See also* Aristotle

"riding the wind," 86, 117

Rilke, Rainer Maria, 1

ritual propriety, 42–43, 45–46, 55, 69–70, 75, 80, 90, 106, 108, 115, 118–19

roaming, 14, 136, 149, 164–69, 171

Robber Zhi 盜跖, 16, 75, 103–13, 125, 128, 142, 144, 147, 156; Maoist interpretation of, 106, 109

Robin Hood, 59

role model ethics, 41, 47–48, 53, 56

Romantic irony, 30–32, 34, 135

Rorty, Richard, 14, 31–34, 169; final vocabulary, 32–33, 169; ironism, 31–34. *See also* Romantic irony; Socratic irony

Rosemont, Henry, Jr., 7–8, 28–29, 42–43, 45–47, 49–53, 55

Roth, Harold D., 158

Ruism, 5. *See* Confucianism

ruosang 弱喪 (exile since childhood), 167, 169

sage, 60, 81, 99, 127; Confucian, 60, 99, 124–25, 127, 131, 144, 156, 174, 182–83; Daoist, 37, 83, 85–86, 92, 96, 106–9, 111, 113, 115, 117, 125, 130, 136–38, 144, 153–54, 156, 164–65, 185; inner sageliness and outward kingliness, 9

sai weng shi ma 塞翁失馬, 141. *See* old man at the fort

sanity, 4, 13, 34, 76, 83–84, 151, 171–74. *See also* insanity

sarcasm, 76, 156

Sartre, Jean-Paul, 32

satire, 66, 72–74, 90, 101, 107–8, 110, 131, 135, 150, 155–56

Saturnalia, 69

scholars, 5, 10, 19, 28, 38–41, 54, 60, 71, 134, 152, 155

School of Names (*ming jia* 名家), 42, 168

Schwermann, Christian, 90, 138

Schwitzgebel, Erik, 72, 82, 154–55, 160

Secret Agent, The (Conrad), 41

Secular Age, A (Taylor), 19. *See also* Taylor, Charles

Sein und Zeit (Heidegger). *See* Heidegger, Martin

self-cultivation, 42–43

self-overcoming, 39

Sellmann, James D., 73–74

sexuality, 65. *See also* Freud, Sigmund

Shang, Ge Ling, 39

Shangjunshu 商君書, 90

Shanhaijing 山海經, 78, 81

sheng ren 聖人, 37, 117, 127, 130. *See also* sage

Shi Qiu 史鰌, 103, 147. *See also* Zeng Shen 曾參

Shiji 史記, 6–7, 74, 105–6

Shu the Discombobulated, 141

Shu 儵 and Hu 忽, 78–81, 94

Sigurðsson, Geir, 50

Sim, May, 28, 54–55

simpleton, 90–91

Sincerity and Authenticity (Trilling), 19–20, 22, 26, 30, 34, 36. *See also* Trilling, Lionel

single correspondence, 44, 49–50, 55. *See also* dual correspondence

sinology, 152–53

skepticism, 11, 16, 32

skill stories. *See* knack stories

Slingerland, Edward, 13, 153–54, 160

smooth operator, 34, 101, 111, 113, 117–18, 124–76

Socratic irony, 30, 91, 112

Sommer, Deborah, 106

Song Rongzi 宋榮子. *See* Song Xing 宋鈃

Song Xing 宋鈃, 116–17

Sophocles, 20–21

soteriology, 12, 79, 83, 153

Spencer, Herbert, 61

spirit, 13–17, 21, 24–26, 39. *See also* Hegel, G. W. F.

spontaneity, 75, 80, 152–54, 157, 163–64, 172

Strickmann, Michael, 172–73

stupidity, 89–91, 138–39, 146

subjectivism, 30

subjectivity, 31, 161

sublime, 161

subversion, 6, 48, 59, 68, 76, 102

surreal, 135–37, 157

Tai Shan (mountain), 107. *See also* Lu 魯 (Chinese state)

Tai xuanjing 太玄經 (canon of supreme mystery), 128

Tao Wangling 陶望齡, 117

Taylor, Charles, 19–20, 25, 27, 29–30, 33–34, 39

teleology, 169, 184

therapeutic, 13, 72, 147–49, 151. *See also* medicinal aspects of Daoism

tian 天. *See* heaven

tiger trainer, 149–50

transitoriness, 5, 120, 129, 176

tree, 110, 117–18, 138, 140–41, 151, 160

tricksters, 76, 91, 99–100, 102, 111–13, 115, 125

Trilling, Lionel, 8, 19–27, 30, 33, 39, 41, 43. *See also* authenticity

True Man, 126. *See also* zhenren

Tünnes and Schäl, 71

uniqueness, 25–26, 31, 36, 40, 127

universalism, 21, 28

useless usefulness, 138–41, 147

Van Norden, Bryan, 49, 53

vanity, 111–12

veneration, 125, 131, 161, 166

versatility, 75, 117, 165–66

village worthies, 49–50, 99, 130, 136–37

virtue, 42–43, 49–50, 52, 78, 82, 97–104, 108–9, 112, 114, 116, 128, 133, 137, 141, 182; as *de* (see *de* 德); ethics, 28; thieves of, 49; and vice, 26

virtuosity, 6, 14, 37, 95, 113, 116, 143, 171,
    173–76
virtuosos, 37
vitality, 87, 95–97

wandering, 37–38, 117, 136, 149, 164–67,
    171. *See also* roaming; *xiaoyao you*
Wang Bo, 13, 33, 73, 78, 89, 111, 115, 139, 160
Wang Deyou 王德有, 111, 140
Wang Fuzhi 王夫之, 89, 116–17
Wang Shu 王恕, 52
Wang Tai, 102
Wang Xiaoyu 王孝魚, 161
Wang, Youru, 32, 73, 76. *See also* Buddhism:
    Chan 禪; deconstruction
Wang Zhang, 49. *See also Mencius (Mengzi*
    孟子*)*
wannabe, 89
Warring States period, 74, 105
Watson, Burton, 126, 164
Wei-Jin 魏晉 period, 33, 135
Weiming, Tu, 6, 23, 28, 55, 190
weltanschauung. *See* worldview
Wenzi 文子, 132–34
wild card, 1–5, 165–67. *See also* cards; joker
    card
wisdom, 41, 53, 104, 138
wit, 60, 65–66, 72, 76, 109, 112
Wittgenstein, Ludwig, 129, 169–71.
    See Philosophical Investigations
    (Wittgenstein)
Wohlfart, Günter, 15, 40, 68, 79, 153–54
Woodworker Qing, 157, 159–60
worldview, 78, 153–54, 169
worship, 123, 131–132, 140, 163
wu wei 無為, 152–53. *See also* nonaction

xian 仙. *See* immortals
Xiao Dong Yue, 72
xiaoti 孝悌, 51–52. *See* filial responsibility
xiaoyao you 逍遙遊, 164–66. *See* rambling;
    wandering
xin 心. *See* heart-mind

Xu Gan 徐幹, 50
Xu, Weihe, 60
Xu Yinchun 徐陰春, 42
xuanxue 玄學, 135. *See also* neo-Daoism;
    Wei-Jin 魏晉 period
Xunzi 荀子, 74, 80

Yan Beiming 嚴北溟, 16
Yan He 顏闔, 149–50
Yan Hui 顏回, 107, 118–19, 141–47, 149,
    157–59
Yang Guorong 楊國榮, 29, 42, 52, 114–15,
    118
Yang Rubin 楊儒賓, 7
Yang Xiong, 128
Yearley, Lee, 73–74, 76
Yellow Emperor, 128, 156
yin 陰 and yang 陽, 79, 148
Yu (sage-king), 144, 147
yu zhi le 魚之樂. *See* Happy Fish (*yu zhi le* 魚
    之樂)

Zaiwo 宰我 (student of Confucius), 45–46,
    118–19
Zeng Shen 曾參, 103, 147. *See also* Shi Qiu
    史鰌
Zhang Hengshou 張恒壽, 16
Zhang, Shi Ying, 40
zhen 真 (true, genuine), 5, 34, 36–40,
    112–13, 127–29. *See also zhenren* 真人;
    zhenuineness
Zheng Banqiao 鄭板橋, 138–39
zheng ming 正名. *See* rectification of
    names
zhenren 真人, 14, 34, 36, 112, 115, 126–37,
    145–46, 161, 173
zhenuineness, 5, 14, 115, 126, 128–29, 134,
    136, 139, 145–46, 173
Zhongyong 中庸, 9, 42, 52–53, 130,
    145
Zhou dynasty, 103
Zhu Xi 朱熹, 46
Zhu, Yang, 104

Zhuang Zhou, 4, 6, 16, 105–6, 129, 139

Zhuangism, 15, 73

Zhuangzi 莊子, 1–17, 20–21, 24–25, 30, 33–34, 36–44, 48, 53–57, 59–121, 124–40, 142–47, 149, 151–58, 160–74, 176. *See also* Inner Chapters (*Zhuangzi*); Miscellaneous Chapters (*Zhuangzi*); Outer Chapters (*Zhuangzi*)

Zi Gong 子貢, 107

Zigao 子高 (duke of She 葉), 147–49

Ziporyn, Brook, 1–2, 32, 85, 141–42; on humor, 76–77; translations of the *Zhuangzi*, 82, 86–90, 93–95, 101–4, 113, 116–18, 120, 131–39, 144–46, 148–50, 156, 158–59, 163, 173, 177, 181, 186; wild card metaphor, 2, 5, 165

Ziqi 子綦, 158, 184

ziran 自然 (self-so), 90, 152

ziyou 自由 (freedom), 38–39

Ziyu 子輿, 120, 133

Zuozhuan 左傳, 78

CPSIA information can be obtained
at www.ICGtesting.com
Printed in the USA
LVOW12s0422040118
561737LV00004B/4/P

9 780231 183994